SNOW DODGING
for umpteenagers

mark newham

Published by MoriartiMedia.com

First edition 2022 published by MoriartiMedia.com
Copyright © 2022 Mark Newham
Cover illustration by Eleanor Holmes

All rights reserved. Without limiting the rights under copyright reserved above, no part of this publication may be reproduced, stored in or introduced into a retrieval system, or transmitted, in any form, or by any means (electronic, mechanical, photocopying, recording, or otherwise) without the prior written permission of the copyright owner of this book.

ISBN 978-1-7396498-0-7

About the Author

After a journalism career stretching back to the days of steam-driven typewriters, telex machines and hot metal presses **Mark Newham** now spends his days marvelling at how anyone can keep up with the white hot pace of technological change while using his quill pen to craft books on issues other writers seem to have neglected.

Published in 2011, his first book – *Limp Pigs* – exploded the myth of a China changing beyond recognition, became an instant Amazon best seller and was equally instantly banned in China.

The BBC called it 'Unique... Inspiring...'

Newham's greatest claim to journalistic fame is through being a recipient of the National Union of Journalists' Trireme Award, an honour bestowed on members receiving the most derisory rate of pay offers for their freelance work and an award which has led to an abiding preoccupation with how anyone ever manages to survive on journalism work alone.

He can (sometimes) be contacted through mail@moriartimedia.com

*To airport baggage handlers everywhere
for a smashing job well done.*

Contents

1. **The Fartherland** – Do you REALLY want to go there?	1
2. **India** – Never a dull moment. Never.	17
3. **Sri Lanka** – The teardrop island. Just so.	41
4. **Thailand** – Eden, gardened to death	67
5. **Cyprus** – Aphrodite has left the building (site)	93
6. **Kenya** – Palms, qualms and Kalashnikovs	123
7. **Cambodia** – Din by name…	157
8. **Camelot** – AKA Scambodia	185
9. **San Serriffe** – A goose, cooked	221

1

THE FARTHERLAND
Do you REALLY want to go there?

No. Not there. THERE. It's taken as read you want to go there. It's been your dream to follow the swallow and leave winter to others as soon as you've the wherewithal to do so.

But now you have, you lucky pensionaire you, are you sure you're really ready to go THERE? Into the land of tripwires, mantraps and viper nests on the road to winter escape perfection? Along a trail booby-trapped with the social equivalents of improvised explosive devices that can quickly turn dreams to the stuff of nightmares?

Thing is, although you might have a list of candidates that could fit the snow-dodging location bill, that's just the start of it. Narrowing the list down means having to either go and see for yourself or rely on the reports of others. Reports that can have those of a nervous disposition abandoning the whole idea altogether and deciding that gathering close to a cosy pub's blazing fireside is an infinitely preferable way of passing the winter months.

After some deliberation it was the former course of action for me. I'd been around. I was no innocent abroad. There wasn't much anyone could tell a world-weary umpteenager like me about trips to faraway places that'd come as much of a surprise. Anyway, in my experience other people's travel horror stories were about as reliable as the average bus timetable and all too often designed more to terrify than to inform. So I closed my ears to such reports and went deaf.

Would that I hadn't. Well, not completely anyway. Had I at least had the sense to lend half an ear to the traveller's tales of others I might have been spared a series of near-death experiences while fighting my way round the steaming Indian sub-continent, any number of dead-of-night multispecies creepy crawly invasions and bomb scares in the heart of darkest Africa, a succession of boredom-gone-bonkers days that felt like weeks on a rain-blasted Mediterranean island and becoming the victim of a chain of hair-tearing lunacy-gone-mad Chinese cheatings in the jungles of South-East Asia. Had I at least kept one ear open maybe I could have avoided all these and completed my quest in the couple of years – three at most – I thought finding my own winter sanctuary would take.

Two decades and any number of revisions on how I should have approached the search later it's abundantly clear I might have over-estimated my own capacity for sensing pitfalls on the road to perfection. Like Paul Simon's boxer it's now clear I failed to resist seeing only what I wanted to see and disregarding the rest.

That failing has a lot to answer for in my search for the perfect place to escape winter and is something I really should have tried to correct before setting out on the quest.

But I didn't and I think I know why. It was too heavily ingrained in me, traceable as it was to a day of revelation in my early teens my shame will never let me forget.

* * *

The day I knew I was destined to spend my life looking for sanctuary from that time of year when the sun, if it does deign to poke its head out from behind lardy winter skies is the colour and consistency of a half-dead oyster, was the day I could and probably should have done more to help put my father's blazing trousers out.

But I didn't. Couldn't. I was transfixed. Mesmerised by a message in the flames that'd left me frozen in time, my mind reeling. Utterly at odds with everything I'd grown up believing, the blaze was telling me it might, just might, be possible that my father could, at times, be wrong.

All my short life until that day I'd believed his word was law, omnipotent and infallible. But this couldn't be right. Contrary to the diktat he'd delivered moments before setting himself alight, there must be an alternative. Where, the flames were challenging me to answer, was it written that you just had to grit your teeth and bear the great winter freeze until Spring arrived? Nowhere.

While the rest of the family scrambled to prevent my father becoming an involuntary burnt offering I was left immobile, wondering how to take this further. Indeed, whether to. Not big on challenges to his proclamations was my dad and when he heard what I had to say he might not be the only one being put out. The front door beckoned for anyone daring to question received wisdom or the status quo. His English-as-tuppence upbringing forbade such heinous acts of family or national disloyalty.

It wasn't the only thing it forbade. Self-immolation was, I'm pretty sure, another thing forbidden in our household. Far too showy and un-English, which rather ruled out any suspicion of my father having done it on purpose. No, if he saw 'doing the decent thing' as the only way of salvaging the family's good name it'd be by the traditional route of going into the library with the brandy and a service revolver.

Trouble was, we didn't have a library. So that final solution was out and so was the only alternative. There were rules prohibiting excessive noise in public libraries and my father would rather die than subject his family to the shame of the inevitable complaints.

So no matter how bad things got, there'd be only one thing for it for my dad – laugh in the face of adversity and, as Churchill would have put it, keep on buggering on.

Big on Churchill my dad was. Old Winnie represented everything he admired, especially the man's capacity for stoicism – something my dad ensured was imported into our household in spades and, as it happens, something that was to come back to almost prove his own personal nemesis the day of the great trouser fire.

The thing that sparked the incident – as it were – was the issue of the temperature of the house we lived in, a house whose only form of heating was a single open hearth fire in the living room.

On a day so cold that ice could be scraped from the inside of the single-glazed windows, as the family gathered eagerly around waiting for him to fire up the coals in the grate someone had strayed into minefield territory. Not only had they'd dared have the temerity to question the paternal axiom that if this house-heating system had been good enough for his parents it was good enough for us but had used the words central and heating one after the other in the same sentence.

The two words' juxtaposition was as incendiary to my father as the twisted paper fire-lighting tapers he spent hours fashioning to save on matches.

'Central heating!' he spat as if trying to rid his mouth of a bad taste. 'Such things are the stuff of cissies and Americans!' Father wasn't keen on either, especially Americans. Apart from just being here during the war they'd left their heinous ways behind when they left. One of which was the concept of central heating, even in bedrooms! My GOD! What sort of spineless culture needs heat in THERE?

Had I been a bit older I might have had the nerve to remind him that the full house central heating concept had actually been developed by the Romans, the sort of disciplined society my father held in special esteem. But this was not the time anyway. Of greater urgency was getting him to notice that his fire-lighting attempts had left his trousers ablaze.

Distracted from his regular practise of getting the fire to draw by placing a page from the *Daily Telegraph* – no other newspaper was acceptable – over the upper half of the fireplace he hadn't noticed that the method had been more successful than usual. Roaring into life, flames from the lit kindling latched onto the newspaper and the ensuing inferno sent flaming bits of newsprint floating neatly into his trouser turn-ups which caught rather quicker than the coal in the hearth.

Waving away any attempt to interrupt his flow as the flames began their determined rise up his tweeds towards the matches in his pocket, he fixed us with an apoplectic stare and went into full turbocharged rant mode. Volcanic wouldn't be wide of the mark given the circumstances.

'Heating! In the bedrooms? Never heard of anything so... so... treasonable! It was cold bedrooms that made Britain GREAT, young man, and don't you EVER forget it!'

We wouldn't have been able to if we'd been subjected to mass hypnotism and collective frontal lobotomy. Apart from the effect the comment and his pulsating beetroot face left on his cowering offspring, there was a reinforcing aspect to the incident which was to go down in family history.

As the tirade rose to its full finger-jabbing climax it was frozen in mid-flow by my mother's speed of thought. As keen as the rest of us not to see him and the house go up like a Roman candle, her action doused both the flames and the tirade in one go.

For a moment time stopped, the whole family in suspended animation. But only until my father realised what had just transpired. Clear from the look of growing horror on his dripping, jaw-flapping, face was the fact that he believed himself to be under attack from his nearest and dearest, the woman who'd hitherto shown no evidence of disloyalty but had now been caught in the act, her trembling hands still gripping the soda siphon weapon of her attack.

* * *

I was still laughing as I braced myself for the breath-depriving crawl between icy sheets that night. Well, part of me was. The other part was still grappling with how to take my father to task over his cold bedrooms making Britain great decree.

I'd tried to see my father's point of view. I really had. But I just couldn't find any justification for accepting the assertion without question. Geography lessons had taught me there were any number of countries around the world equally as well-qualified as Britain to attach the 'great' superlative to their names, many in far warmer places than the land of my birth. Places where I suspected bedrooms would never be cold and where you'd only don winceyette pyjamas if you wanted to break a fever or blend in at a West African knees-up.

In the end, after any number of talks with myself, I decided it wasn't worth it. There wasn't much an early teenager could say to change his mind. In fact, anything I did say on the subject was quite likely to have the reverse effect, the man having been the victim of an acute terminal conditioning. That's not a misprint. It's a form of mind manipulation some parents feel is quite acceptable for their offspring having been subjected to it themselves, apparently with no ill-effects.

'You've been born in the north where it gets cold and wet and dark in winter,' was the standard response to family gripes about this particular season. 'Get over it.'

'... like I did,' was the unspoken sub-text to the command from a man who'd clearly received such a heavy dose of the conditioning that even the experience of Indian sub-continent warmth during the war years hadn't been able to eradicate.

That conditioning had resurfaced with venom on his disembarkation back on home shores. Worried that winning the war might have put paid to the great British trait of suffering in sullen silence, his relief on finding gritted teeth and the frozen stiff upper lip hadn't been replaced by smiles and grins as the standard British facial expression was palpable. Now he could relax. What he found was a post-war rationing blitz in progress to ensure they hadn't.

My father was in his element during rationing, embracing the culture of make-do-and-mend with a gusto that would impress Old Man Steptoe and ensuring there was no relaxation of it in his own household even years after rationing ended. It was, as he never tired of reminding us, the British way. A way which put Britain in a different league to the rest of the world and which should be preserved and defended at all cost.

So devoted to king, queen, country and everything Britain stood for he wouldn't have known disloyalty if it stabbed him in the back he'd duly signed up to help stop Hitler in his tracks and had returned to the land of his birth with his mind made stolidly up.

He'd seen 'abroad' and it was as his parents had told him. Nothing was better than Britain unless it was England. Here was a country around which the cosmos undeniably revolved. Or if it didn't it should and, for their edification, the rest of the world should be forced to learn every word of every song ever written by those embodiments of Englishness Gilbert & Sullivan and Flanders & Swann.

If my father had had his way they'd have had one Flanders & Swann song in particular printed on their retinas. The one that contains the immortal line 'the English, the English, the English are best'.

Whether my father realised the song was a parody of Englishness I never discovered. But I suspect not. Had he, I doubt very much he'd have been heard muttering it whenever there was even the mildest criticism of England or Britain on the radio (wireless in our household) or television.

Commentators questioning British values and those who dared poke fun at Englishness were at best unpatriotic, at worst out and out bloody traitors and it wasn't much different with things newer than Victoriana. New fangled devices – especially those emanating from the USA – were regarded with extreme suspicion bordering on outright contempt. We'd got by well enough without them before and there was no reason to adopt them now unless there was an exceptionally compelling case for doing so.

The wireless and, late in the day, television both fell into this category on the grounds that they had one clear and unarguable benefit. They were invaluable tools for disseminating that sentiment contained in that line of that Flanders & Swann song.

But few modern devices received such grudging acceptance which somewhat put paid to there being any likelihood of being able to listen to the wireless or watch television in centrally-heated comfort until the time came for me to move out of the family home. It was not an enticing prospect.

If all that sounds begrudging it's not meant to. I attach no blame to my father for his attitude towards modernity, foreign influence or child management. Like so many others of his day he was simply a product of his time, eking out scarce resources and doing the best he could in trying times. He wasn't a mean man – far from it – just one who had difficulty keeping up with a rapidly changing post-war world.

In fact, now I come to think about it, I actually have a lot to thank him for. Not least for being the unwitting source of the revelation that it wasn't carved in stone that people born in the higher latitudes had to stay in the higher latitudes year-round. There was another way and the seed had been sown by my never-ever-venture-beyond-these-shores-ever-again father of all people. There was a big world out there and a place just waiting to welcome me in as a refugee from the frozen wastes.

But where? After that revelation I knew my fate was sealed. I'd never be satisfied until I went to find out.

* * *

Easier said than done. No matter how ambitious or honourable one's intention, of one thing I was certain even at an early age.

Nothing gets achieved without money, a commodity that as a young man in his teens I had little of, wasn't ever likely to have much of unless my fortunes changed dramatically and without which I'd be left high and dry in Blake's green and pleasant land, lyrics that could only have been written in summer.

Something had to be done. But what?

It took some years for the answer to come. But when it did it came with such blinding intensity I knew I'd look back on that day as the day I discovered dreams didn't have to stay that way.

Staring out of the classroom window as the teacher tried unsuccessfully to retain my attention inside it, I remember hearing a word that even the rumbustious goings-on in the school's courtyard below couldn't drown out.

That word was 'expenses' and when combined with the subject of the day's lesson – geology – it snapped me back into the room like knicker elastic snagging on barbed wire.

The day was a Friday, the day when all thoughts of pupils and teachers alike were tuned to whatever extracurricular activity they had planned for the weekend.

The geology master was no exception. Having got bored with trying to instil in his daydreaming charges the procedure for remembering the sequential stratification of the Cretaceous period, he'd turned to reminiscing about his own life as a geologist, alighting on how being constantly abroad had ironically provided him with the means of escaping a career he'd come to realise was the civil equivalent of the Foreign Legion.

'Geology's not for everyone,' he warned. 'Sign up to work in the field and you'll find yourself shipped out to some of the world's most inhospitable places for months on end – something that can seriously affect your home and your social life,' he reflected ruefully, 'and even your health.

'But at least the perks are good. When you're on the job everything's covered by expenses. You can leave your salary untouched in the bank.'

Suddenly I was right back in the room, ears pricked and my whole attention on the man who, whether he knew it or not, had just shown me my own future. If his experience was anything to go by, this, I knew, was the path I'd been seeking. A path that would put me on the road to adventure and places where bedrooms needed to be cooled, not heated, where there'd be mango not lumpy porridge for breakfast and where someone would actually be paying me to be there. It was all too good to be true.

Fast forward ten years and that's exactly the way it turned out. First came a succession of lengthy geological tours to the swamps of Africa and deserts of the Middle East and then, on realising I was becoming about as civilised as the silverback gorillas I as good as found myself sharing a tent with in the Congo jungle, a change of direction. Rather than doing it, I began writing about it – a neat compromise on the realisation that I wasn't that keen on regressing to Neanderthal level. This way I could visit the self-same places but not become trapped in them for months – years – on end.

Journalism offered the quick in-out, the story in the bag and on to the next place. And still I didn't need to suffer sub-zero northern bedrooms for too long. Returns to the UK chill lasted but a matter of days. Bliss.

Fast forward again another twenty-five years and what had started out as a dream existence had started losing its allure. The constant travel had taken its toll, long-suppressed tropical health problems were getting harder to ignore and the so-called developing world was doing its best to prove it was beyond developing. In short, it just wasn't fun any more.

But I was addicted. And it took just one complete winter back in the UK to realise the extent of the addiction... to bedrooms with mosquito nets and fans and air conditioning in particular. Somehow I had to re-fashion my life to be able to slow down, get out of hard news yet avoid being condemned to trudging to the pub through slush and snow to stay just this side of being labelled a professional social outcast.

I'd tried to adjust to life back in Britain, I really had. But all evidence showed I'd somewhat over-estimated the speed at which things were changing in the northern latitudes.

Guiding my decision to return had been reports of global warming happening so quickly that, sooner than anyone thought, the peoples of the north would be living amongst groves of olives, fields of maize, vineyards dripping with grapes and enjoying shirt-sleeved mid-winter strolls on village greens overrun with boule-playing old men quaffing pastis after dining al fresco in their bougainvillea-festooned gardens.

They lied. Even with greenhouse gas emissions out of control and rising you still needed to cover your ear tips when the north wind blew, still needed the woolly vest your mother wouldn't let you go outside without and still needed to jig around to speed the metabolic rate before even thinking about leaving the house.

So where was all this global warming? Not where I was living, that's for sure and slowly the realisation dawned that either my return had been a tad premature or I hadn't done enough to help the climate change process along.

I was sure I had. But no matter how much wood and coal I burned in the most inefficient woodstove I could find, no matter how far I drove at high speeds alone in a large gas-guzzling car, no matter how long I kept the fossil fuel-fired boiler running when I had no need of hot water, no matter how many old-style lightbulbs I kept burning when it wasn't dark it clearly hadn't been enough. Still the chill wind whistled through the windows and roof I'd ensured had been left un-double glazed and un-insulated on the greenies' promise of imminent climate change making such fripperies both redundant and unnecessary.

So, as the clock ticked over to a new century, there I was, shivering in my layers, reflecting on all this wasted effort and facing having to make a decision.

The next bout of sub-zero weather made it for me. 'Get thee

gone,' it said. 'Fly in the face of thy father's diktat and give in to the simpering wimp in thee.'

Wise words well received. Enough of all this waiting around. Enough of living in hope of never again having to wear a coat in my home country. And enough of cold feet, in both the physical and metaphorical sense. The time had come to take matters into my own frostbitten hands and find somewhere to chill out – metaphorically not physically – until it really was safe to come in from the warm.

But where? That was the problem. After a lifetime on the road I already had a long list of rejects. Places that satisfied some of the items on a growing list of requirements for a winter freeze avoidance retreat but not all. That was the place I had to pin down. The one I could flee to every year until the toes of the feet I was so desperate to put up turned permanently up and where I could lie back smiling smugly at the thought of my countrymen shivering at home, safe in the knowledge that nowhere I'd found was better than this.

It was going to be a long search.

I hadn't expected it to be. A quick trip round a small number of places I thought might fit the bill should be enough I reckoned.

Miscalculation number two. Saddled with a list of Shangri-La selection criteria that grew exponentially longer with each place tested and rejected my quest went from one year to five to ten and by the time the twenty-year figure loomed the search was looking increasingly like the definition of the fool's errand.

Could it be possible that *the* place didn't actually exist? Was there no golden fleece to be found? It was beginning to look very much like it.

But since I'd started I thought I'd better finish and on I searched convinced that the perfect place was just around the next corner.

Which was when realisation number two struck. On the road I'd met any number of people searching for the same thing I was. Some were closer to finding it than others, some just starting out, but all had one thing in common. Every one indulged in the intense picking of fellow seekers' brains for news of places that might fit the bill.

With nearly twenty years of research under my belt, my brain became one of the most picked and frankly it was becoming a tad tiresome recounting the same stories over and over.

So why not put it in a book, someone said?

Ting! Yes, that was the way to do it and here, for the edification of anyone in a similar position and just starting out on their own quest for an escape from their winter wonder-what-I'm-doing-here-land, is the book in question.

Not everyone will agree with either the criteria or the conclusions drawn from my own quest because not everyone works to the same parameters. Enjoyment and acceptability are subjective, not least when it comes to choosing a likely winter escape hatch. Everyone has their own criteria but, for what they're worth, please find below a list of the initial parameters I started out with, a list that's found itself being refined and added to in subsequent chapters every time a new, critical issue bit me in the bum and demanded to be included.

Did I find what I was looking for? Don't really expect me to reveal that at this stage do you? But one thing I can reveal is that during the quest another epiphany occurred – quests of this nature are a process of evolution, not unlike the relationship I had with my father.

Before I grew a mind of my own, his word was law, my world was his world and that world was the fatherland.

Then, as more light entered my life it began illuminating something I'd not previously imagined existing. As my eyes opened it became clear something had been lost in translation. It was the 'Aaah!' factor and when included in the text what was revealed was a land I knew would suit me a whole lot better than the one of my father.

MY land, the one I knew I was destined to return to whenever

British summer time ended, the clocks went back and English teatime wasn't possible without turning the lights on, was undoubtedly the one where swallows went for the winter. The one that, on asking my mother where they were going, had come to be known affectionately as the faaartherland.

PRIMARY PRE-QUEST WINTER SANCTUARY CRITERIA

CRITERIA	ITEM	REASONING
Affordability	Cost neutral	Including all costs – travel, accommodation, subsistence, entertainment etc – location should be as close to cost neutral as possible compared with the cost of remaining in the UK for the same length of time.
Location	Warm/hot	Rather defeats the object of the exercise if it isn't.
	Not wet	Places where it's dry season during the northern winter. Flood/pest/health risks rise in wet season.
	Beachside	If possible. Not too far to access if not. Best for catching cooling sea breezes and sea is vital for cooling off in during the day. Anyway, being by the sea is nice, good for the soul and offers the best prospect of acquiring fresh seafood.
	English-speaking	As first or second language but also French if not. Makes miscommunication – which can lead to serious problems in faraway places – less likely.
	Not dry	Places where alcohol is banned/frowned upon makes sundowner activity difficult. Anyway, such places can't be regarded as civilised.
Accommodation	Self-catering	Crucial. For stays of longer than a week or so it's vital to be able to cook for oneself. Eating out the whole time is limiting, boring and expensive. And catering for oneself brings you into contact with interesting activities in the local market.
	Utility-connected	Not being connected to mains water and electricity supplies is seriously inconvenient and can be health-threatening.
	Communications	Preferably equipped with internet connection (for work purposes mainly) but definitely close to public internet-connection facility if not.

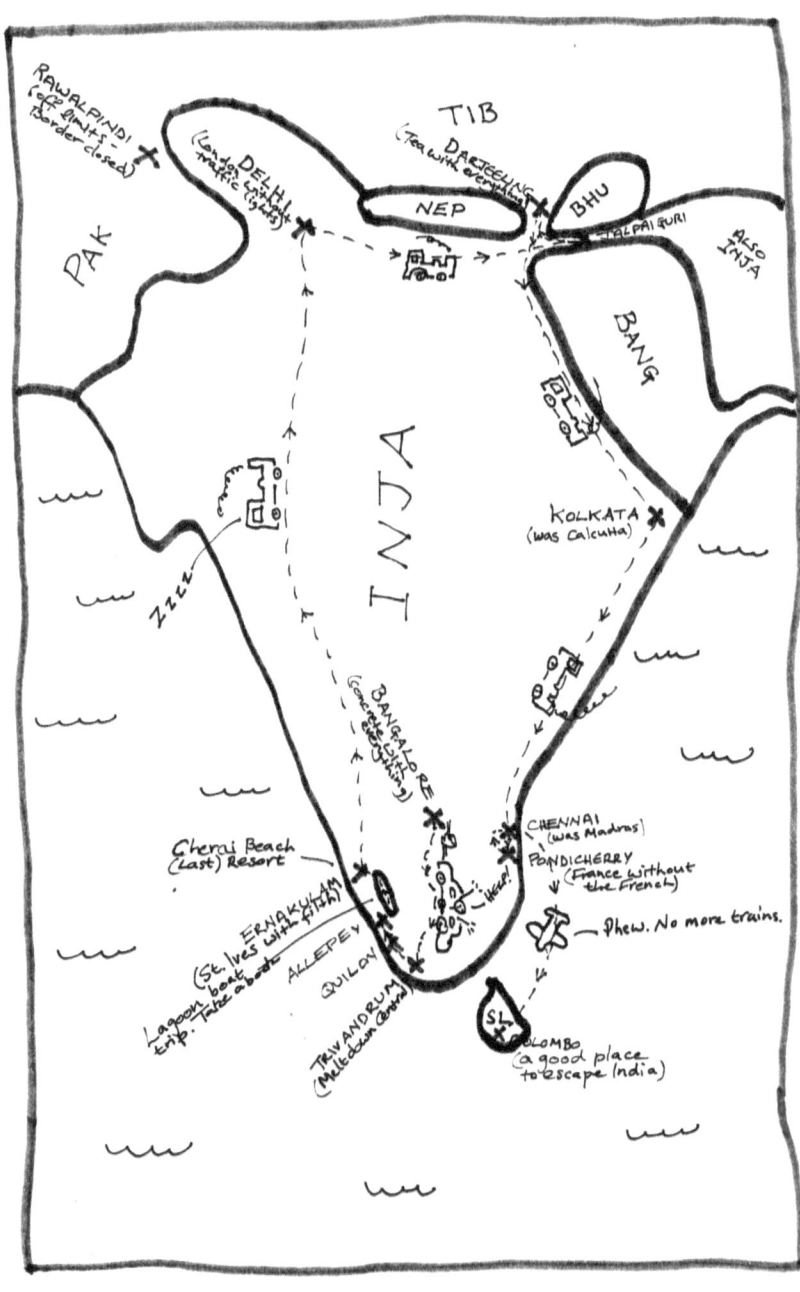

2

INDIA
Never a dull moment. Never.

India, although I didn't realise it at the time, is where the quest for the holy snow-dodging grail started. A quest that began with curiosity and ended in enlightenment.

The year was 2001, the year the dotcom bubble burst, planes smashed into the twin towers and I received an unignorable message that I wasn't as immortal as I'd thought.

A full decade of criss-crossing Africa without a break can make a bloke think he's indestructible. I'd withstood everything the place could throw at me. What more could it do?

A great deal, as it turned out. Starting with catching me off-guard.

Just when I thought I was starting to develop an ability to pre-empt Africa's less-than predictable nature, up steps the lord of misrule to remind me who's boss. Two near-death experiences in as many days provided a rude reminder that Africa and all its 'majesty' can never be taken for granted. And that to survive the place you need to leave from time to time to view it from afar.

So that's what I did. First to the UK to see how it was faring without me, then to India on realising Britain was doing OK on its own and that I'd missed the English cricket season.

There are many reasons to visit the UK, many of which to the uninitiated are of somewhat greater priority than spending five days watching twenty-two men knock a ball around without any certainty of a result. To many, the idea of being trapped inside a cricket ground is the rough equivalent of being locked in an immobilised train in a tunnel until the end of time with nothing to read and no signal on your phone.

Well, each to our own I suppose. Personally, after ten tempestuous years of having to hold my mental faculties together under what can generously be described as trying African conditions, the prospect of gazing mindlessly across a cricket field for days on end with no concern other than how low the beer in my glass was getting wasn't only appealing, it was something I felt my doctor would very likely order.

Disinclined to argue with him, I duly presented myself in the UK for the required therapy only to find that not only had the England cricket team left for India but that autumn was doing a good impression of winter. There was only one thing for it. The therapy treatment had to be relocated to Bangalore.

I'd always wanted to visit what was known as the garden city of India but had never had the chance. Now there was nothing stopping me. I'd awarded myself a long-overdue holiday, suspended all assignments for long enough to allow the recovery process to take effect and built a bit of a holiday fund to tide me over. So I did the sums. Since the tiding-over was based on the British cost of living and India's was reputed to be a great deal lower, even with the airfare taken into account I could still make the fund last the full term.

So the decision was made, visa arranged, flight booked and I was on my way to a country where cricket is the one religion no Indian has any problem with. And as I boarded the flight I wondered why Mahatma Gandhi hadn't realised it.

With sectarian violence breaking out all around him in the run-up to India's independence in 1947 he went on hunger strike, threatening to let his fast go the distance unless the fighting stopped.

But who should stop it first, asked those around him, the Hindus or the Moslems? Which are you, they asked?

'I'm a Hindu and a Moslem and a Sikh and a Christian and a Buddhist and a Jew,' he responded with characteristic impish mediation skill.

As sagacious and Yoda-like as the answer was, it didn't please everyone and I couldn't help thinking that the bestial brutality might have been brought to an end a lot sooner had he added the words 'and a cricketer'.

* * *

It wasn't the only irreverent thought I had during a trip that was to take me round the entire periphery of this vast country, starting at Trivandrum on India's southernmost tip and running up the west coast, across the top and back down the east side to finish in Chennai, formerly Madras. Thoughts of similar ilk were also directed at another of India's quasi-sacred icons, the railway, and at the Indian tourist board for the fine job they were doing of luring the unwary to places tourists would otherwise give a wide berth through the attachment of wholly misleading monikers.

To describe the concrete jungle that is Bangalore as a garden city is to make you wonder if you'd been misinterpreting the word 'garden' your whole life and whether the fault for the misinterpretation lies at the door of the country's earliest British colonialists. Well known for lifting Indian words and adding them to the English lexicon, could it be possible that they'd mistranslated the Indian word for 'place of absolutely no vegetation whatsoever'?

As I made my way to the dehumanising block-built bowl that serves as the Bangalore cricket ground from the god awful Airlines Hotel whose name bore as much relation to VIP lounges as 'garden city' bore to natural beauty, I began to think that it was. Indeed, had to be. Not only that but that their mistranscribing of 'garden' wasn't the only thing my forebears were guilty of. They'd done it with 'curry' too.

If there's a bog standard word for chicken madras in any of

the myriad of Indian languages I missed it. Not just in Bangalore but throughout my entire tour of the country. Yes, I was well aware that Indian food in the UK bears little relation to the real thing and that all the names of the various curries in British curry houses have been invented to tempt the English palate. But I did expect the Indians to know the word 'curry' and to see it somewhere on regular restaurant menus. More enlightenment added to the great à la carte of life. Roti? Yes. Samosa? Of course. Papadum? Naturally. Curry? Pardon.

In the end I began to think it was a little Indian joke known to all and played throughout the land on English tourists. And that I was the only one not in on the jest. The only one not knowing it was a way of getting back at the English for occupying their country for close on two hundred years and leaving without even saying thanks for all the words they'd filched and made their own.

Which would account for some of the smirks, gawps and wobbly head grins that seem to follow the tourist wherever he goes. There's no escape and in the end you just get used to it. But to begin with it's a tad disconcerting. It gives the impression that everyone's your friend and everyone's eager to help.

But then you encounter it with the bureaucratic officialdom India has made into an art form and suddenly the scales fall from your eyes.

'Oh, absolutely sir!' the nods and grins seem to be saying as the clerk inspects your application for a train ticket. 'That is most easily accomplished. Especially for such a VIP as your good self, sir.'

It's only on close inspection of the ticket issued after hours of queuing, waiting and form filling that you find it's in the wrong class, on the wrong day and going to the wrong place. Which of course means having to start all over again.

OK, that didn't happen every time I went to get a train ticket but often enough to give the distinct impression that the English, the English, the English weren't necessarily best at the bureaucracy game. In India, they've taken it to their hearts, quadrupled it, given it a prominence in Indian society English bureaucrats would drool over and finally added their own unique 'charm' to it. Witness my attempt to trade in an unused ticket for a replacement after missing my train at New Jalpaiguri station.

First to the ticket office to be told that refunds and replacement tickets were the sole responsibility of the station master. Onwards then to locate said master of the station. After an hour of searching I finally found him giving some poor underling hell. Deciding to let him get it out of his system before adding yet another problem to what was clearly not his best of days, I lurked close-by until the hell-giving subsided. Only then did I gingerly approach a man who'd plainly modelled himself on the Fat Controller in Thomas the Tank Engine.

Looking down the full length of a nose that'd clearly been designed for the purpose he deigned to give me a moment of his time, listened impatiently to my request, thought for a moment, wobbled his head, grinned a malicious grin through voluminous whiskers and ushered me with great ceremony into a scabby office housing an equally voluminous collection of filing cabinets and clutter where I was then given the third degree.

After my meeting with this man I now know why such inquisitions are so-called. In the wake of two hours of form-filling and being required to write in longhand, in triplicate without the benefit of either carbon paper or a cup of tea what was effectively a thesis on why I failed to arrive in time to board the booked train, I reckoned the adding of a third to the two degrees I'd already sweated blood over was no more than I deserved.

Yes, I could have simply turned on my heel and left. He could hardly have me arrested for failing to make the train on time (or could he, this was India after all?) and it wasn't as if the outlay on a new ticket was going to bankrupt me. But with several hours to wait for the next train and nothing better to do, I thought I'd go along with the performance for the craic that was in it.

It would, after all, make a travel horror story paragraph or two and anyway, now it was personal. The man whose gain was clearly other people's pain had thrown down a gauntlet and I was damned if I was going to give this supercilious sadist the satisfaction of winning without a fight. OK, I had about as much chance of beating him at his own game as I had of catching up with the train I'd just missed but I reasoned I could at least get a score draw out of it. There was the small matter of honour at stake.

In the end the honour of both participants was satisfied and as he handed over the precious replacement ticket there was a definite degree of respect in his eyes that hadn't been there before.

Or was it a 'this ain't over yet' look? In hindsight, judging by subsequent events it could hardly have been anything else.

As I stowed my bags on the next train to my desired destination, due to leave in a few minutes, my newfound 'friend' materialised outside the unopenable window beckoning to me. Unsure what he wanted I got out onto the platform to find him at a nearby kiosk buying two cups of tea, one for me it seemed. Pleased that all enmity was about to be ended in such an amicable way, I ventured to the kiosk to collect it and found myself engaged in friendly conversation about my impressions of India, my back turned to the train and looking into eyes that had now developed a mischievous twinkle.

That was the man's big mistake. In the twinkle I sensed movement behind me, glanced round and to my horror saw the train silently beginning to slide out of the station without warning. Slow enough at first to allow me to walk back and hop on but then swiftly picking up speed before I reached the door. No matter, there was another within reach. But with unexpected acceleration, that door shot past before I could gain a foothold and with growing alarm I found myself sprinting along the platform to catch up with my bags that looked destined to arrive in Kolkata unaccompanied.

That's when the train started playing games. The faster I went, the faster it did and people started taking bets on who'd get to the end of the platform first. The smart money was on the train. How could it fail to beat a sweating middle-aged man in flipflops, leave him breathless in the dust and disappear with all my belongings aboard, never to be seen again?

It was just the incentive I needed to hurl myself Buster Keaton-style at the handrail of the last door of the last carriage as twenty grinning Indians stood in the door and laughed.

It took a while for compassion to kick in but eventually a hand was thrust to haul me on board, much, I suppose, to the disappointment of the Fat Controller whose crestfallen face I could see rapidly disappearing into the Jalpaiguri smog.

* * *

I wasn't disappointed to be leaving either behind. They were a rude reminder of the real India I'd returned to after a delightful diversion into the Himalayan foothills.

I hadn't intended to go off-road and venture north to Sikim province – far too cold at this time of year – but someone in New Delhi recommended Darjeeling and getting closer to it I found myself being magnetically drawn to the town. There was something in the name. Something buried deep in the data banks but for the life of me I couldn't recall what.

It needed to get close to the place for a distant memory to stir. My parents, I found myself remembering, would sometimes be overheard reminiscing about Darjeeling, a place they both knew from respective postings to India during the second world war.

But just what was it about Darjeeling that made it stand out from the myriad of other Indian places mentioned? For the entirety of the three-hour white knuckle jeep ride up to the town along and nearly over the side of the barrier-less mountainside track that was the town's only means of access while its narrow gauge connecting railway was being repaired, I wracked my brains.

Little came apart from recalling my mother once telling me it was hilly, chilly and surrounded by tea plantations which, considering the circumstances, wasn't altogether surprising. I was a tad preoccupied with the very real prospect of death by imminent mountainside plunge as the jeep roared past lumbering trucks on blind bends in dense hillside fog.

That fog – both within and outside my head – only started clearing on my second night in Darjeeling, a night of glorious recovery from the first night mistakenly spent in the forlorn shambling wreck that was the Pineridge Hotel. Picture waking stiff with cold after the last of the three lumps of coal limit has burned away in the room's pitiful fireplace and emerging from your single-blanketed bed to find you can't even wash the memory of the night out of your hair and you have the Pineridge in one. The water trickling from the shower head wasn't warm enough to trouble a baby let alone thaw the hotel's generously-provided single sachet of frozen shampoo.

Fleeing almost screaming from the place I couldn't help but reflect that the Pineridge would have suited my father well. I wonder if he stayed here.

The answer only came when, unable to think straight, I'd let my nose do the talking and had followed it to what turned out to be nirvana, a beautiful wood-panelled room with a roaring fire, a huge comfortable double bed, an inexhaustible supply of hot water, a balcony with a breathtaking view of the world's third highest peak Kanchenjunga and my own personal bearer. In short, after stopping thinking and letting instinct do the work, I'd been guided by some cosmic force to the wonderfully old colonial Planter's Club and full recall of my mother's words. THIS, I could now hear her telling me years and years back, was where she and my father spent their honeymoon. Not THIS room, surely!

With mother's spirit voice going oddly silent on the matter, there was only one way to find out. The club's guestbook for April 1945 would reveal all.

Yes and no. Yes the club undoubtedly had the records for that time, I was informed by Bharat, my cheerful and faithful self-proclaimed bearer who was included in the amazingly affordable price of the room and who made both the fire and my early morning tea which he delivered to me in bed whether I wanted it or not. But no, the only person with the key to the records room was on leave.

So there I was, gin and tonic in hand on one side of the door, the answer to a burning question stowed securely away on the other and no means of connecting the one with the other. It was almost too much to bear. No less so when I discovered that the man with the key, the club secretary, had gone to watch the cricket in Bangalore. Who knows, I might have been sitting next to him. Aaaargh.

No one I met in India seemed as disconcerted by this turn of events as me, least of all the man who got me thoroughly pie-eyed on tongba, a hot millet beer drunk from a bamboo mug through a bamboo straw, at ten in the morning and did no more than grin philosophically as the story unfolded.

Frozen to the marrow after visiting the snow leopards in the almost humane Darjeeling zoo I found myself outside the nearby ramshackle Hot Stimulating Cafe and couldn't resist the temptation to discover how hot and stimulated I'd feel on re-emerging from its dilapidated depths.

Kiran, the cafe's Nepalese hippie proprietor, was clearly intent on ensuring I wouldn't leave disappointed. Emerging bleary-eyed from his quarters he first grinned at the sole customer in the place, informed me breakfast might take a few minutes, fired up the hifi with the Doors' 'LA Woman' and then delivered the first of three complimentary mugs of tongba to keep me going in the meantime.

Only history will recall if any breakfast actually arrived. I certainly don't. All I do recall is Kiran joining me with another tongba for me and one for himself and then replenishing mine as I recounted the story of how I'd found myself retracing my parents' footsteps around India without realising it.

Listening intently to the increasingly slurred tale all he did was grin. A grin that told me everything I needed to know.

'What the hell did you expect?' it said. 'From the moment you decided to come to India your parents' spirits were guiding you. They led you to a place whose memory they treasured so you could share in it.

'But there are limits. Would you want your offspring knowing which of the rooms contained the marital bed? Anyway, the beauty of it is that not only did you not resist but allowed them to bring you to Darjeeling... and to my place. Had it not been for them you might have left India without having had the chance to sample the delights of my famous tongba!'

Said delights not only followed me back to the Planter's Club for a lengthy lie-down but stayed with me for the rest of the trip and finally re-emerged to take up permanent residence on arriving back in the UK. Hidden amongst the contents of my backpack was a keepsake I have only a hazy memory of acquiring – a Buddhist scarf I vaguely remember Kiran tying round my neck with eight symbolic good fortune knots he said should never be untied.

Whether they've worked or not I'll never know. They've remained untied to this day and it'd only be by undoing them that the claim could be tested.

It's one of several unknowns carried away from Kiran's cafe that day, not least the worry of not being able to recall if I paid for the breakfast I may or may not have had. If I do owe you anything Kiran, sorry mate. Some day I'll try to get back to check and make amends.

There aren't many places in India I'd say that about. Very few warranted even one tick on my winter sanctuary requirements list. But Darjeeling was special. It was, after all, the place I now believe to be the inspiration for my quest. The place where, thanks to the Planters Club, Bharat and Kiran, I realised for the first time that I *was* on a quest.

Boarding the jeep for another harum scarum plunge down the mountain to catch an onward train two things came to me. First that I'd felt more at home in this grubby little town than I'd felt almost anywhere, and second that that is what travel is really all about – finding places like the Hot Stimulating Cafe. Places you can see yourself returning to time after time without getting bored.

Or is that the tongba talking? Yes, Darjeeling was wonderful. But get real. Could you really see yourself spending each winter in a place where you need a roaring coal fire to keep warm and the nearest palm-fringed beach is a thousand miles away?

On sober reflection, nah. Don't take it personally Darjeeling and everyone in it but somewhere there has to be another Kiran in his cafe where hot and stimulating refers as much to the climate and lifestyle as it does to the cafe's ambience and alcoholic offerings. But where?

* * *

In a way I'd already started answering the question. Without knowing it the criteria list was already forming in my head the moment I'd decided to go to India and I'd already applied it to quite a few rejected-out-of-hand places on the way from Bangalore to Darjeeling. Bangalore was one, Trivandrum at the southernmost tip of India another and pretty much everywhere in Kerala province a third.

To be fair I didn't really do Trivandrum justice. My few days there were mostly spent recovering from the manic, homicidal, seventeen-hour straight through taxi ride to it from Bangalore after discovering all flights and buses were booked by people fleeing to the coast for the Christmas holidays.

Christmas? In a Hindu/Moslem/Sikh dominated country?

Some mistake here surely. What were these folk doing indulging in a Christian festival? Christians don't do India's big festival Diwali or Ramadan or Eid or any of the country's hundreds of other excuses for a religious knees-up. So what would India be doing celebrating Christmas?

The same as everywhere else in the world it would seem, be they any of the above or Jewish, Buddhist, Zoroastrian, Rastafarian, Satanist, Pagan, Animist or just plain born again atheist. Extensive research has produced the inescapable conclusion that everyone everywhere does Christmas and that it's the amazingly successful end-product of a global corporate hallucinogen production machine project initiated to cash in on a money-making opportunity not to be missed.

And who's at the top of this great Christmas opportuni-tree? The religion-deprived communist Chinese of course. Or more precisely, an anonymous grouping of state-owned Chinese companies with a monopoly on the manufacture of Santa hats.

It took only one visit to China one December to discover this. At that time of year if you can find anywhere not drowning in garish Santa-themed tinsel tat you've discovered time travel and been transported back to the days of the cultural revolution. These days, if you're a devotee of plasticated flashing-nose fluorescent reindeer bearing the gritted teeth rictus grin of stubbed toe pain and of grossed-out rosy-cheeked Santa blow-ups with dewy oversized puppydog eyes that follow you around with Mona Lisa eeriness, you'll love Beijing.

Not so those who prefer a more traditional Christmas. The only nativity tableau I saw featured the usual cast of characters clad in white-trimmed crimson tunics and hats using the last word in Huawei phone technology to take selfies of themselves with China's latest and most audacious scientific development to date, the virgin birth.

Actually, no. I didn't see that. I made that bit up. The selfie phone wasn't in common use back then. But with its advent and in the light of something a Chinese friend told me, one can easily imagine it happening today.

Asked why the Chinese are so big on Christmas and what he knew about the event my friend first looked at me as if I was mad then softened on realising it was a genuine inquiry.

'You don't know?' he said with incredulity. 'I thought everyone knew. It's to celebrate the birth of Santa in Bethlehem.'

Now it was my turn to look incredulous. But only until I realised he was being serious. That really was the story doing the rounds. And not only in China. From Cambodian check-out girls to Congolese coolies the Santa hat has become such a global symbol of Christmas that one might easily suspect it's all a highly successful Chinese plot. One that's become so successful that not joining in the fun is regarded by some Santa fundamentalists as tantamount to blasphemy.

Don't believe me? Try getting served in a Beijing confectioners at Christmas without a Santa hat on. In the end I gave in and donned one. But on offering round the purchase I'd made, I did get the last laugh. Out of politeness the shop's staff were obliged to take one each and put in their mouths the closest thing they have in China to the humbug.

It wasn't quite as bad in Trivandrum but close. Being in the most Christian part of India at least they had a rough idea of what Christmas was all about. Not that I saw much of it. I was in therapy after the terror taxi ride with a drugged-up driver through a rainstorm to the coast. Seventeen hours of holding your breath as your driver roars past all-comers forcing oncoming traffic off the road while holding the wheel with one hand and reaching out of the window with the other to sweep torrential rainwater from the windscreen with a detached wiper blade can have a seriously unsettling effect on your psyche.

So I probably didn't do Trivandrum or the Wild Palms guesthouse justice and being struck down with what I was sure was ebola didn't help. Most of my week there was spent hacking up phlegm and sweating like a stoker in the sanctuary of my room. Or it was until Hilda, my amazingly patient hostess, decided enough was enough and that I wasn't going to miss out on a Christmas Day trip with all the other guests to the beach.

Disgorged from her minibus at a clapboard fishing village an hour from Trivandrum the guests did their best to stay on their best behaviour as the Santa hat-clad locals drank themselves into oblivion, plied us with paint stripper cocktails and started fighting when one side of a tug-o'-war contest put on for our entertainment accused the other of cheating.

Retreating hastily to the guesthouse we discovered that the day's entertainment wasn't yet over. Christmas dinner was accompanied by a singing bank manager and his dancing daughter to a karaoke selection of Abba songs. At which point I made my excuses and retired to my room to catch up with the coughing and hacking I'd been trying to suppress the whole day.

Whether it was retiring early or the noise coming from my room I don't know but suddenly Hilda's patience with me disintegrated. The next morning I was informed she needed the room for another guest and that she'd be 'obliged' if I'd make alternative arrangements. Something in her voice told me I wasn't the only one thinking it was ebola.

Thankfully it wasn't. I was just enough recovered the next day to move on, first by train to the unremarkable towns of Quilon and Allepey then a nine-hour 'pleasure' cruise up the mosquito and water hyacinth-infested lagoons/swamp of inland Kerala to Ernakulam, a jaunt that was about six hours too long for someone trying to shake the tropical shakes.

Yes, they were back. This time with a vengeance and after suffering it through a succession of vile, rubbish-strewn Kerala towns I decided I needed help. It was time to seek out someone with the skills to beat it out of my system.

I don't use the word lightly for that's exactly what happened.

Look up ayurvedic medicine on the web and it'll tell you it's a thousand year-old system of curing ills through the use of herbs and gentle massage. What it doesn't tell you is that in India there are ayurvedic hospitals staffed by brawny muscle-bound women skilled in the art of pummelling victims to pulp while simultaneously water-boarding them with hot oil and calling it medicinal therapy.

Maybe I was just unlucky. Maybe there are ayurvedic treatment centres where more humane therapies are available. I don't know. I didn't try anywhere else. Not because I'd lost faith in the whole thing but because, to my amazement, the pummelling and drowning therapy actually worked.

After subjecting myself to it for a complete week and diligently holding my nose while swallowing the disgusting 'doctor'-prescribed herbal medicine that looked and tasted like the residue of an engine oil sump, I was back to somewhere near normal. Whatever was in my system causing the ebola-like symptoms had been unceremoniously banished and after two weeks of having my sleep pattern interrupted by a hacking cough, catching the remains of my lungs in a handkerchief and seeking a dry patch in my sweat-drenched sheets I was back to more normal interruptions – having to deal with the surfeit of beer imbibed too late in the evening for a middle-aged bladder to handle.

Detractors of naturalistic medicine might argue that over that sort of time span the bug could well have worked its way out anyway without the intervention of what they'd describe as costly non-efficacious hocus pocus remedies and they may well have a point. But I'd reached the point of grasping at straws and was too weak to resist the sales patter of the ayurvedic 'doctor' who was also the co-owner of the guesthouse I'd parked myself in at Cherai Beach and who'd decided to make me a case study to promote his hospital on its website.

That wasn't explained upfront of course. Only later – and under duress – when he drove me through the gates of the hospital for my final treatment. There to greet us was a man with a video camera recording our every move, up to and including following me into the changing room where I was to strip down to my underpants in preparation for the oil water-boarding and pummellation experience.

It was at that point that I regained enough strength to query the premise of the ayurvedic treatment prescribed. How, precisely, did the videoing fit in with the treatment, I found myself enquiring of the 'doctor'?

It was the only time he failed to meet my eye. Under its penetrating glare he was eventually persuaded to mumblingly admit it was more for his benefit than mine. His hospital didn't get too many European patients – none, in fact, before me – and more might be tempted to come if they saw one on the pummel block.

'So let me get this straight,' I said. 'You were intending to video me virtually naked on the massage table drenched in oil and being worked over by your massage ladies and then put the footage on your website without consulting me. That about right?'

It was.

'And you still expect to get paid for the treatment?'

Yes.

'I think you and me need to have a little talk.'

The look on his face suggested he thought I was going to hit him, with either my fist or a law suit. The latter I was seriously considering but then on reflection realised there was mileage in this. Backed into an embarrassing corner he could hardly refuse me a serious discount on both the treatment and the accommodation at his guesthouse. Having paid not a red rupee yet on either I was seriously considering withholding payment altogether but there was the little matter of getting back to the guesthouse. The 'doctor' was my only means of transport to and from a place too far away for most tuk tuk drivers to contemplate.

In the end a deal was struck which satisfied both parties. He'd get payment for the accommodation and me off his back while I got the treatment free of charge and the right of unlimited video editing of any footage revealing the identify the near-naked torso on the massage table.

Both parties remained faithful to the deal except the 'doctor'. Despite daily requests, the footage was never produced for review and in the end, as he dropped me at the station for my onward train ride, I was forced to accept the 'doctor's' assurance that he'd ensure my identity would be protected in the final cut.

It'd been a strained car ride to the station. Apart from the lack of a review of the video certain little unexpected extras had appeared on my 'discounted' accommodation bill. Enough, in fact, to cover quite a lot of the cost of the hospital treatment.

Once again I considered refusing payment. But with a train to catch and only the 'doctor' to get me to the station, this time it was me backed into a corner. There are times when you just have to bite your lip and accept your fate.

But there are also times when fate is a double-edged sword, something the 'doctor' was about to find out when he checked his establishment's guest comment book. If my little contribution to it didn't have him biting HIS lip and tearing the page out before anyone else saw it then he's more a man of honour than I'd given him credit for.

It wasn't just vengeful malice driving me into crafting such a coruscating review of a place that the 'doctor' would have to pay people to stay there when they saw it. It was a genuine attempt to be helpful. Unless he did something to stop the guesthouse waste-water draining neat into the lagoon, he'd soon be finding it'd been reclaimed by something that'd make future guests' comments about the place make mine look positively glowing by comparison.

The thing is, Cherai Beach Resort sells itself on the uniqueness of its location and architecture. Occupying a sliver of land separating the beach from Kerala's lagoons, the resort features thatched huts perched on stilts rising out of the lagoon's landlocked waters. All sounds quite idyllic doesn't it? That's what I thought on first hearing about it. Could this be the sort of place I'd be happy returning to year after year to escape the northern winter? It could well have been but for a couple of issues that had me crossing it off the list within days of arriving.

Not only did the absence of decent outfall plumbing result in all the huts' grey water draining straight into the lagoon with the inevitable polluting result but the beach lacked any of the charms you'd normally associate with tropical strands. No friendly bar/restaurants in which to while away the hours. No coral reef to protect against the ferocious surf. And worst of all, no shade. Not a coconut palm or a bush or a casuarinas tree along the entire unwaveringly straight strip of sand making it as bleak and unforgiving as an African desert abutting the Atlantic or Indian oceans.

It was a feature I'd noticed wasn't confined to Kerala in India. Unless I was very unlucky in my choice of beaches it seemed that when the Indian sub-continent broke away from Gondwanaland, India found itself deprived of the horseshoe-shaped palm-fringed cove with protecting reef normally associated with tropical beaches. OK, I didn't try them all (Goa in particular, said by some to be becoming India's version of Blackpool) but I did give it my best shot in the time available, even braving a train, two buses and a tuk tuk to check out the beach at Pondicherry, a short hop (by Indian standards) from Chennai on India's east coast.

* * *

Reputed to be an unreconstructed remnant of France's colonial presence in India, Pondicherry had to be checked out. If it was as French as people said maybe this could be the place I was looking for. At least it'd have decent wine and cheese.

Imagine my elation on arriving to discover French colonial

architecture ranged around garden squares housing little bars and bistros, the whole lot patrolled by Indian gendarmes wearing the traditional kepi hat and looking like they'd stepped straight out of a Pink Panther film. Strolling the French-named streets I began to believe that for once on this trip hope was not going to be trashed by actuality.

Then imagine that elation evaporating on the subsequent discovery that not only was there nothing in the bars and bistros except the regular selection of beer, arak and Indian fare but that the beach was as much of a desert as any I'd tested around the country. Its only saving grace was the locals who invited me into their beachside hovels to share their meagre rations and looked on with unabashed fascination and longing as I rolled a post-prandial cigarette.

One cigarette rolled for my host led to another for his brother, his cousin, his cousin's cousin and by the time tea was served, half the village. By way of showing gratitude every one of them issued invites to return anytime to share their repast. Naturally all invites were smilingly accepted even though I'd long since decided this was to be my first and last visit to this neck of the woods. But if ever I do find myself back there I'll make sure of two things. I'll pack a great deal more tobacco and make damned sure my cholera shots are up to date.

I'll probably not live long enough for that to be a necessity, a reality that very nearly arrived sooner than expected after ticking off the last bar on my list that evening.

Inside the bar I encountered a small gaggle of Europeans engaged in heated discussion over some local issue or other and, without expecting it, got drawn into the conversation. As the evening wore on the group shrank until in the end it was just me and a rather theatrical Brit doing his best to emulate the star of the West End hit 'Jeffrey Bernard is Unwell'.

Fuelled by several more glasses of arak, he then attempted to outdo the play's perpetually pissed anti-hero by insisting we go on his motorbike to a 'real Indian bar' on the other side of town.

Intrigued and with defences lowered by my own attempts to keep up with my new tour guide's drinking capacity, I found myself being driven through trash-strewn alleys at packdog avoidance pace until amazingly, we reached our destination unscathed.

We emerged rather less so several glasses of 'real' arak later and with the last of my intact brain cells demanding that I be delivered back to my guesthouse forthwith.

There then followed a series of events so bizarre that even now I wonder if they were the product of an arak-fuelled hallucination.

The scars on my leg suggest not.

Racing through the alleyways back to our start point, our way was blocked by what from a distance looked and sounded like a fairground amusement attraction. Mounted on the back of a human-drawn trailer was a tableau of such outlandish illuminated garishness and eardrum busting distorted volume it left Chinese Christmas decorations and the cheapest of level eleven amplifiers in the shade. Without realising it we'd become part of the festival of some Hindu deity or other and were not about to be allowed to forget it by our fellow drunken revellers. Garlands were found, baptismal arak poured on our helmetless heads, powder of every colour hurled all over us and even the motorbike was blessed with flaming incense sticks stuck in the chassis rather too close to the fuel line for comfort.

But at least the tableau had forced my driver to slow down, enough to allow my addled brain to stop worrying and wonder about things other than how painful my likely imminent motorcycle accident demise would be. Things like what the hell was powering this travelling shebang.

I was soon to find out. Spotting a passing place not far ahead my companion booted the bike to turbo revs and shot past the tableau to squeak through the narrowing gap between the alleyway fence and the huge generator neither of us spotted being hauled on an even larger trailer in front of the tableau. At the speed we were going it could and should have been carnage. But as we exploded through the gap it also occurred that any slower and we'd never have made it, ending up as a surprise offering to the god on the trailer.

As it turned out that's exactly what was also going through my tour guide's mind. And was the reason he kept accelerating away from the mania continuing serenely behind us when sense suggested it was time to slow down.

In the end it wasn't sense that put paid to the hellboy flight to the dark side but a rickety fence lining a sharp bend and the rubbish-filled trench of some piquancy beyond.

Lying there wondering how much of me had survived the crash I politely enquired of the reason for the hurry. From my driver's response it was clear he'd travelled way beyond the alcoholic stage I'd reached, arriving body and soul at the doors of booze-fuelled paranoia.

'Shit man! Had to get away from that. We were being lined up as human sacrifices!'

If I'd had my way I'd have marched him straight back to ensure his paranoia was fulfilled. But by the time I staggered to my feet he was legging it away along the alley without so much as a wave goodbye leaving me scrabbling to escape from the garbage heap with a badly gashed leg and the less-than appealing prospect of having to face the rapidly approaching music alone.

With no idea of either where I was or what to do next the only choice was to throw myself at the mercy of the god on his pedestal and his wailing human sacrificing acolytes coming at me like Christmas light-bedecked Dervishes smelling blood.

In a flash they were on me dribbling and drooling and tearing off their turbans in hysterical excitement. Unable to resist being pushed to the ground by the milling throng all I could do was wait for the daggers to flash and prepare for the subsequent coup de grâce.

It never came. Opening my eyes after giving myself the last rites it became clear the only sacrifice they had in mind was that of their turbans, ripped into strips and used to bandage my leg wounds.

'Do not being concerned, sir,' said the one doing the bandaging. 'I am doctor. Recently failed from most excellent medical university of Borsetshire.'

Oh great. I sustain life-threatening wounds and the only medic for miles is one who can't even complete the course at a mythical college in a non-existent English county invented by the writers of 'The Archers', the BBC's long-running radio soap opera.

But at least the treatment staunched the blood loss and amazingly didn't lead to gangrene. The strips of turban looked like their normal use was to wipe the last remnants of curry from the cooking pot.

Maybe that's what did it. The food in this part of the world was fiery enough to kill any infection.

Even so I was glad to get back to my guesthouse to treat the wound properly. Having bandaged it so tightly I could feel my toes going numb, the 'doctor' yelled for a tuk tuk and I was delivered safe and sound to the door of my hostess who turned not a hair at being roused from her bed in the middle of the night by a drunken, coloured powder-covered guest in a torn shirt stinking of garbage and wearing a turban on his leg. Just a regular night in Pondicherry it seemed.

And a regular night in India. Say what you like about the place but one thing's for sure. It's never boring. Yes it might be polluted to hell, noisy as a newborn baby with colic and as difficult as a dyspeptic donkey but it's always absorbing.

How could it be anything other? If there isn't a political crisis there's a religious riot. If there isn't a feast day there's a wedding festival. If there isn't a drought there's a monsoonal flood. In short, even though India does have a wealth of cinema and TV choice, there's actually little need for either. You can get all the entertainment you need by simply stepping out of your front door.

And on those rare days when there's nothing much of note happening to grab the attention there's always cricket.

Always.

If ever I doubted it, all I need do is recall the ride back from the ayurvedic clinic to my Kerala guesthouse. Gazing out of the 'doctor's' car window over a landscape yielding nothing of particular interest I was yanked out of my reverie by one of the most extraordinary cricket spectacles I've ever seen.

Underway on a lagoonal island no bigger than a medium-sized marquee was a full-scale cricket match in progress complete with scoreboard, umpires, two batsmen at the crease and eleven white-clad fielders ranged around the island periphery. Even a half-hearted connection with the bat would see the ball sail over the fielders' heads and out into the lagoon, never to be seen again.

So... why? Were they on a mission to lose cricket balls?

The 'doctor' just shrugged. 'Who knows,' was all he said. 'This is India.'

It surely was.

POST-INDIA WINTER SANCTUARY CRITERIA ADDENDA

CRITERIA	ITEM	REASONING
Location	Medical	Definitely needs at least passable medical facilities, conventional if possible. Witch doctors need not apply.
	Sanitation	If environment isn't at least making an effort to be sanitary, forget it. Health is more important than sunshine.
	Beachside	There are beaches and there are beaches. Some are just extensions of desert. Avoid. Beach needs to be horseshoe shaped with healthy protective reef, shade and at least some refreshment facilities.

↑ INDIA

× JAFFNA

× VAVUNIYA (Do Not Pass Go...)

× TRINCOMALEE

× ANURADHAPURA (Ruins inc. Grand Tourist Resort)

SRI LANKA (was Ceylon)

× BATTICALOA

× KANDY (Temple of the Tooth Fairy)

× COLOMBO

× ELLA (Surrey in the Tropics)

GALLE
× UNAWATUNA
× TANGALLA
MIRISSA × × MATARA

ANTARCTICA ↓

3

SRI LANKA
The teardrop island. Just so.

Beautiful beaches, wonderful weather, fabulous food, affordable accommodation. Put those together with tremendous transportation links to an astounding array of ancient antiquities and you have all the alliterative attributes you'll ever need for selecting the perfect paradise in which to while away those wearisome winter weeks.

Agog over such reports reaching me about Sri Lanka in 1992, this was a place that had to be checked out. And to my amazement, apart from the transport description, back then it was all generally true. Well, for the southern half of the island anyway. Forget about the little matter of a savage civil war tearing the north apart and here really was somewhere that had it all.

Well, the bits I had time to check out on a two-week flit in and out of the country did and by the time I reluctantly had to leave I knew I'd be back to take a longer, closer look. Only then could I put to the sword a lingering suspicion of having been guided by a fellow traveller to the one place on the island that had so far escaped the mutilation of mass tourism.

Call me an old cynic but it wouldn't have been the first time I'd followed up on a recommendation only to discover that their idea of heaven was my idea of something, well, else. Enough times, in fact, to lead me to develop a not altogether popular theory to go with the whole idea of travel: rather than broadening, it can have the effect of narrowing the mind. Bear with me while I try to explain.

Take a group of travellers unknown to one another and put them in a bar. Ply them with drinks and listen in as the stories unfold. If they're not novices at the travel game, sooner or later you'll hear this: 'Oh, THAT place. I've been there. But it wasn't anything like you say. I found the natives to be friendly.' At which point a heated discussion will ensue over the relative merits of place X culminating in the realisation that travellers A and B had been there at different times of year with different levels of health, finances and reasons to be there and that anyway, their visits were five years apart.

To which A and B will often respond 'so what?' Regardless of the evidence there's a tendency for travellers to get quite defensive about their own findings, scrabbling around for something – anything – that'll support their own thesis which, in the process, exerts a reinforcing effect on that particular traveller's mind. Ergo, not broadened, narrowed.

The upshot, of course, is that those unfamiliar with place X can be left with a misguided impression of it and it's not just fellow travellers who're to blame. Long lead times between guidebook research and publication can result in failures to alert readers to often swift and alarming changes to a place, changes such books can help bring about themselves. One good review is all it takes for acolytes of certain guidebooks to descend on a recommended place like flies and there's one range in particular which might consider a change of name, responsible as it is for making some places so popular they end up becoming the very definition of the crowded planet.

Got a lot to answer for that guidebook range has.

Take Sri Lanka for instance.

* * *

Despite good intentions it took a full ten years for me to go back. Ten years in which a lot had happened, not least that peace had broken out in the north. Solid it was not but at least, under the auspices of a Norwegian truce brokering team, it did seem to be holding. Well enough, in fact, for reports to emerge that it was now possible to travel all the way to Jaffna on the extreme northernmost tip of the island.

If that was true, I knew the journalist still in me would not be satisfied until the route was travelled and I had no excuse for not travelling it. There were still a few weeks left of my 2001/2 Africa recovery holiday after 'doing' India, just a hop, skip and jump from Sri Lanka.

A hop, skip and jump and three varieties of smile, as it turned out. On the short flight from Chennai to Colombo I went from delight at the prospect of returning to a beach that'd put all others in the shade in 1992 to relief at having got round India more or less unscathed to the twisted smile of reluctant congratulation grudgingly awarded to the perpetrator of the last parting gift laugh India had had at my expense – a con that'd left me rather shorter of funds than anticipated.

After overnighting in a hotel near Chennai airport I emerged brain dead and not at my most attentive for an early morning onward flight.

It was just what the hotel clerk was waiting for. Presenting me with a bill for nineteen hundred Indian rupees he leaned close and whispered that he could reduce it to seventeen if I paid cash, didn't need a receipt and didn't hang around. The boss was due any minute.

Deal duly done I headed for the airport without looking back and without doing the sums. When I did, I had to applaud the scam. The cost of my one night stay shouldn't have been more than thirteen hundred rupees.

I was still laughing, almost, over what some might describe as the very definition of karma – you get what you deserve – as

I checked in at the magnificent colonial Galle Face Hotel on the Colombo seafront.

Cheap the Galle Face is not. But after six weeks of dragging my bedraggled butt from Indian flop house to Indian flop house (with the exception of the wonderful Planter's Club in Darjeeling) I reckoned a reward was due. Just for a couple of nights, but a couple of nights I knew I needed, deserved and would never forget.

The Galle Face did not disappoint. With all the wood-panelled gentility of a country house library, the hotel sucked me in, calmed me down and enveloped me in its capacious bosom to transport me back to a time that would have been familiar to Somerset Maugham and Ernest Hemingway, just two of the famous guest names engraved in the hotel's sweeping staircase panelling.[1]

'Maybe yours will join them one day,' the receptionist grinned on spying my Press card lodged next to the credit card I was using to cover the room deposit and instantly applying a healthy media discount to the bill.

Already being some way beyond the 'best before' date modern day editors privately attach to their selection of prospective correspondents, I somehow doubted it. But it didn't stop me dreaming over the avocado with masala prawn starter to my sumptuous Galle Face seafood meal that night, gazing mindlessly out over the glittering Indian Ocean from the hotel's moonlit dining verandah. Hell, I told myself, even the luminaries whose names adorned the staircase had had to start somewhere.

But probably not at Mirissa, the place I HAD to get back to without further ado. While the Galle Face was a glorious not-to-be missed experience, Mirissa – the south coast beach I'd been directed not to miss back in 1992 – was where my heart was.

---

[1] *Sadly, all staircase panelling and guest name engravings at the Galle Face Hotel were either removed or painted over in a criminal 'restoration' of the hotel in 2015. One can but hope that one day they'll be replaced with the names of those responsible and the terms of their jail sentences.*

For once the glowing report given it by a wandering Dutchman met in an Australian hostel back then did not disappoint. This was perfection personified and well worth the jolting snail-pace train ride to get there.

Changing trains at Galle, I'd started having my doubts. Drowning in sweat from the interminable cattle truck rail trip from Colombo I was about ready to give up. But then the onward train arrived and I found new resolve. This time there were so few onward travellers I could choose my seat or just sit on the steps of the open carriage door being cooled by the breeze coming off the Indian Ocean, glimpsed through the beachside palms all the way to Welligama, Mirissa's closest stop.

It didn't matter that the trip seemed to take days. Helped by the smiles and grins of my fellow passengers who seemed as happy as I was to be trundling away from the mania of Sri Lanka's big towns, I relaxed into a kind of contented trance somehow knowing I was in for a treat at Mirissa.

Two weeks later and my suspicions had been confirmed. Paradise – my idea of it at least – did exist. It consisted of lotus flower coconut milk curry dished up in prodigious quantities by the happy-go-lucky family running the lone crumbling guesthouse in Mirissa's horseshoe cove while cheering the Sri Lankan cricket team on in the World Cup screened on a shaky black and white TV after body surfing all day in the silky Indian Ocean waters with my host's five other laid-back traveller guests. Apart from the odd fisherman we really did have the palm-fringed, reef-protected, unadulterated white sand beach to ourselves, waited on hand and foot by the man from the bakery delivering hot bread straight from the oven, a pot of Marmite, a bag of cucumbers and a crate of beer.

For the pittance we were being charged for all this we could have stayed months. So why, I hear you quite reasonably ask, didn't you?

Well, for one the monsoon was due. For two, every one of our little gang of Marmite and lotus flower curry-addicted beach bums had greasy career poles to get back to. But as we drifted away there wasn't one of us who didn't vow to return one day.

I can't speak for the others but for me the opportunity to fulfil the vow didn't arise until my round-India odyssey was done with in 2002.

Would it be the same?

'Course not. Ten years is a long time in the life of anywhere finding itself included in certain travel guidebooks. More than enough for it to move out of obscurity and succumb to the horrors the touristic limelight brings.

To begin with, all the ease of booking a train seat to get there had vanished. Now it was a sweat-drenched scrum at Colombo station, foreign travellers climbing over one another to grab any seat overlooked by locals using the windows as carriage entry shortcuts. One glimpse of the mayhem was enough to convince me there had to be a better way.

Fortunately there was. With air-conditioned buses now a feature of the Sri Lankan landscape (presumably as a cash cow response to the pleas of foreigners finding themselves the victims of rail travel madness) it was now possible to go pretty much door-to-door to Mirissa, avoiding both Galle and Welligama in the process.

There was a reason why Mirissa was now a regular stop. Seven more guesthouses/bars/restaurants had been added to the single one there in 1992 including the imposing Paradise Beach Club built to attract a more upmarket punter to the beach. But at least the new places were generally in keeping with the environment, mostly low level affairs hidden by the palm groves they nestled in.

Oddly, the biggest sore thumb in all this beauty was the very place I'd stayed ten years earlier. Not only had the owners expanded outwards but upwards. At three floors high, the concrete block they'd thrown up had all the architectural charm of a Stalin-designed multi-storey car park and if I expected the guesthouse's ambience and menu not to have changed I was in for a shock. In the time I'd been away Sri Lanka's version of sophistication had arrived. Small individual plastic tables had replaced the big communal wooden one and now everything seemed to come with chips. Except the lotus flower curry. That'd gone altogether.

So had the bakery and the beach's seclusion. In their place was a bar/restaurant run by an itinerant Irishman and rank upon rank of sun worshippers protectively claiming their own patch of sand under the coconut palms as their own. It was almost too much to bear. Or it was until one sun worshipper narrowly missed getting a coconut on the head. Does anyone ever get killed by falling coconuts, I asked my guesthouse host? 'Oh, yes,' he grinned. 'Eighteen every year. All German.'

Buoyed by this news I decided to hang around for a while to witness the spectacle. I was glad I did. Although there were no more falling coconut incidents it was clear that all the development hadn't totally emasculated the ambience I first felt at Mirissa. Seclusion was still possible if you looked for it, the water was still clear and best of all, the turtles hadn't abandoned the beach. Despite the bar and restaurant lights and music now polluting the beach environment you could still have a close encounter with a turtle laying her eggs. And if you were there at the right time, to witness the end-product of the egg-laying performance.

I was one of the lucky ones. Three-fourths cut and about to retire for the night after falling about to our genial Irish host Jimmy's story of the Irishman shipwrecked on an island of cannibals who used the skins of their victims to make canoes and pricking himself all over with a fork so they couldn't use his, the entourage at our outside table on the beach simultaneously shrieked and leapt onto their chairs.

'What der fock is dat?' squawked Jimmy flashing his torch under the table to see what was tickling our feet.

'Jayzus! Would you look at dat?' We were being attacked by baby turtles. Not just one or two but hundreds and all going in the wrong direction. Or rather, any direction except towards the sea. Something had to be done and after a brief drunken discussion on the ethics of interfering with nature, we did it. To prevent the little fellas becoming beach dog food we scurried inebriatedly around gathering buckets of turtles and carefully depositing them into the lapping waves where they were instantly gobbled up by pointy-toothed predators lurking offshore. Not really. Or at least I hoped not. The thought of it wouldn't have done much to augment the warm glow of smug self-congratulation as we settled back down and ordered more celebratory beers.

'Anyone get a picture of dat?' asked Jimmy.

The entourage just looked at one another.

No matter. We had the memory. One that helped sustain me through any thoughts of Mirissa being on its way to being finished as a tranquil retreat for weary travellers. I'd keep coming back as long as the turtles did and as I packed for a trip upcountry I could put off no longer, I knew it wouldn't be long. Or it wouldn't be providing the immigration authorities didn't have other ideas.

* * *

When it comes to extending visas in a place like Sri Lanka the guidebooks have a habit of outlining the process but then failing gloriously to give you the full flavour of the experience. Had they done so I might have been more prepared for what was about to hit me at the visa extension office in Colombo.

So hot and humid inside that even the fans were melting, I was confronted by what seemed to be the entire population of the East Bloc trying to do the same as me but with rather less grasp of English, Sri Lanka's working language. Within minutes it was clear that unless I could come up with a cunning plan for circumventing the system the office would very likely close before my rapidly dehydrating presence was called to the counter.

Thank God for the Press card. It'd already got me into a sold-out cricket match in Chennai, won me a healthy discount at the Galle Face Hotel and I had no qualms about abusing it again now, this time for the sake of sheer survival.

Even so, I was surprised at the speed with which it worked in a government office. If this had been Africa its use would undoubtedly have led to me being abandoned in an airless cell-like waiting room while the minister who didn't want to see me legged it into the bush.

Here, I was in to see the big cheese in minutes, got the visa extension in moments and even got a scoop out of him. As frustrated as me over the antediluvian visa extension process he'd been charged with supervising he wasn't backward in urging me to give it the full coruscating review treatment. It might help win him the funds to bring his department out of the dark ages.

I never did find out if it worked. With the nightmare of that office fresh in my mind when planning a return to Sri Lanka in 2007 I paid through the nose for a longer-term three month visa at the country's London embassy before booking the flight.

One thing I did find out though in 2002 was that reports of the rail line being open all the way to Jaffna at the northernmost tip of the island were, as Mark Twain might have put it, a trifle exaggerated.

Dragging myself away from Mirissa to fulfil the journalistic challenge I'd set myself I wondered whether I'd be the first western Pressman for years to make it further than the mid-island tourist town of Anuradhapura.

Yes, it turned out, and no.

Yes, I got to within sniffing distance of Jaffna but no, the barricades across the rail line at Vavuniya, fifty kilometres north of Anuradhapura, were a pretty good indication that once again I'd been misinformed. Neither was there a bus service going any further, something made very clear to me by the crisply uniformed military man whose eyebrows nearly shot off the top of his head on seeing a westerner get off the train from Anuradhapura.

It was a reaction I'd got used to on this part of the trip. First from the ticket office clerk at Anuradhapura on trying to get a ticket all the way to Jaffna, then from the ticket inspector aboard the train and finally from the seventeen other passengers. Male without exception, my fellow travellers spent the entire two-hour rickety ride through swathes of abandoned farmland turning to jungle trying not to meet the eye of any of the others and sweating in the way men about to hand themselves into the police after being promised an amnesty they weren't sure they could trust would sweat.

The silence of that trip was deafening, rising to a thunderclap as we pulled into Vavuniya station where a heavy military presence at a desk separating us from the exit eyed the new arrivals through narrowed slits. But only until they spotted me. Unable to disguise their astonishment, the slits turned to twin full moons and the silence was shattered by the collective thud of military jaws hitting the ground.

Unlike my fellow travellers queuing nervously to present their credentials at the checkpoint desk – and, I think, much to their relief – I was suddenly the centre of attention. The one given the fast-track treatment to the front of the queue where the man in the crisp army uniform greeted me with the frozen, stone-eyed look of one expecting to have his day ruined.

Mine in return was intended as one of reassurance that I had no such intention. That all I was was a stupid middle-aged western tourist blithely unaware of having blundered into a war zone. Presenting him with my Press card, I surmised, wasn't likely to be quite as well received as at the visa extension office.

'What you do here?' he managed at last.
'Visiting the town.'
'Why?'
'I heard the line to Jaffna is now open... or that there's a

bus service,' I said, glancing beyond him to the barbed wire encrusted, firmly padlocked level crossing gates preventing any further progress up the warped and heavily rusted rail lines.

If you've ever been on the receiving end of someone thinking you've lost your reason, you'll know the look that comment got.

'No train. No bus,' said the man without smiling.

'Oh dear. Have I missed it?'

Damn, still no smile.

'Yes.'

'By long?'

'Yes.'

'How long?'

'Nineteen years.'

At last, just the hint of a smile.

Gotcha, I thought. The man does have a soft centre. Let's see how far we can go with this.

'Hmmm. Can you tell me when the next one will be?'

Stony face returns. It tells me everything I need to know plus the information that the next train back to Anuradhapura is in an hour. 'Be on it,' the look says.

'Could I take a look at the town while I'm waiting?' I venture cautiously.

A brief discussion with other military types later and he nods his approval – with the addendum that I have one hour. No longer. He doesn't need to tell me what will happen if I miss the train.

Only problem is my bag. It's big and heavy and I don't want to have to haul it round town. Any chance of leaving it here?

To my amazement he casually indicates to leave it under his desk. Well, at least it's unlikely to be tampered with there... unless it's searched for explosives while I'm gone. That wouldn't come as much of a surprise.

What did was that the town wasn't especially militarised. Most people seemed to be going about their business normally and the only military presence I came across was in the form of an army driver dozing at the wheel of his parked truck and two heavily-armed squaddies wobbling down the road on a bicycle checking the numbers on their lottery tickets. In fact, if you didn't know there was a war on you'd have assumed it was just another day in a provincial Sri Lankan town.

That's obviously what my 'friend' at the station thought too. Arriving back in time to catch the return train I dragged my bag out from under his desk to discover no sign of it having been moved or opened. With the padlock still in place and no evidence of forced entry I was left with no option but to conclude that either it'd been carefully replaced under the desk after being x-rayed or that no one was too bothered about being blown up by the bomb it may or may not have contained.

If there was one thing that left me anxious to get away from the place without further ado it was that. With security so lax anything could happen, as the train pulled out I breathed again. They could keep Vavuniya and everywhere else in the north if that was a realistic reflection of the public protection measures in operation.

After a couple of nights in Anuradhapura at the grossly misnamed Grand Tourist Resort where the water tasted like it'd come neat from the nearby lake and where I narrowly escaped severing an artery when my foot went straight through the plastic shower tray, I decided they could have that as well. Well, most of it. The ancient Buddhist monuments at nearby Minitale were worth the trip as was the evening spent at Sri Lanka's holiest Buddhist spot, the Bodhi tree, at a time of the Poya Day full moon celebration.

Grown from a cutting from the very tree under which the Buddha gained enlightenment in India I expected there to be a modicum of commercialisation of the site but nothing could have prepared me for what I encountered.

You didn't need to join the hordes of pilgrims trudging

joyously towards the tree to find it. As the sun went down the lights of the monster shrine built to almost obscure the actual tree lit up like Piccadilly Circus and in case your eyesight wasn't up to seeing it the illuminations were accompanied by the sort of noise that'd ensure there'd be no Buddha-like enlightenment for anyone that night. Except, oddly, for me.

Ducking into the biggest of any number of shrines surrounding the tree I almost tripped over a carpet of devotees lying prostrate on the floor frantically genuflecting and praying to a vast ornate Buddha built against the tree's trunk.

I'm not sure what I did expect but it wasn't that. Surely praying was reserved for gods. And since the Buddha himself said he wasn't a god – or so I'd read somewhere – didn't that make all the praying and genuflection a bit contradictory and futile?

With all others in attendance too preoccupied to enlighten me I was left to draw my own conclusions. One of us had surely got the whole concept of Buddhism wrong. And since, from the minimal research I'd done on what some erroneously call a religion I considered it wasn't me, all I could do was walk away shaking my confused head.

I was shaking it again the next day as I arrived back in Kandy. Coming into the town the bus I'd taken had to stop to let what looked like a demo march across the road. Only on seeing the banner at the head of the march did it become apparent this wasn't a demo as such. 'World's First Ever Twins for Peace March' the banner read, behind which were about two hundred sets of twins happily tramping off to a rally somewhere.

The full significance of this escaped me until alighting from the bus. There on the pavement was a man wearing possibly the most tasteless T-shirt ever – a cartoon of a plane crashing into the twin towers. It was, I suddenly realised, exactly six months since 9/11 and definitely time to hit the beach again. I'd been away too long.

* * *

Which beach though? Mirissa was the obvious candidate but after seeing what had happened to it in my decade-long absence it didn't have the draw it used to. So how about the east coast? With the ceasefire still holding, maybe Trincomalee would suit my needs. Out of bounds while the fighting was going on, there was no way it could have been touristised. Could it be like stepping back in time to the Mirissa of the nineties?

Sadly, despite three attempts to get there, I was never to find out. Before leaving Anuradhapura I'd tried to check out buses to Trinco only to be met with a bus schedule I couldn't read and local reaction to my presence at best described as cautious.

Under normal circumstances in the more under-developed parts of the world I've found that adopting the lost lamb look in bus and train stations usually attracts sometimes too many offers of help, frequently with a gawping audience and always with conflicting advice from all quarters. It's then a case of putting your faith in your inner Jedi and trusting your instincts to choose from the panoply of suggested possibilities. It never ceases to amaze how often the method works. Allowed the freedom to do its thing the force is a powerful guiding instrument.

But it only works if there's a range of options to choose from. In Anuradhapura there were none. Not one offer of help from fellow local travellers and I couldn't help but wonder if it was the product of word being put round by the owners of the Grand Tourist Resort that the writer of the excoriating review that had appeared in their guestbook the day I left was to be denied help in leaving town until he recanted and said something nice.

Was it my imagination or was that a collective look of disappointment around me when, after thirty minutes of dehydrating unaccosted in the blazing sun, I abandoned all hope of finding a bus to Trincomalee and boarded one clearly marked to be going to Kandy? Imagination if subsequent events were anything to go by for it was the same in Kandy. The surprise solitude I once more enjoyed in their bus station was suggestive of the reaction you'd expect from a group of people finding a leper in their midst. The look on the faces of those close-by when I gave in and headed for the railway station was clearly one of relief, not disappointment.

Illumination, when it came, had me slapping myself for not seeing it and thanking the railway ticket clerk for being kind enough to put me straight.

Intending to abandon all hope of seeing the east coast and heading straight back to Mirissa via Colombo the clerk was about to issue the ticket when I realised the narrow-gauge train up into the Sri Lanka highlands was due out. That, I thought, would make an interesting diversion. Word was that the highlands were high enough to have a climate not unlike London's gin and tonic belt, the reason why British colonialists had built a series of English village lookalikes there to retreat to during the steaming monsoon. If that was true it'd be worth a look and I could probably get a bus down to Mirissa, avoiding the horrors of Colombo in the process.

Or maybe, just maybe, I could find a bus from the highlands to the east coast. Did the clerk know?

'Which part of east coast, sahib?'

'Well, I was hoping to get to Trinco but I've had trouble finding the right bus.'

'No bus from Kandy, sahib. Maybe from Anuradhapura. You want ticket go there?'

A-ha. A cue to recount the strange events of the past few hours.

Listening intently with head wobbling as I related how I'd failed to find the right bus at either the Anuradhapura or Kandy terminus's and how unusual it was for no one to step up to help at either location, the man's grin transformed into the knowing look of one who was about to impart a great secret.

'You asked go Trinco?'

'Eventually, yes.'

'You have this thing when ask?' he said, indicating my bulky backpack.

'Yes.'

'Well, that is problem,' he said as if that explained everything.

'Sorry. Why?'

'Big bag, sahib. Problem for people.'

'But I was happy to buy two tickets, one for me, one for the bag. Like on other buses I've been on.'

'Not problem of bag on seat, sahib. Problem of what in bag.'

'It's just clothes. What did they think was in it?'

'Bomb, sahib. You carry big bag on bus to Trinco. Maybe you Tiger suicide man.'

* * *

I was still in a state of shock as I settled into my seat on the narrow-gauge train trundling up to the English village film set that was the town of Ella in the high country. I'd been compared to a lot of things in my time but this was a new one. Tamil Tiger suicide bomber? Really? Were they recruiting ageing westerners now to do their dirty work? Or had my time in the sun left me more dark-pallored than I thought. The absence of a decent mirror in recent days had made close scrutiny impossible and my clothes hadn't seen a washing machine for a while. Could I really pass for a local?

It was left to the embodiment of ethereal elegance who'd materialised in the seat next to mine to put my mind at rest.

Austrian by birth my neighbour fixed me with her drown-in-me deep blue eyes for rather longer than felt altogether comfortable and gave me the assurance I was seeking with one word.

'Unlikely,' she said. 'Ze clothes need to vizit zer laundry, ja,' she opined with a twinkle of mock disdain, 'but ze eyes say vesterner. Zey could never be mistaken vor Asian.'

Sucked down into the vortex of those deep blues for the

entirety of the six-hour train ride into the highlands I only started coming up for air as I was disgorged, stunned and disorientated, onto the platform at Ella, the train disappearing from view with my new friend gazing impassively back at me through the panoramic window of the observation car.

Left helpless and floundering in a whirlpool of other-world connectivity with someone who'd seemed capable of seeing well beyond the eyes she never stopped looking into, as I struggled to get my bearings at Ella I wondered when the accompanying shortness of breath would subside.

Not for a while, as it turned out, not least because Ella was a good bit higher and chillier than expected. High enough for tea to grow and cool enough for my tropical coast-acclimatised respiratory system to rebel.

Shrouded in mist for the entire two days I stayed at a ramshackle tea plantation guesthouse, the weather could not have been a better reflection of my fogged state of mind. The altitude, the chill dampness of the thin air, the utter absence of warm clothing and the out-of-body trip up the mountain with someone who seemed to know me better than I knew myself combined to turn both body and brain to mush.

Starting with a streaming nose the moment I reached my room, within the hour I was shivering with the sort of fever only previously experienced at the onset of a bout of malaria in Africa and I knew there was only one thing for it. Abandon the search for buses to the east coast and flee from this bloody mountain forthwith. Only the silky warm waters of Mirissa could cure this.

A lengthy expensive taxi ride later in which the driver put the fear of God up me by stopping at a roadside shrine to pray before hurtling fatalistically round hairpin bends on the plunging mountainside road down to the coast and I was back in the warm bath of the Indian Ocean, miraculously cured after just a couple of dips.

Restored to health, I considered a resumption of the quest

eastwards but quickly thought better of it. My flight out was imminent and another period of mindless beachlife seemed the more sensible option. It'd allow time to ponder on whether I'd had the best of Mirissa and whether it was time to move on, resuming the search for a regular winter retreat further afield.

* * *

By the time I got back to the UK the decision had been made. I'd give Sri Lanka one more chance to prove it could resist the ravages of tourism, but not immediately. Work assignments for the following couple of winters would mean a temporary suspension of the quest for a regular winter retreat. But I'd be back, probably for the winter of 2004/5.

I was well into planning my return when everything changed. A work assignment came up forcing me to shelve the trip and instead face the dubious pleasure of spending the winter of 2004/5 in Beijing. It was an assignment that probably saved my life. While I was shivering through the Chinese winter deep-freeze reports started coming in of a massive subsea earthquake off Indonesia triggering an enormous tsunami wave that'd swept across the Indian Ocean and decimated Sri Lanka's southern coast, Mirissa in particular.

As reports of the numbers of dead and missing continued to climb into the hundreds of thousands, so did the feelings of personal guilt. I should have been there when the wave struck. I too should have been a victim. But the only victimhood I could claim was of being a victim of circumstance. A circumstance which had undoubtedly saved me and one which meant only one course of action was open to me. A pilgrimage had to be mounted to plead for absolution for surviving through an accident of timing. Only then was I likely to shake the feeling of the tsunami victims' eyes being forever on me.

As despicably self-centred as that sounds it's as nothing

compared with a truly disgusting parallel thought I couldn't shake no matter how I tried. If Mirissa had felt the full impact of the wave, would that mean this former paradise on Earth might had reverted to the way it was in the nineties? Might all that vile touristic excess have been swept away leaving a once more pristine, untouched beach in its wake?

As heinous as the thought was I couldn't help it occurring. Nor that the disaster might be regarded by some as divine retribution, nature's vengeance on Sri Lanka's inhabitants for the way they'd disrespected their paradise home. Hadn't something similar happened to Adam and Eve?

It was to take until the winter of 2007/8 for an answer of sorts to come. Delayed for various reasons, by the time I did fulfil my pilgrimage, if it had been regained, paradise had been lost again. In my absence the whole south coast had not only rebounded like grasslands after a bushfire but with a vengeance that'd have shocked even the first inhabitants of the Garden of Eden. Sri Lanka's tsunami survivors had taken full, gleeful advantage of the massive reconstruction funds on offer and not only rebuilt but, in the absence of any development constraint, seemed intent on outdoing the jungle for feverish chaotic growth.

Concrete monstrosities – funded by the donations sent to help Sri Lanka recover from what some locals had allegedly re-named the Golden Wave – had sprung up everywhere, not least at Unawatuna near Galle where new buildings seemed to have been constructed on the wreckage of their pre-tsunami predecessors without much apparent attempt to clear the rubble.

Stopping at Una for a few nights to take in the first international cricket match in Galle since the wave decimated the city's unique cricket ground, I wondered whether they'd taken the time to clear all the corpses. At the speed the reconstruction was going it seemed entirely possible that the new Unawatuna was quite literally being built on the backs of those who hadn't run fast enough. In fact, despite all the lights and noise of the beach bars at one of Sri Lanka's premier tourist hotspots, there was a definite creepy feeling walking on the beach at night and although I desperately wanted to, I just couldn't bring myself to go in the sea. Three years just didn't seem long enough for either the spirits or their mortal remains to have dissipated.

It was a feeling I saw reflected in the eyes of those who'd lived to tell the tale. Some were still so in shock that the tale could only be told through the look in those eyes. Words to go with it could simply not be formed.

It was a look I desperately hoped I wouldn't be seeing again at Mirissa.

But there it was. Mirissa hadn't escaped the wave and the evidence was all around. The fishing harbour area in the next bay along had been especially hard hit and as I wandered dazed along the quay I looked for the place I'd considered buying during my last trip here. With a bit of fixing up it would have made a fine winter retreat.

Gone. That and a host of other small houses along the port's front were no more. In their place a barren wasteland looking like it was being readied for some large development scheme. Cleared on purpose or simply a victim of the tsunami? I'd read that the Chinese had arrived in Sri Lanka to start a surreptitious colonisation of the island. Had the Mirissa harbour been singled out for special attention? It didn't take long to find the answer.

After stumbling on a sign containing Chinese characters I wandered though the village streets looking for more evidence of oriental incursion. None was immediately apparent but there was plenty that the harbour had felt the full force of the wave. Any number of houses had been reduced to rubble and half a kilometre inland I discovered two large fishing boats gradually being swallowed by the jungle. Had I gone through with the house purchase that could well have been me.

Wandering back to the beach in a daze I found myself drawn to a small school with children's voices chanting a Singalese song.

Stopping to listen, a teacher beckoned me inside. Immediately the singing stopped. I apologised profusely for the interruption and made to leave. No no, said the teacher showing me to a seat at the front, tapping her baton on the desk and prompting the children to start again from the top. I was, it turned out, both the audience and the guest of honour.

By the time I emerged an hour later I was almost in tears. The plaintive songs the children were singing were a rehearsal for the imminent anniversary of their collective parents' deaths. Every one was a tsunami orphan and this complete stranger who'd missed the tsunami by a hair's breadth had been honoured with a command performance of their repertoire. It was almost too much to take.

And almost too much to prevent me avoiding a nasty bout of rabies. With my mind more on the there-and-then than the here-and-now I found I'd wandered blindly into the midst of another group of tsunami orphans – a pack of snarling dogs left to run wild when their owners failed to come home. With a jolt I was back in the present whirling desperately around looking for a tree to climb.

In the end I didn't need one. Seeing my plight a group of young boys raced at the dogs with sticks and drove them off. So that was twice in one day the direction of my life had been guided by children. Was this going to be the general tenor of this trip?

In a way it was. By the time I left the country my future had once again been dictated by children but not in a way they'd have looked on with any degree of pleasure. With so many left parentless, this part of Sri Lanka had become a magnet for every disgusting paedophile with an overactive libido and that alone was enough to leave no doubt this was not the place for a regular winter hideaway.

* * *

On first arriving back at Mirissa I hadn't immediately spotted the paedophile link and there was certainly nothing about it in the guidebooks. Put generously, perhaps, like me, their researchers were too busy bemoaning the other changes to notice what was happening behind Mirissa's reconstructed façade.

While parts of the beach had obviously taken a tsunami pounding, other sections had escaped virtually unscathed. But every bit had been subjected to another, equally devastating, disaster – indiscriminate slapdash development. Now there was hardly a square foot of beachfront not developed, every guesthouse and bar/restaurant lit up like Christmas and draining its waste straight into the sea. No wonder the water was cloudy and those braving it suffering eye infections, sore throats and upset stomachs.

And that wasn't all. With the newly-equipped fishing fleet taking to dynamite fishing, the reef had been all but destroyed and with it, ironically, protection of the cove from the waves. Result: the surf was definitely bigger and more dangerous than before, something that had attracted the attention of both the worldwide surfing community and those intent on cashing in on the surfing dollar.

Now, Mirissa was booming in every respect. With all the surf money pouring in the bars now had the money to invest in bigger and boomier amplification, much of it starting up in the latter stages of the evening and lasting right through til breakfast. No wonder I saw not one turtle on the beach during the whole of my stay. They had more sense.

It didn't take me long to follow their lead. With most of the hullabaloo gravitating to the centre and one end of the beach I fled to the other to take up residence in the sprawling traditional Giragala guesthouse. Here at least one could just about sleep without earplugs.

Could it last? Judging by the pace of change at Mirissa I'd have put money on this last bastion of relative tranquillity being overrun in months. It was time to look reality in the face and go in search of an alternative. But where? With 'development' coming in from the west – in both senses of the word – moving east seemed the only possible escape route. During my 2002 visit I'd noticed a couple of places east of Mirissa that seemed to have so far escaped the tourist mauling. It was time to take a closer look.

It didn't take long to discover I was too late. Someone had been there in my absence and set up camp. The smallish town of Matara had sold its soul to the Chinese devil and the beach outpost of Tangalla seemed to have collectively decided to become a bankers' retreat.

It was the absence of local produce in the Matara market, now replaced with Chinese fruit and vegetables, and the soaring prices of Tangalla's accommodation that gave the game away. Tasteless applied to both in equal proportion.

Although Mirissa wasn't much better, at least you could still buy locally-dynamited fish there and I fled back to the beach to while away the remainder of my visa. When it finally ran out, I fled from Mirissa and from Sri Lanka *per se*.

It'd taken just fifteen years to go from outback paradise to inback purgatory and I knew that that was that for me and Sri Lanka. Whoever named it the teardrop island didn't know how prescient the description was. Now, it wasn't just the shape the description applied to... and it was partly my fault. Having vowed not to in 1992, the name might have slipped out over drinks bought for me by those who'd yet to develop a healthy suspicion of travellers' tales.

Shit. Another lesson learned.

POST-SRI LANKA WINTER SANCTUARY CRITERIA ADDENDA

CRITERIA	ITEM	REASONING
Location	Not a war zone	Additional visa and insurance conditions apply and packing a flak jacket pushes you into excess baggage territory.
	Not guidebook featured	Following good review, seclusion is almost guaranteed to be impossible. You're not the only person reading it.
	Security conscious	Lack of makes relaxation unlikely.
	Earthquake-free	Almost impossible to guarantee but steering clear of primary tectonic belts helps.
	Paedophile-free	Ditto above. What is it about earthquake zones that attract these vile people?
	Chinese influence-free	Places not resisting Chinese economic colonialism unvaryingly become flooded with tasteless food imports in both senses of the word.
Accommodation	Honest management	Good luck with that.
	Good storage	Crucial for storing the bulky unnecessary winter clothes you left home in.

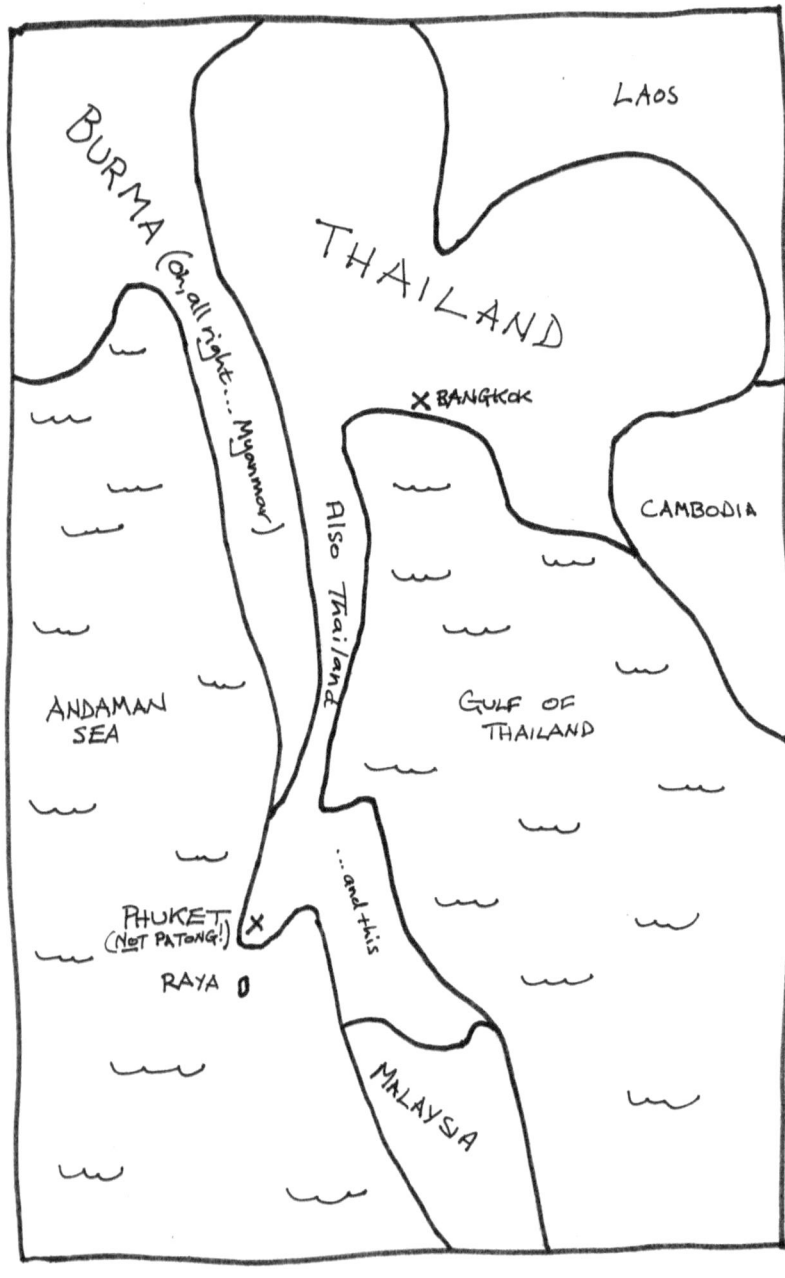

4

THAILAND
Eden, gardened to death

War can seriously ruin your holiday. Take my word for it. After the Sri Lanka truce collapsed, a spate of bombings prior to my 2007 trip had put all but the south coast beaches off-limits and the place I'd chosen as an alternative – Thailand – looked very much like going the same way a year later.

Just days before I was due to fly out violence erupted between the country's red and yellow shirt political groups, one lot occupied Bangkok's main airport, someone was killed and tourists started fleeing the country in drug-fuelled droves. It looked like Thailand was on the verge of disintegrating and I was about to arrive for a three-month fact-finding stay. Good timing Newham.

Had there been a chance of getting my money back I might well have cancelled. But with the UK Foreign Office yet to issue a 'don't go near the place' advisory and both airlines and insurance companies refusing to consider reimbursement until it did, it looked like I was stuck with it. Ah well, in for a penny I suppose. Too mean to give up a paid-for ticket I headed for the airport. Anyway there could well be a story in it.

I'd tried to kick the journalism habit in favour of seeking out less newsworthy winter sojourn backwaters, I really had. But journalism obviously hadn't finished with me. 'Just one last little story,' it was taunting. 'You know you want to.'

Did I? Hadn't I had enough of adrenalin rush? And what about that dodgy knee picked up in Mirissa's cartilage mangling surf? Could be the difference between getting a scoop and getting caught in crossfire, my inner voice was nagging. You sure you want to risk it?

Fortunately Thailand answered the question before I had to. The flare-up lasted about as long as the Sri Lankan truce and by the time I arrived in Bangkok it was as if nothing had happened. Street riot was now limited to food vendors fighting for trade and the mad traffic stinking the city up.

Even so, I wasn't taking any chances. White shirts only for me, I decided, hoping there wasn't a white shirt political party as well. For all I knew the white shirt faction could be the one so universally hated by all the others they'd abandon their internecine fighting and unite to attack. Ah well, done now. No other colour packed.

* * *

After my 1992 and 2002 trips to Sri Lanka I'd pretty much decided I need look no further for a regular winter retreat. Where else could fit the bill so snugly?

My return to Mirissa five years later answered the question. Almost anywhere.

'So why not Thailand?' said a German layabout met in a guesthouse near Galle. That's where he was heading.

Too popular and commercial, surely. Thailand had been on the map too long for it to have escaped the worst ravages of budget airline-fuelled tourist incursion.

Not so, said the layabout. Like anywhere, Thailand had its fair share of tourist hotspots but it was still possible to find sanctuary. 'Come to Phuket and I'll show you what I mean.'

With my traveller's tales scepticism antennae yet to be fully grown as the 2008/09 winter loomed I found myself booking a flight. What was the worst that could happen? It might not be the tourist backwater I was seeking but at least cuddly little peace-loving Buddhist Thailand was hardly likely to lapse into the sort of violence Sri Lanka was experiencing. Yeah, right.

By the time I got to Bangkok all seemed quiet but even so I decided not to tarry too long. The city's 'delights' were well known and needed little additional investigation to know it could be added to the list of winter retreat rejects without further ado. So, after a couple of nights in a city centre hotel to get over the jet lag and the shock of nearly busting a tooth when Gulf Air decided to have a laugh at my expense and hide bones in the lamb curry, it was back to the airport for a super cheap Air Asia flight to Phuket on Thailand's west coast. After the glowing reports the German layabout had given it a dim memory had surfaced. This was the magical paradise some good friends went to get married in the eighties. Their pictures showed nothing but deserted palm-fringed beach after deserted palm-fringed beach skirting untainted azure waters where they'd skipped and played unaccosted in much the same way I had in Mirissa in the nineties.

OK, I wasn't blind to the fact that things might have changed since then, but even so nothing prepared me for what I was about to encounter. Three minutes in Patong, Phuket's prime tourist hotspot, was enough to tell me that wires had become tangled in the German/English translation. 'A good place to unwind,' had been the GL's review of Patong. Was 'unwind' the German for 'wind up'?

As the airport bus lurched into town there was every indication that it was. My first memorable view of an otherwise unmemorable sprawl was of a roadside bar heaving with fat white middle-aged semi-naked men drunkenly pawing diminutive Thai hostesses. And it wasn't even lunchtime yet.

Now no one's ever accused me of being a prude – well, not to my face anyway – but the spectacle spurred a puritan spirit in me I didn't know I possessed and as I got off the bus at the Chinese-owned hotel where the GL was staying another alien feeling stirred. From nowhere I suddenly knew how the first missionaries into Sodom and Gomorrah must have felt.

Bars like the one encountered on Patong's outskirts punctuated the town like rotten teeth and where there wasn't one there was a 'massage' parlour you couldn't pass without being ambushed. The throngs of 'available' masseuses milling like under-sized underfed vultures outside made making it to any of the local restaurants unmolested all but impossible and the torture didn't stop on reaching them. Finding something to eat that hadn't been poaching all day/week under the burning Patong sun became a nightly argument ritual and by the end of the third night when one of the town's infamous ladyboys all but dragged me to see the 'spectacular' in which (s)he was appearing I knew I'd exhausted all the pleasures Patong had to offer. It was time to move on.

But where? I needed somewhere to recover my senses and hopefully discover the unadulterated Thailand the GL had assured me still existed.

'Raya Island. That's the place for you,' he ventured.

From his description it sounded ideal. But this was the GL talking. The man who'd parked himself in Patong declaring it to be 'my sort of place' and the man who'd also raved about Sri Lanka's Unawatuna, one of the most debased, overpopulated tourist hotspots in the country. Maybe, I was beginning to think, his 'good place' criteria and mine weren't in perfect symmetrical alignment.

So the Raya Island recommendation was approached with extreme caution. If it was anything like his other recommendations I wouldn't even bother unpacking.

My face must have betrayed my thoughts because at that very moment the hotel's Chinese owner intervened.

'Why not check out with day trip?' he suggested. 'I get you good discount.'

It took some persuading but in the end I found myself

crammed into a minibus with a thousand Chinese tourists all getting discounts far better than mine to spend a day speed-boating out to Raya and back in time for the nightly hunt for something salmonella-free to eat.

On first sight I wished the boat would turn straight round and take me back to the mainland. Beyond the quay was a beach overrun by the sort of humanity that knew the price of everything and the value of nothing basking in front of the kind of tourist resort that to any self-respecting real traveller would qualify as the last resort.

Fortunately, this time I'd been forewarned about what to expect and how to avoid it. Spotting a face that didn't fit the regular overfed tour group passenger profile one of the deckhands had taken pity on me. Or was it taken advantage of? I wasn't quite sure. Knowing a representative of the non-tour group genus when he saw one he'd recommended I walk straight past the quayside resort and check out a place on the far side of the island run by his cousin or mother or great grandfather or someone. His English was as bad as my Thai.

'Take it for word, sah. You place that like better much.'

With any recommendation from anyone being received with narrowed eyes after the GL's last two 'good place' reviews I had a mind to do the exact opposite of what was being suggested. But since I had a good three hours to wait in this tourist hell before the boat left on the return leg I thought I might as well give the deckhand's half-understood directions a go.

I was glad I did. Thirty minutes later, just as I was beginning to think about retracing my footsteps back through the tangled jungle that had swallowed me up without me realising it, voices up ahead made me think again. These weren't the voices of equally lost tubby tourists. These were the singsong sound of Thai island locals skipping through the mess of vegetation towards recognisable habitation and something told me to follow their lead.

Minutes later I emerged from the forest to find myself staring at the sort of bay I'd begun thinking didn't exist in Thailand. It was the spitting image of Mirissa in the nineties, a horseshoe-shaped white sand cove flanked by tree-shrouded headlands with a surf-breaking reef ranged across the entire mouth and nobody on it. I rubbed my eyes and looked again.

Yes, it was still there. But this time small thatched huts had been added to the vista. Huts that could only belong to the guesthouse of the deckhand's cousin/mother/great grandfather and without any help from me my legs propelled me excitedly towards them.

This cannot be happening, I kept telling myself. It's EXACTLY the image I was carrying in my head of the place I could return to time and again without getting bored. Who could EVER get bored with such perfection? There had to be a catch. It was too perfect not to have one. A catch like being full and without an opening for months, years, ahead surely.

But even getting closer to what was clearly the restaurant/bar/office I bumped into no one. Was it deserted? Not by the looks of the neatness of the place. Tables on the stilt-perched restaurant terrace had tablecloths, dust-free magazines and books were arranged in a rack and there was no sign of invasive vegetation. But there was also no sign of whoever was running it. I had only one option. I sat down at a terrace table overlooking the stunning beach and waited.

Mesmerised by the gently lapping clear blue water below I could have sat there forever, gazing into its hypnotic depths and hardly worrying whether anyone noticed I was there or not. If this wasn't nirvana, nirvana didn't exist.

* * *

With time seeming to stop during the trance I'd slipped into it's difficult to tell how long it took for someone to notice me. All I do know is that when I eventually snapped out of it I found a large green coconut with the top sliced off and a straw stuck in it placed in front of me. That someone had thought better of interrupting my reverie – something that just served to amplify my love-at-first-sight relationship with the place.

Three absent-minded sips of fresh coconut milk later and I'd re-entered sufficiently from my low orbit around reality to be able to scan the place for the source of the refreshment. At first I saw nothing. Then, as my eyes adjusted to the inner restaurant gloom, I spotted a set of pearly whites grinning at me from the shadows. My host was enjoying my moment of revelation as much as me.

With words seeming somehow superfluous all I could do was grin back and return his enthusiastic thumbs-up. Lines of communication had been established.

But what now? Somehow I had to convey to him that I wanted to book a room – HAD to book a room – for the foreseeable future. But how? Without much Thai, would I have to resort to the old sign language standby? Thankfully not.

'Fresh fish coming. You like?' he said from the shadows.

Thank God. Not only did we have a language in common but he had something fresh on the menu. After Patong I'd begun wondering if I'd ever find anything in Thailand not retrieved from a display stand ranged over an open sewer alongside a polluted highway or from the nether regions of an ice-encrusted deep-freeze, age, identity and antecedents unknown.

Here at what turned out to be called the Seaview Resort, An the owner would have no truck with that. If there was fresh food to be had he got it and his guests thanked him for it. As I was to discover later, most were doing exactly as I was – escaping from places like Patong to recover their senses of both wellbeing and taste.

But where were they? It was almost lunchtime and I was still the only one in the restaurant.

'Is Tuesday,' said An as if that was enough to answer my question.

'Most come weekend,' he added when my quizzical look told him it wasn't.

'So you have free rooms now?'

'No free.'

'Oh. Are you full up?'

'No full up. Have own meal later.'

Bemused look then enlightenment. I needed to be more precise in my questions.

'But have rooms?'

'Yes. Many,' he said sweeping his hand around some dozen thatched huts on the compound.

'But no free.'

'No free. All price same same.'

Ah-ha.

'And some available now?'

'All available always.'

Right. Time to cut to the chase.

'Can I see one?'

'Which you want?'

'One that's free.'

'No have free.'

'I meant one that's available.'

'All available always.'

Aaaargh. OK. Time to change tack.

'So can I see number, er, twelve?' I said choosing the first number that came into my head.

'Twelve? But you are one.'

'Yes. Just me.'

'One too small for four room.'

'I said twelve, not four.'

'You are twelve?'

'If that's OK.'

'No have twelve room. Have six two room. OK? When you want?'

It took ten more minutes in this vein to realise that although we had a language in common it wasn't a common language and that signing would've been quicker.

But finally we got there and An got the key to hut number five, one of the two-person rooms he thought I wanted six of. Unless I was serious about taking the whole of the four-person room twelve for myself, he said with a twinkle in his eye. I could tell that An and me were going to get along fine. Providing we didn't muddy the waters by trying to talk to each other.

Hut five turned out to be the very hut I first saw on emerging from the jungle behind it. A simple clapboard one-room plus shower room affair on stilts with a fair-sized veranda and steps up to it sited high up at the rear of the compound where it benefited from the best view of the bay and the cooling sea breeze. With a large slatted double bed, a working fan and a mosquito net with holes only where they were supposed to be it was perfect and I booked it on the spot once we'd settled on the price of a long-term rental.

At first An was obdurate, refusing to budge from the regular daily price times the number of days I wanted it for.

'But I want to stay several weeks,' I whined. 'Surely there's a long-stay discount.'

No. The concept appeared not to compute. Maybe he'd misunderstood.

He hadn't. No matter how differently I put it to him the price remained the same. Not expensive by western standards but not cheap either and the total would stretch the budget a bit.

But I was determined. THIS was the sort of place I'd been looking for for God knew how long and I wasn't about to see it disappear from view for the little matter of a few Thai baht.

Then a brainwave. Since the hut had no cooking facilities I'd have to have all my meals out. What if I had them all at An's restaurant? How about a hut discount then?

Ting! That got his attention. A guaranteed customer in his

restaurant every day would more than make up for a small reduction in the hut rate and realising this he duly bit my hand off.

So now I was obligated, tied to taking all my meals there regardless of what he had to offer. It was a risk but only a small one. If they were all as good as the fish I'd just wolfed down I had nothing to worry about and after we'd ironed out one or two more glitches in the translation regarding the precise meaning of the word percentage I agreed to return in a couple of days to take up residence.

After shaking hands on the deal I dreamily began retracing my footsteps through the forest back to the boat humming a happy song. At long long last I had my winter berth sorted out, not just for this winter but for many to come I hoped. It'd been a long, uphill haul. But now, please God it was over and I raised my head to the forest canopy to celebrate.

Big mistake. Eyes off the track for a second I found myself coming down to earth in both senses of the word. Face down in the forest litter I scrabbled to see what it was I'd tripped over. Eye to eye with a monitor lizard as long as I was tall I froze as it mirrored my startled look then flicked out a forked tongue to taste my face. Was what had had the audacity to interrupt its afternoon doze edible?

From the undisguised look of disdain on the beast's face as it turned and scuttled off into the bush, presumably not. I didn't know whether to be relieved or insulted. One thing I did know though was that I wasn't alone in this forest and that not looking where one was going was likely to have consequences. That could have ended a lot worse.

So could the trip back. Pancake flat on the way out, a squall bounced the boat all the way to the mainland and even the deckhands looked relieved on making it to the quay in one piece. It was a look of relief that turned to unfettered disgust for all tourists on being confronted with what they were now being expected to clean up. Unlike the boat's green-gilled passengers, significant quantities of the food they'd tucked into on Raya had failed to make it back intact.

With the headline lunch lost at sea etched on my retina another mental note was made. Don't eat too much before boarding the boat, don't underestimate these waters and do keep a weather eye out on the forecast when you're ready to leave. It could mean the difference between making it to the airport in time for your eventual trip back home and having to shell out for a new ticket.

But that was for another day. The immediate need was to get my bags from the Patong hotel and enough cash to pay the Seaview rent for a month at least. If what I'd just experienced was an example of Thailand's climatic unpredictability, once on the island I didn't want to have to leave it more than a couple of times during my stay. I valued my own lunch too much.

Three days later I was back. It'd have been less but with the Thailand's ATMs as fickle as the weather, several trips to the machine were needed to accumulate enough to pay for a month on Raya where neither ATMs nor Mastercard machines had yet to reach.

But at least the delay gave me the chance to appreciate what it was I was about to experience. The comparison between Raya and Patong was the rough equivalent of my daytrip speedboat rides to and from the island. One was an utter delight.

Disembarking back on Raya with my luggage, only now did it occur to me why not many chose the Seaview as a long-term base. Getting there was an expedition. The forest had not become more amenable in my absence and by the time I struggled luggage-loaded out of its shadows I was showing the early signs of terminal dehydration.

An's grin grew exponentially wider on spotting someone doing a fine impression of Robinson Crusoe dragging himself into camp from a hunting expedition. Was it the simple unadulterated pleasure of seeing I'd made it or, I caught myself thinking, something more? During our accommodation discount discussion An had shown himself to be more canny than he looked when it came to money matters. Could he be calculating how much in bottled water profits he'd make out of the bedraggled dehydrated wreck that'd just emerged from the undergrowth?

Surely not. What a heinous thing to think. But still the thought nagged. Was it possible that the friendly grin belied a money-grubbing opportunist enshrined within? Getting to know him better over the coming weeks might produce an answer.

It didn't really. Although we eventually got to the point of being able to communicate better through a mix of rudimentary English, awful Thai and waving our hands about a lot, he remained about as enigmatic at the end as he had in the beginning. Only rarely did he allow himself to address my questions directly and not once did he provide chapter and verse as to the future of Seaview.

It was something I needed to know. The plan was to make it my regular winter haunt. Was his to keep the place as it was? New developments were creeping ever closer and Seaview was a prime candidate for 'modernisation'. Could he resist outside pressures forever? Or was he likely to up sticks and ship out when the price was right?

Answer came there none and over the weeks I eventually gave up alluding to it. The last thing I wanted was to make him think I was in the pay of the developers sent to feed news of his thoughts back to my employers. That was a sure way of making him clam up even more.

So instead I contented myself with just watching and listening and the tactic paid dividends. As some form of familiarity grew I gained the distinct impression that An had little time for anyone who would spoil everything he'd worked to build, least of all those from further east.

Responsible for the building of a resort at the other end of the bay, any mention of China and the Chinese was met with a glass-eyed stone-faced stare which told me everything I needed to know. To An, the Chinese were the equivalent of a troublesome demanding guest he'd have no hesitation in showing the door if it wasn't for the baubles they brought to the party.

Loaded down with newfound trinkets the nouveau touristique Chinese hordes had earmarked Thailand as their personal playground and were busy pumping gazillions into transforming it into a place that could only be distinguished from their motherland by the climate. With scant regard for environment or tradition they'd fallen on Thailand like dogs on a bitch in a determined attempt to produce offspring in their own image and it was clear that An was less than whelmed by their arrival.

So when someone asked about the book I was writing within his earshot, for a while it looked like An's frostiness wouldn't just be confined to visitors from the East. The look I got when China was mentioned would have chilled our steaming curries.

It softened only when I took great care to explain that the book was a critique of China's expansionist ambitions and that I was singling out Thailand for special mention.

In truth I hadn't intended to give Thailand any more prominence in the book than anywhere else but a white lie seemed prudent on this occasion. Keeping An onside was vital if I wasn't to be made *persona non grata* from the place I'd chosen to become my personal winter sanctuary.

* * *

Although that decision had effectively been made the first time I set eyes on the place, the not-to-be-silenced, ever-present, inner professional sceptic in me kept demanding to be heard urging caution. Wasn't it just a bit too perfect? Apart from the higher-than-expected room price there seemed nothing I could fault it on. Give it time, the sceptic said. There has to be something.

If there was, after a few days there I'd yet to find it and told a fellow resident so. Was I being too starry-eyed about Seaview I asked Herman the German techie escaping here for a week from his London base. Absolutely not. He'd 'done' pretty much every Thai island and this was the one he returned to time after time.

'Trust me,' he said. 'None can better it. I know what I'm talking about.'

Now where had I heard that one before? Oh yes. From another German. Result – although Herman's comment had the effect of muting the inner sceptic, it refused to be gagged outright. He's just a butterfly, it continued to whine through its muzzle. A flitterer from flower to flower staying no longer than it takes to collect the nectar.

'And his needs are nothing like yours. He's still young enough to be looking for stimulation. That's why he only comes for a week or so. As soon as he starts to feel he's being sucked into the vortex he moves on. Unlike yours, there's no grass allowed to grow under his feet.'

'Pardon?'

'C'mon. Accept it. You're getting slow old man.'

'Well, I might have a year or two on Herman but hardly old.'

'A year or two?'

'OK. A decade or two. But I'm not in my dotage yet.'

A raised eyebrow was all the sceptic thought necessary to answer that one.

'OK, OK, you've made your point. He's me twenty years ago. But I'm not ready for the care home yet.'

'So what is it you're looking for then? A place in the sun to put your feet up, you said. What's that if it's not a care home?'

'Steady on. Somewhere to avoid the British winter is hardly a care home.'

'Not far off.'

'Rubbish. A care home assumes I need care. Given enough facilities I could look after myself. Especially If I had a kitchen.

Give me one of those and I wouldn't be reliant on theirs.'

Ting! OMG. Now I saw it. THAT was Seaview's shortcoming. I knew there was an unticked box. I'd allowed all the resort's other perfections to mask it and now I came to think about it, it was going to be a problem. Apart from having nowhere to cook, I couldn't even make a cup of tea if I woke up later than daybreak.

With no gas in the kitchen that didn't exist and open fires banned, tea-making was only possible through the use of my trusty old electric travel water heater. But since there was no grid power on the island and An switched the Seaview generator off at six in the morning that meant waking before dawn to switch the heater on. Miss the deadline and it meant waiting until An opened the restaurant for breakfast. Result – one of life's great hitherto untapped pleasures denied, the one I'd taken to with alacrity once earning a crust was no longer necessary and I could lie back conscience-free sipping at a steaming mug in bed until I, not they, decided it was time to get up.

So yes, no power after daybreak was going to be a problem and having realised it, it then occurred that tea in bed wasn't the only thing being denied. Daytime work on my computer would be limited to its battery life – about four hours on mine even set to full power saving mode – and the fan would be rendered redundant.

For anyone else staying there this would hardly present a problem. Other snow-dodging island hoppers at Seaview spent their time in either the sea or the restaurant.

But I was here to write and with my trusty antiquated typewriter long stashed away in the loft back home that meant being reliant on electrical power. And even while the battery lasted if there was no decent sea breeze to cool me no fan would mean melting in my hut. The prospect did not appeal.

Neither did being denied access to the internet. Even if there had been power there was no internet to use it on. Wifi was as foreign to Seaview as choosing an imaginative name. There was nothing else you COULD view.

These days you could of course access the web with your phone but not back then. In 2008 smart phones were an exotic luxury restricted to oligarchs and the Microsoft mafia and even if you had won the lottery, at the glacial broadband speeds available the phone charge for downloading anything bigger than a flea byte could bankrupt you.

It wasn't that much different with simple phone calls. Although Raya had a mobile phone connection anything more than a cursory 'come and get me' call to the speedboat company meant seeing your credit disappear faster than the boat in a following typhoon.

That's when you could get a signal, the absence of which regularly scuppered the resort guests' attempts to call the speedboat company except, oddly, An. He seemed the only one at Seaview who never had a problem, either with connecting to the boat company or with charging through the nose for his boat-ordering services.

All of which rather put An and Seaview in a new light and forced a much-suppressed thought to rise to the surface. Here on Raya I was more heavily dependent on him, his staff and his services than I'd anticipated and it wasn't long before I found myself grudgingly agreeing with my inner sceptic.

Bugger it, I thought. He was right all along. This WAS a version of a care home.

* * *

Once out, the thought refused to go back in its box and as time passed seemed determined to bring me back to hard reality. Looked at without rose-tinted specs it was now becoming obvious that Seaview wasn't the incarnation of perfection I'd willed myself to think it was. For one, the restaurant meals were hardly the Michelin star quality one might have expected from the price, the breakfasts in particular.

When bread was available, all that came with the scrappy portion of scrambled egg was a couple of pieces of tired baguette and the coffee was rarely strong enough to defend itself. With no bakery on the island and, so far as I could see, no chickens or coffee plantations it was unsurprising that all the requirements for a decent breakfast were in short supply. Everything had to be ferried from the mainland and since neither the ferries nor the weather were what Germans might describe as 'reliable', shortages were the rule not the exception.

But surely that shouldn't also have applied to fish. Surely they were all around us just begging to leap onto our plates and make all the imported foodstuffs unnecessary.

Yes and no. Yes there was a wealth of fish but no, they weren't destined for our plates. Most ended up in China's factory ships hoovering up everything they could find in SE Asia's waters and it wasn't just Thailand's fishermen who were suffering. Every country in the region was being affected to the point of little Vietnam – a particular Chinese target – almost setting its warships on China's fishing fleet.

End product – fresh fish on my plate, when it was available, cost at least half as much again as chicken thanks to there being hardly a fishing boat on Raya.

On first arriving I thought they must all be out catching my dinner or taking tourists on day trips round the island. But no. Sight of one during my whole three-month stay was so unusual it was enough to prompt comment and, from the look on An's face when I did, it was clear that China's resort construction takeover wasn't the only thing getting his goat. The only fresh fish he ever got his hands on these days came from locals supplementing their meagre incomes by going on speargun fishing expeditions out on the reef.

But even that was rare and I found out why on snorkelling out that far. Both the reef and the bay were virtual fish deserts. During an hour in the water I saw three and they seemed lost.

Was it just over-fishing or was there something else? The water didn't seem polluted and there was no sign of excessive reef damage. Yes it had suffered a bit during the Asian tsunami but that was four years ago, surely enough time for nature to repair itself.

The answer presented itself at the first Spring tide. Exposed as the waters retreated, what had once been unadulterated sand was now coated with a brown-tinged film of sludge across the entire bay, sight of which made me begin regretting having eaten anything caught within a mile of it.

The fault, of course, was the lack of water treatment facilities included in the island's tourist resort construction plans leaving the bay a classic case of how short-term cost cutting can destroy any project's long-term prospects.

Prior to being confronted with the bay's impending pollution catastrophe the issue of how the waste was dealt with had already crossed my mind. In the absence of any waste-water treatment plant it was obvious that whoever was behind the bay's development had deemed natural filtration through soil and rock adequate protection.

By and large such soakaway techniques work well enough for small population clusters. Subterranean microbes hungrily devour the waste rendering it harmless to life. But even they can't deal with the amount of crap being pumped into the rock by larger conurbations and the result is what I'd seen beginning to build up on the bay's bottom. Just a few more years of this and a bay with little natural water circulation thanks to the blocking reef would be little more than a dilute cess pool.

My heart sank as I sat nursing a beer in the restaurant that night. For the time being the water was still swimmable. Neither I nor anyone I'd come across there was complaining of seawater-induced stomach problems. But for how much longer? The bigger, Chinese-owned, resort along the beach was clearly being earmarked for rapid expansion. Would this be the point of no return? Would its completion leave the water unswimmable? There was only one way to find out. Come back next year and see.

* * *

From a distance with the tide in eleven months later all seemed exactly as I'd left it. But that might have been the jet lag talking... and the brain-withering experience of trying to make it through the chaos of Mumbai's airport in time for my connecting flight.

Choosing the Indian-owned budget airline Jet Airways for the round trip wasn't just a mistake, it was lunacy gone mad.

'You get what you pay for, you get what you pay for' kept reverberating through my head as I punched the ticket booking button. Then, 'don't tell me I didn't warn you' as my money disappeared out of my account and into the airline's coffers.

Yes it was cheap and yes it was popular – too popular – but I could have afforded better and just one look at the queue to get through the packed sauna they called Mumbai's transit security area was enough to convince me that had I, I'd definitely live longer.

The four hours of standing wilting in line with no food, water, toilet facilities or seat to sit on while shuffling towards the single working scanning machine operated by an Indian jobsworth minutely scrutinising the bags of three simultaneously arriving planeloads of unfortunates left me on the verge of making my peace with my maker.

I'd often wondered how it would all end, imagining all sorts of possible scenarios. But somehow the likelihood of dying of dehydration in an Indian airport madhouse, caught in limbo between the twin hells of an Indian airline's battery hen class and the purgatory of the airport's no-man's land transit area never entered the equation. A death of such ignominious anonymity was simply too horrendous to contemplate.

I'd obviously been away from India too long. Long enough for the memory to subside of it being run by people defining mortal existence in terms of the amount of inconvenience it's possible to inflict on those they're officially employed to serve. It all came flooding back in those hours of almost fading unnoticed, ignored and forgotten into the ether and prompted the thought that even a demise by Chinese water torture would be better than this.

And that was just the outward flight. In a month's time I'd have to face it all over again and another winter getaway criteria priority was added to the list – take direct flights only or, at the very least, apply a great deal more care in choosing countries through which to transit.

With the thought of the return journey just too horrific to contemplate as I boarded the onward flight to Bangkok I willed myself to park it in favour of visualising what I devoutly hoped would be a final destination restored to its natural beauty by an outbreak of common sense. Or at least showing signs of those targeting Raya as a tourism hotspot seeing the error of their polluting ways in my absence and beginning to make amends.

Dream on.

If anything they'd just exacerbated the problem. New buildings had appeared with no thought given to design or impact on their surroundings and a jetty now jutted out into the bay where none existed before. And when the tide went out a blocked toilet smell permeated right up to my shack at the rear of the Seaview compound.

But that wasn't all. The bay now seemed set to become a battleground between opposing cultural forces. While I'd been away it'd been discovered by genus English football supporter keen to educate anyone within shouting distance as to the superiority of their game, club, country and race. Whether anyone was being swayed by the message wasn't clear but I suspected not. The look on the waiter's face as he made trip after trip to the bar on our new visitors' behalf suggested he was more likely to be swayed by Islamic fundamentalism.

In fact, as time passed at Seaview it started becoming increasingly apparent that maybe that was exactly the direction he was heading. Whether it was the shaven heads and tattooed torsos of our footballing friends or the cavortings of their bare-breasted female companions that prompted it I knew not but one day he simply refused to touch anything with alcohol in it. He was willing to carry bottles and glasses to the table on a tray – not doing so was more than his job was worth – but the bartender now had to put them on the tray and the recipient had to remove them. To the waiter, even touching anything that had been in contact with alcohol had become haram.

A bit extreme I thought. But then, the lad wasn't the brightest spanner in the box and there were reports of Islamic extremism infiltrating up into Thailand from Malaysia in the south. Being not too far from the border area where non-Moslems had been attacked and killed, could it be long before Phuket, Raya and all the other islands in the vicinity found themselves similarly targeted? As hotbeds of infidel tourist excess they were surely prime candidates for attracting the attention of Islamic insurgents. You only had to think back to the Bali bombings of 2002 and 2005 to imagine what could easily happen here.

The thought led to a series of uneasy nights' sleep and a new item being added to the winter retreat location criteria list. The chosen location must not be in the vicinity of any form of religious nutcase activity… not guaranteed in the case of Raya Island which was far from protected from landings by anyone taking an exception to ongoing infidel activities there, especially at night when the football supporters club was at its most vocal. If they didn't decide to move on soon I wondered if I'd be getting another night's uninterrupted sleep before I left.

Fortunately they did, eventually deciding they'd drained the bay of interest and it was time to move on and leave me in the company of another resident who'd gone quiet during their stay. How pleasant to hear the uh-oh gecko again issuing his sundowner call from the treetops.

Correctly called the Tokay gecko, I'd originally thought it was a bird so shy it never showed itself. Put right by An, one of the best moments of the day was to settle down with a beer at dusk to wait for the little chap's evening chant. Each up-down uh-oh was repeated three times and the whole sequence as many as seven times, always ending in the gradually fading 'that's it, another day over, goodnight' reassurance that all was well with the world. Sounding like something he had to get out before falling asleep and only just making it, one could imagine his eyes drooping as he valiantly tried to stay awake and the whole performance never failed to prompt a smile and a sigh. We had a whole night and day to wait before hearing it again.

It'd be something I'd miss greatly on quitting Raya. Not so much Seaview's lack of electricity and wifi. I'd tried to adapt by bringing my own small gas stove and supplies from the mainland to keep my early morning tea habit satisfied. But neither the gas canisters nor the longlife milk lasted long and for at least half my time at Seaview I was left dependent on the restaurant. Likewise, I was left dependent on the one place on the island with a rentable wifi connection, a small hotel inland. But with a connection as dependable as the people who'd rented my house in my absence, I almost missed their email informing me they were leaving without giving notice.

That alone was enough to convince me that Raya probably wasn't an ideal winter retreat. Fine if you don't need to keep in touch with the outside world, don't mind shelling out for all your refreshments in the restaurant, couldn't care less about the quality of the seawater and the wildlife that wasn't in it, like the idea of having rowdy drunken neighbours to keep you entertained 24/7 and can go blind to the possibility of finding Islamic insurgents arriving on your doorstep in the depths of night. But if you're averse to any of the above, it's probably not for you. Me neither.

In truth it didn't need a whole month to realise it and I'd most definitely have left earlier if it wasn't for two things. Reports received via my little shortwave radio – my only link with the outside world in the absence of an internet connection – told me the UK was in the grip of a torrid winter backlash and I still wasn't ready to face Mumbai airport again. Even Raya's football supporters' invasion was preferable to that.

Support for my decision re. Raya and Thailand in general came from a surprising source. Recently arrived in the shack next to mine was an elderly British woman seeking almost the same thing I was. She too thought Thailand might offer an affordable retreat from the UK winter's chill and gloom and had decided to take a look during a year-long trip round the world she termed her geriatric gap year.

With all three of her children taking a year off to travel before going on from school to university she'd begun wondering why the gap year should be restricted to young adults. Me too, she'd decided, and had let her house and invested some of her life savings in a round-the-world ticket.

So might Thailand fit the bill? Probably not. Her reservations pretty much echoed my own.

So where might?

Nowhere she'd been so far. And if there was one thing she'd learned on her travels it was that you needed to be a young fit adult to be able to get by in the third world. So no, she was heading for Europe. Somewhere there had to be a place that was both warm enough in the winter and affordable for someone on a limited income.

Ting! Another revelation. Having spent half my life in the tropics the idea of there being such a place in Europe never crossed my mind. But now... maybe I too should take a look. Just to rule it out. I'd get the atlas out as soon as I got home.

If I ever got home. First there was the delight of the Mumbai airport transit area to look forward to.

POST-THAILAND WINTER SANCTUARY CRITERIA ADDENDA

CRITERIA	ITEM	REASONING
Location	Not too remote	Being too far from civilisation can be problematic in making it to the airport in time for your home-bound flight.
	But off regular tourist routes	For a better chance of encountering the more discriminating variety of traveller.
	Direct flights to UK	After the Mumbai airport experience, crucial. Transit lounges can kill.
	Religious nutcase-free	If you value an untroubled night's sleep, let alone your life.
Accommodation	Self-catering	The Raya Island experience served to reinforce just how essential this is.
	Easy access to shops/market	No good having cooking facilities if there's nowhere to stock up.
	Internet connection	Crucial if you need to keep in touch with the outside world.

TURKEY (100km) ↑

CY (SOUTH) **R US** (NOT SOUTH)

POLIS (Little Paphos)

NICOSIA ✕ (The Peace Line)

SYRIA (100km) →

CORAL BAY (Costa Geriatrica)
✕ PAPHOS (1)
✕ PAPHOS (2)
(Home of Aphrodite ...and Andrew)

✕ LARNACA (Noise with everything)

✕ LIMASSOL (Under construction)

Catch anything?

Nope.

AFRICA (more than 100km) ↓

5

Cyprus

Aphrodite has left the building (site)

Luck, as it turned out, was with me. Flying back from Thailand I hit Mumbai airport at one of those rare times when India's bureaucratic tide was at a low ebb and even the transit area scanning machines were cooperating. So, contrary to what I'd not only feared but pretty much planned for, I didn't miss the connecting flight home.

Even so, with flashbacks to the horror of that outward trip giving me sleepless nights for months afterwards there was no way I was ever going to subject myself to another experience like that. If it didn't result in my actual demise it'd certainly kill the traveller in me and there were still bits of the globe needing to be checked out. Starting with somewhere closer to home I could get direct flights to with no need to transit.

But where? A reworking of the location criteria list for my next trip might help narrow things down.

Narrowed with laser-beam precision as it turned out. After adding 'must be less than four hours direct flight from London, be within the Euro zone yet still be warm enough to swim in winter' to the list, anywhere north of the thirty-fifth parallel was effectively ruled out leaving just three candidates out of the whole of western Europe. Just the Canary Islands, Madeira and Cyprus remained and there was a still a problem with the first two. Stuck out in the Atlantic I knew their waters had a habit of cooling to suspended animation levels in winter, something a friend once discovered to her medical cost. Glittering under a burning sun, the sea around the Canary Islands lured her into an icy embrace and a nasty subsequent case of double pneumonia.

So that, in reality, just left Cyprus. Yes, the waters there would likely also be off limits for the coldest weeks of the year but for the most part they should be fine. Well, that was my assumption. The only way to confirm it was to go and find out.

Where in Cyprus though? Easy. As far south as possible. So Limassol, Larnaca and Paphos were duly selected for investigation, not least because there were direct budget airline flights to the last two from a number of UK airports and because northern Cyprus, after Turkey had walked in uninvited and occupied it in 1974, wasn't only not in the EU it wasn't even a proper country.

With the Gatwick-Larnaca route found to be the cheapest all others were unceremoniously rejected and my maiden voyage on easyJet booked. It was a flight that transported me in more ways than one. Besides taking me to my chosen destination it took me back to Africa in the seventies and any number of best forgotten experiences with various local airlines.

EasyJet's every-man-for-himself seating policy in 2011 was every bit the measure of the likes of Nigerian Airways a quarter of a century earlier. As the departure gates opened, previously civilised passengers shape-shifted into snarling hyenas jostling ferociously for position as they tore across the tarmac to get the best seats. The only difference between this and the average Nigerian Airways experience of those bygone days was that you'd presumably get your money back if you missed getting a seat on the easyJet flight. In Lagos if your elbows weren't sharp enough it wasn't unusual to pay large sums for a seat on a heavily over-booked flight only to find yourself bounced back onto the scorching apron to face the dubious delight of tracking down the only, highly elusive, airline official with the power to issue refunds.

Africa, it is said, is a young man's game and there's a very good reason for why they say that. Elbows lose both flexibility and sharpness with age. But while that left me at somewhat of a disadvantage in Lagos it was just the opposite at Gatwick. I was but a callow youth compared to a good half of my fellow passengers en route to Cyprus, a comparative youthfulness and mobility I confess to using unashamedly to secure one of the better seats.

But even as I settled in the recent memory of a disquieting security check prior to boarding intervened to mute any over-celebration of my disgraceful victory. Discovering something unidentifiable in my carry-on bag the truly youthful security scanner operator demanded it be unpacked and in the process confirmed something so unpalatable I'd refused to acknowledge it. I was closer to joining the ranks of club geriatrica than my ageing brain could accept.

'Ah-ha. I think this might be the problem,' grinned her older colleague on unearthing the little shortwave radio that had travelled with me for years.

'Why? It's just a radio.'

'Yes,' he whispered conspiratorially back with a what-can-you-do roll of the eyes. 'But the girl operating the scanner's never seen one.'

The message in the clarification was clear. Technologically, things were moving on way faster than either he or I could keep up with and both of us – but mostly me – were viewed by people her age as cobwebbed fossils who should have been consigned to the scrapheap of anachronistic coffin-dodging bed-blockers long ago. To a girl who saw radios as the rough equivalent of steam locomotives, 78rpm shellac records and milk delivered to your door in bottles I was obviously about as with it as her granddad and as soon the thought struck I realised she could well have a point. Using the term 'with it' just confirmed what she was thinking.

The only consolation was that my research on Cyprus had revealed that there it'd be her, not me, who'd be regarded as out of their time. The former British colony was apparently steeped in age-old traditions that would render the girl and her ilk social outcasts and have her begging for lessons in how to use a radio. So as I stepped off the plane at Larnaca airport it should have felt like coming home.

For a while it did. Unlike British airports, machines had yet to start replacing humans and even the immigration man issued a cheery greeting as I waved my European Union passport at him and passed through unchallenged.

Then things changed. First it was the sniff of disdain from the foreign exchange desk clerk on being asked to change pounds for euros and then the scarcely-veiled contempt the taxi driver showed for his passenger.

It might have been the argument we had before I'd even got in that did it. Nowhere, not even in Africa, had any taxi driver ever demanded extra for my bags. Here, he tried to assure me, it was normal practice. Here, I as good as told him back, the only thing normal about it was the taxi driver tradition of trying to take flagrant advantage of a new arrival's lack of local knowledge.

The staring contest that followed ended with the driver conceding wordlessly that I wasn't as doolally as I obviously looked and loading my bags with an 'OK, you win' sort of look.

I hadn't of course. The only thing I had done was misread a look that was really saying 'OK, you win the battle but this ain't over mate. You won't win the war.'

Never a truer word not said. Arriving in central Larnaca after a thirty-minute drive of glowering conversationless tension, the driver brusquely dropped me off in a dead-end street he said was as far as he could get towards the hotel.

'Eez just round corner,' he said without looking at me and roaring off in a cloud of diesel and dust.

Game, set and match. Not only had he legged it with my change but the hotel, when I finally found it, was a twenty-minute heavily-bagged walk further on located above a noisy bar which the owners thought not worth mentioning on their website.

OK, I thought, lesson learned. Cyprus and me were beginning to understand one another.

* * *

The problem, of course, was that this was the fag-end of the tourist season. That time of year when tourist town locals start getting heartily sick of having to keep a plastic smile glued to their faces as lobster-coloured loudmouth foreigners staggered drunkenly around town with their pot bellies hanging out issuing commands SLOWLY AND LOUDLY in whatever non-local language they were speaking in the belief that the delivery would assist in their comprehension. COMPRENDAY AMIGO?

So perhaps I shouldn't have been surprised at the indolence of the hotel staff or the man demanding money for a sun lounger on a beach that owed more to military regimentation than holiday relaxation. The scowl on the man's face when I moved my sunbed out of line with the others told me everything I needed to know about Larnaca. The folks here were itching to close up for the winter and sit back to enjoy their tourist season takings without that face-achingly awful smile etched into their features.

Would Limassol be any different? If anything it was worse. At least Larnaca had done most of the reconstruction needed to accommodate the foreign invasion. Limassol seemed to have only just realised that any reconstruction was necessary.

Passing through to investigate the town's residential opportunities, as I stepped warily through the building site wreckage that was Limassol's epicentre it was clear I'd need to speak Russian to find anywhere suitable. Blocks of flats were materialising everywhere with Stalinesque lack of consideration for those behind, every other one plastered with Russian language 'Apartments for Sale' signs and if there was a restaurant without borscht on the menu I failed to find it.

And was that a car showroom selling Volga, Zil and Moskvich models? Probably not. No self-respecting member of the Russian diaspora – for want of a better word, mafia for example – would be seen dead in anything less than a sizeable Merc these days.

With mafioski not being numbered amongst my linguistic achievements, perhaps Limassol isn't the place for me I concluded as I fled from its ruins. Speaking SLOWLY AND LOUDLY to make myself understood might not have the desired effect and could well end up in me becoming an integral part of one of the apartment blocks. If a proxy involvement in the construction industry was necessary to take up residence in Cyprus I'd prefer it not to be as one of the construction materials.

So how about Paphos? Surely it couldn't be as bad as my first two stops. It was time to roll the dice and hope to hell it wasn't. There was nowhere else to go.

Or that's what I thought. Only on arriving did it become apparent that there were, in fact, two Paphos's to choose from – Kato Paphos and Ktima Paphos, also referred to as Pano Paphos.

Confused? Me too. And the discovery that almost everyone in the town(s) was called Andreas didn't help.

It was the first Andreas I came across who was largely to blame for the confusion. Staring out of the panoramic window of his lovely old world Axiothea Hotel lording it high up on a hilltop overlooking the built-up coastal plain and the Mediterranean beyond, I asked him what the habitation below was called.

'Paphos.'

'I thought this was Paphos.'

'Is.'

'So that's a suburb of Paphos?'

'Ochi – No.'

'But you said we're in Paphos and that's also Paphos.'

'Right.'

'So how come it's not a suburb?'

'Is other Paphos.'

'The other Paphos? There are two?'

'No.'

Maybe if I just looked at him.

'Is Kato Paphos. New Paphos. Also called Nea,' he eventually ventured, not altogether enlighteningly.

'So this is old Paphos.'

'No.'

'So what is it?'

'Pano Paphos.'

'Sounds like that means "old".'

'Is.'

'Right. No. I'm confused.'

'No confused. One is New Paphos, other is Pano Paphos, also called Ktima. What is to be confused?'

OK. Time to give up on that one. But Pano Paphos definitely sounded the more interesting of the two. What was its history?

'Histories? Yous wants histories? I gives you histories,' he said picking up the phone and speaking rapidly to someone in Greek.

'OK. Histories man coming.'

'Oh. Thanks. Who is it?'

'Cousin.'

'What's his name?'

'Andreas.'

* * *

Three coffees, two plates of unripe olives and one interminable over-detailed lecture later I'd had all the histories I could take for one day and made my excuses to leave. I needed to go shopping and hoped desperately that my 'informant' had better things to do. As educational as cousin Andreas was on the subject of Paphos, I could tell by the smirk on hotelier Andreas' face that given the chance his cousin could talk the toga off Aphrodite, the Greek goddess of love and beauty whose birthplace Paphos mythologically was.

Wandering the traffic-clogged streets of the old town I wondered what she'd make of it now. Unless she had a somewhat warped idea of beauty, the almost complete absence of foliage and over-abundance of dilapidation would likely see her wishing she'd been born elsewhere. Even so, there was a certain idiosyncratic charm to it, something that had obviously not escaped the attention of UNESCO and the European Union. Paphos had been selected to receive their coveted World Heritage Site and European City of Culture designations.

The more I investigated, the more I found myself grudging agreeing with UNESCO, warming to the town and its maze of streets and alleyways which never failed to produce a surprise. Here, hidden quietly away, a small market bustling with locals thrusting fresh produce at you as if your few coins meant the difference between life and having the wherewithal to pay for their funeral. There, a neighbourhood of noisy metalwork workshops fizzing with acetylene torch fireworks wielded by grime-faced men who seemed to view the wearing of welding masks as the stuff of wimps and EU health and safety regulations as best for lighting acetylene torches.

As the days went by I gradually began to work the layout out but still the surprises kept coming. How had I missed that coffee shop with a fabulous view of the ocean or the real estate agent window advertising local flats at prices that made me think they must be a misprint? Clearly because I'd been captivated by the print shop opposite in which an antique hot metal linotype machine clunked happily away oblivious to the anachronism that computer technology had made it.

Second time around and now knowing what to expect, this time it was the letting details grabbing my attention and before I knew it I was inside the agency being cajoled into signing a four-month lease.

After explaining my requirements to the agent, he picked up the phone and barked an instruction. Then he selected three flats from a fat file and handed their details to a man who'd magically materialised at the door.

'This man will show you these places, all perfect for your needs.'

I'd yet to see the details but that seemed superfluous.

'Thanks. Are they close?'

'Not far. Andreas will drive you.'

Two hours later I was back at the agency signing the lease. After seeing and quickly rejecting two grubby flats with little natural light and no view tucked away in a corner of Kato Paphos I braced myself for the third. If the first two represented what could be got on my budget it seemed unlikely the last would be any different.

But once again Paphos was determined to keep the surprises coming. Occupying the top floor of a three-storey building perched halfway up the hill separating old from new Paphos there was no shortage of either view or light with this place. The lounge doors opened onto a balcony with such a panoramic view of the Mediterranean that the only problem I could see was the distraction issue. I had a book to write and the view wasn't going to help.

'You like?' asked my grinning driver. My flapping jaw must have given the game away.

'Like?' I managed back, forgetting for a moment that we'd yet to start negotiating the rent. 'It's amazing.'

'Yes. Perfect for you,' he said. 'And has two bedrooms.'

I could hardly believe it. The other two flats barely had one each and although I wasn't planning on having visitors, the spare one might come in handy when I was forced to reveal my find to friends and family back home. Another great way of putting off writing.

Back at the agency I could hardly wait to get my signature on the lease. But with reason finally getting the whip hand over enthusiasm I refrained until certain little details were sorted out.

Little things like having to agree to put both water and electricity accounts in my name and pay some quite hefty deposits for the privilege. A raised eyebrow for each of the deposits left the agent in no doubt as to my feelings on the matter. With holiday lets utility accounts normally stayed in the name of the owner.

'Ah,' said the agent, 'but this not holiday let. Is normal let. I only let less than six months because I like you.'

Smarmy bastard, I almost told him. It's because you're having trouble letting it. Its close proximity to the local cemetery would, in a manner of speaking, spook most local renters.

Initially blinded by the view, I'd only noticed the closely-packed shiny granite slabs poking up from the ground below the balcony out of the corner of my eye. Evidence of a disused stonemason yard, my brain told me until it returned to planet Earth. But why, it enquired, would a black-clad crone be weeping uncontrollably over a lump of polished rock? In grief over the demise of a stone working business? Unlikely.

The realisation of what I was actually looking at left me both frozen in mid-gaze and metaphorically punching the air with joy. This was the exact same scenario that'd won a friend a stunning apartment in Hong Kong at a peppercorn rent. If local Cypriots were as spooked as Hong Kongers by the prospect of living close to a boneyard I could almost name my own price.

But before I got too carried away maybe best to take a breath. What else had the fabulous view blinded me to?

Not much it seemed. Judging by the flat's general grubbiness it hadn't been lived in for a while and the furniture could hardly be described as either stylish or underused. But otherwise it seemed to have most of the basics and with a good deep clean it could scrub up well.

This would do nicely, I thought in the end, especially since I'd never be lonely. I'd have the ever-present company of the local ghosts to commune with. My inner ghoul could hardly wait.

In fact so keen was it to move in that it didn't even argue the rent. At three hundred euros a month it was a snip compared to UK prices and without further ado I signed the next few months of my life away.

Halfway to the agency's door with the contract and the keys in my hand I realised that in my euphoria I'd missed something. The agent's name.

'Petros,' he said.

Thank God for that.

'But people call me by my first name... Andreas.'

* * *

A week and a healthy dose of flat-cleaning elbow grease later and I was pretty much settled. Cupboards were stocked with produce from the nearest market a fifteen-minute walk down (and a half-hour heavily-loaded stagger back up) the hill, bed linen – found to be non-existent in the place – had been borrowed from the amazingly compliant Andreas at the Axiothea hotel, a signal booster had been purchased to connect to the community wifi service and I'd had a surprise visit from Sophia, agent Andreas's substantially larger-than-life mother.

Arriving unannounced and greeting me in French for no accountable reason while bustling past me into the flat, a woman I'd not been made aware existed and who'd clearly sampled the best that Europe's capitals could offer stood looking me up and down imperiously until I got the message and offered her a chair.

'Andreas m'a diré vous avez demandez un lit nouveau. Pourquoi? Le lit est cassé?'

A blank look while the memory banks dredged up bits of underused schoolboy French I hadn't expected to have need of on a Greek-dominated island nowhere near France. What was she saying? That my book was broken? How the hell did she know?

'Pardon madame. Ma française n'est pas bon...'

'Zut alors! Vous etês Anglaise? Zen vee hass a problem. Eengleesh eez zuch crap language. French you must learn. Only Grik better. Language of ze Gods!'

I decided to take her word for it despite a/ not knowing who on Earth she was and b/ Cyprus having a long history of being under British, not French, control. Maybe that was the reason for her language preference. Things hadn't ended exactly harmoniously between the Cypriots and their British 'protectors'.

Ah well. Out now. Now she knew both my antecedents and my grasp of French and all I could do was hope she wasn't from a family which had backed Napoleon and later come off second best during Cyprus' independence campaigns against the British imperialists. Maybe if I kept her talking she'd give me a clue.

'Sorry. My Greek's a bit rusty too.'

'Muzt learn! How can understand zer vonderful vorks of Zocrates if no spik Grik? You have read?'

'Not yet. But it's on the list.'

'Incroyable! You go to school?'

'For a while. But Socrates wasn't a contemporary.'

'Big loss. Muzt catch up while stay here.' It wasn't a question.

'Maybe. Once I've made some progress with my own book.'

'You writer? Andreas no say. But how can write without know Zocrates? Incroyable. What you write?'

Ah-ha. A way in.

'Books about China. Andreas didn't mention it?'

'Useless boy. More interest in shooting than reading. If wasn't my son I find someone good to run agency.'

Blimey. No wonder she'd barged in as if she owned the place. She did. Well, as long as I had my landlady's undivided attention – and some grudging admiration over being a writer, albeit one lacking in certain aspects of what she'd call a classical education – I might as well make the most of it. There were a few things about the place that needed sorting. Not least the lack of a toilet seat, an aerial for the TV and a bed so hard it was breaking my back.

'I see what can do,' she said after I'd manoeuvred the conversation around from books and philosophy to more worldly matters. 'Muzt keeps writer happies. Maybe great works written in my apartment even if eez in Eengleesh. Better in French or Grik,' she threw in for good measure as she rose to sweep dramatically out. 'Will send Andreas to arrange.'

Sitting alone after she'd gone wasn't unlike experiencing the aftermath of a tsunami. Although all was quiet again the air remained full of Sophia's presence and something told me it wasn't just the ghosts I now had for company. The spirit of Sophia would now be ever-present, tapping me on the shoulder every time my mind strayed from the act of book creation. It was a feeling much like I expect her son had to live with at his mother's real estate agency.

If he did, he had a funny way of showing it. If I expected a rush of attention to my requirements now his mother was both on the case and in his ear I was to be disappointed. Even his mother's intervention couldn't compete with the universal law of AC/DC, the temperature-regulated Activity Capacity Deferment Coefficient those in the tropics use to predict the degree of staff activity at different temperature levels. With activity under AC/DC unerringly inversely proportional to rising temperature, and temperatures still in their high twenties in Paphos (eighty degrees Fahrenheit plus to those on the wrong side of the Atlantic), the law predicted sluggish response from a man whose help I could not live without.

Once again AC/DC did not disappoint. Andreas's reaction time clearly showed he had no intention of taking issue with such a manifestly incontestable law of the universe even though Cyprus wasn't even truly sub-tropical and had officially shed all right to the term 'developing'. As a Mediterranean member of the European Union wasn't it reasonable to hope that its inhabitants might have adapted to European standards by now?

Dream on. Lesson one in Cyprus living is that regardless of

its location and how warm it is or isn't, hot climate syndrome still applies. Time on Cyprus is considered more an abstract hypothesis for dialectical discussion than an instrument for regulating daily life and the only way to deal with it is just to get over it. Patience-challenged tut-tutting timepiece tappers who can't, don't last long in Cyprus.

Would I had known this before calling the agency. Five increasingly irate messages left on Andreas' answerphone with no reply later and the time had come to doorstep the bugger. Twice. The first time I lurked outside his closed office so long I was in danger of dying of thirst or getting arrested for loitering. So the second time I went prepared. Tooled up with bottles of water, a wide-brimmed hat and the expression of a lost tourist to win over any policeman drawn to my suspect behaviour I was ready for all eventualities. Except for him actually being in. To find the door open and Andreas at his desk was almost disappointing.

Whether it was the look on my face or the threat to withhold the rent until I got some action I know not. But I suspect his final acquiescence to my demands and his surprise keeping of his promise was more down to my parting shot as I left the office. I threatened to tell his mother.

It proved a masterstroke. Two days later and I had a seat for the toilet, a TV that worked and a bed that was almost too comfortable for my own good. Staying in it while there was a book to write was a temptation too far at times.

So was spending too much time watching Cyprus's side-splitting television programming, personified by the insertion of a commercial for a Greek cruise ship package in the middle of a screening of 'The Poseidon Adventure'. But even such mirth-making distractions began to wane after a week and the wall-to-wall bouzouki music programme alternatives weren't helping. Within days Cyprus's god awful TV drove me to instigate plan B, the search for entertainment diversions beyond the flat's confines.

Up to Christmas there was a lot to choose from. Both Paphoses were so well-endowed with bars and restaurants it looked like I'd have no trouble avoiding repeat visits over my four-month stay unless I found somewhere I particularly liked.

But then Christmas came and went and with it about eighty percent of the choice.

Deep down I sort of knew this would happen. But I'd buried the horror of Paphos turning out to be the Cyprus equivalent of Margate so deep that while the town still buzzed with tourist activity the paranoia was restricted to little more than a scarcely noticed itch on an otherwise untroubled psyche.

Then the festive season descended and the itch morphed into full scale panic. Like a caterpillar, what had been a bustling bastion of cosmopolitan activity disappeared up its own chrysalis and entered a state of suspended animation. Shutters adorned anything that wasn't vital to keeping the place from a descent into full-blown rigor mortis and I was suddenly faced with an alarming truth. Now there was nothing to distract me from the damn book. It was all too depressing to contemplate.

But just as I was about to submit to the inevitable an alternative distraction appeared out of a clear blue sky. A not altogether welcome one. Temperatures plummeted, heavy clouds appeared in that clear blue sky and it started raining. With a vengeance.

Once it got the idea it went for it. Not for decades had Cyprus seen anything like it. Drains not built for deluge conditions failed to cope, roads and basements flooded and plants that hadn't bloomed for years grew metres overnight. So incessant was it that I awoke one morning to the sight of flood prevention barriers going up around the cemetery below my balcony, presumably in an attempt to stop the dear departed departing even further from mausoleums built more above than below the burial ground's wafer thin soil making it more cementery than cemetery.

I hoped to hell the barriers held. If they didn't we could soon be faced with the storm drains having to cope with something rather more full-bodied than mere floodwater and the danger of the already over-topped reservoirs becoming the source of something else Cyprus hadn't seen for decades – cholera.

As concerning as that was, for now it could be filed away as something to worry about later. Of far greater urgency was the need to deal with a more immediate threat to life and limb. Keeping from freezing.

With a brisk north wind blasting down from Siberia the good burghers of Paphos huddled round wood fires with their nearest and dearest leaving me to the vicissitudes of an electric heater fabricated circa the time of Thomas Edison and looking like that's when it was last used.

For about five seconds it had me thinking it was going to cooperate. Then it emitted a cloud of acrid smoke, sighed and blew all the fuses leaving me scrabbling to restore the power, swaddle myself in a blanket and light the gas oven. The electric heater could go hang. I preferred to be asphyxiated than incinerated.

Well, at least it's probably too cold for the cholera bacteria to survive, I reassured myself through chattering teeth.

But what if it wasn't? The thought had me checking flights out, just in case, and just as I was closing in on finalising a plan of action, what I thought couldn't get any worse did. The ceiling sprang a leak. Right over my computer.

With a screech all thoughts of disease, cold and the means of fleeing it were forgotten, all sensitive electronics gathered up and stashed beyond the reach of the rising tide and all attention focused on contacting the elusive Andreas who, to my immense surprise, answered the call immediately. He was in his office doing much the same as me.

Even more surprising was that he'd already got a local builder on the case to fix his own roof and was willing to redirect him to fix mine.

But the biggest surprise of all came with him actually doing it. Not a permanent repair, of course. That'd be stretching things a bit far for Cyprus. But at least a patch-up job until the rain relented long enough to allow more concerted leak-proofing.

Within a couple of hours of my call to Andreas not only had the leak been fixed but the builder had promised to twist Andreas' arm to sanction work on a couple of other remediation jobs. I'd narrowly escaped having my toes severed by falling tiles while taking a shower, the kitchen sink was stoically refusing to drain and the washing machine had developed a nasty habit of chewing my clothes to shreds. All were on the list to bend Andreas' ear with once the roof leak was fixed. Could the builder circumvent the need for what would undoubtedly be a tortuous exercise in frustration?

'Sure. Leave to me.'

If he wasn't acting on Andreas' orders to take the heat out of the situation by making rash promises unlikely to be kept this was all too good to be true. Who was this man?

'Cousin of Sophia.'

Somehow it was so obvious the question hadn't really needed to be asked.

Neither was asking his name. I was already mouthing it before he told me.

* * *

In the end the rain did stop, the north wind relented and Andreas the builder astoundingly proved as good as his word. As soon as the sun returned he was back to effect a more permanent roof repair, replace the fallen tiles, unblock the sink and give the washing machine a good talking to. And as he left he did what I'd thought would be the unthinkable. He gave me his phone number and told me to call if anything else needed fixing.

'Shouldn't I be going through Andreas first?'

'Useless boy. Forget him. You call me straight. I fix with

Sophia.' Birthdays seemed to be showering down on me.

With my newfound friend's departure I thought they'd dry up but things just kept getting better. Neighbours in the two flats below started delivering gifts as if it really was my birthday. After weeks of thinking they were ignoring me I suddenly found I was flavour of the month.

First came a bicycle from the Pakistani family directly below who said they no longer had need of it and this was quickly followed with plates of fiery curry from the Filipino girls on the ground floor. To what did I owe this sudden recognition? An Irish bartender in one of the few bars still open offered what he considered to be the only possible explanation.

'Dey tink yous one o' dem,' he whispered conspiratorially when I mentioned the sudden change of sentiment. 'An illegal.'

I'd been compared to many things in my time but never to one of the waves of economic migrants arriving illicitly on EU shores and wasn't sure I found it altogether flattering. Where did they think I was from? The mirror showed no evidence of Oriental, Asian or African origins and I couldn't recall speaking any East European language to anyone. Maybe they thought I was fleeing from some Middle Eastern conflict. There were plenty to choose from.

In the end I never did find out because one day they were there, the next they weren't and in their absence I found myself the owner of a bicycle and some additional crockery by default. Whatever the reason for their rush to leave it was urgent enough to prevent them coming to reclaim them.

Or to warn me. If they'd been tipped off about an imminent illegal immigrant sweep, as was the obvious assumption, it'd have been nice if they'd thought to pass the news on to someone they thought was one of their number. The fact that I'd been left out of the loop first left me disappointed, then suspicious. Was it a strategy for putting the authorities off the scent? For giving them a fall guy so they'd leave satisfied they had the illegal they'd been tipped off about at this address?

If so, the plan would have failed. Apart from holding an authentic EU passport and having every right to be in Cyprus I was out and about on 'my' bike when my neighbours high-tailed it leaving me to face the music. If there was an official hammering on my door I knew not and the only person who might wasn't saying. All I got out of Andreas the flat agent was the hint of a smile and a change of subject that gave the distinct impression he knew more than he was letting on. If anyone knew the status of the people renting the flats it was the one who'd rented it to them and I left the office vowing to be a tad more circumspect about people I had dealings with in future.

Not that there were that many. With weeks to go before the tourist season began again the last thing most Cypriots seemed to want to do was be communicative with out-of-season strays like me, particularly on Sundays.

This was the day I dreaded most. At least for the rest of the week regular, if desultory, life went on. Shopkeepers and bartenders continued studiously ignoring customers, their feral children bunked off school to help their parents ignore customers and both acted in harmony to pile garbage on pavements in what I came to believe was a deliberate strategy to force pedestrians into the path of Paphos's manic drivers.

Playing chicken with the traffic became a regular feature of life in Cyprus but somehow I avoided coming into serious contact with it, even on Sundays.

Starting on Saturday afternoons, Sundays were the exclusive reserve of the family and the roads filled up with carloads of squabbling children driven by fathers with eyes more on the back seat than on the road. On Sundays, avoiding becoming roadkill could be counted as much of a triumph as getting a table in one's favourite restaurant. If one did make it there without incident it wasn't unusual to find them full to overflowing with those self-same families and after the third time my food arrived so late it was past its sell-by date it was clear an alternative strategy would be needed to survive the regular Paphos Sunday. Unless I could persuade a local family to adopt me or manage to inculcate myself into some group or other I'd be cooking for myself every seventh day.

It was time to get proactive.

* * *

Having discounted insinuating my way into Sophia's family on the grounds that I felt it best not to mix business with pleasure and wasn't over-keen on being subjected to a lecture on Socrates in French every Sunday, the seeking out of some disparate group seemed the more favourable option.

But who and how? I knew nobody and the only groups making themselves obvious were the ragtag assortment of layabouts, ne'er-do-wells, grifters, pimps and Filipino maids who gravitated to the nearest thing Paphos had to a town park every Sunday.

First sightings of the park-dwellers generated little optimism that they were there to indulge in intellectual dialogue on the social condition. They seemed more interested in passing round cans of strong drink, gabbling incoherently into mobile phones and leaping in and out of cars driven by lone males cruising the strip. And judging by the amount of litter being strewn around it didn't seem likely that this was a meeting of environmental activists out to save the world.

But I could have been wrong and before passing premature judgement I resolved to shelve all preconceptions and try to make contact, at a prudent distance at first with my nose in a book to avoid arousing suspicion, then gradually closer where I could pick up snippets of conversation.

It proved a forlorn tactic. The closer I moved the more murmured the conversations got until, by the time I was all but sitting on their laps, it ceased altogether and they started edging away. Something told me they had a problem trusting people twice their age who lurked nearby pretending to read.

Fair enough. The lurker could have been a government snooper snooping on suspected subversives. But even though I wasn't what I suspected they were suspecting I was, there was clearly little mileage in pushing things further and after a few minutes of tense silence I gave up and wandered off in search of more accommodating folk. I'd noticed a flea market underway close by. Maybe a more communicative community could be found there.

Yes and no. Yes I found people willing to talk. But almost exclusively about things they missed about Britain, how they struggled to get by on their niggardly UK state pensions and Paphos's dearth of public toilets. Without realising it I'd stumbled on the answer to something that'd been bugging me ever since my arrival in this town – where did all the British retirees hang out? Cyprus was a popular retreat for pensioned-off Brits, that was well known. There were bars full of them, mostly ex-service personnel glued to English football matches on satellite TV. But where were the ones with – how can I put this – more varied interests? There must be some.

One day a week they were here, gathered at the flea market partly to supplement those niggardly pensions by flogging off scant possessions and partly to gossip and reassure one another that giving up everything in the UK and moving here really was the best move. It was all truly depressing.

Where the joyous sound of jovial residents celebrating their escape from the British weather? Where the glee of the work-free incomer enjoying having a new culture to immerse themselves in? Where the happy clack clack of backgammon tiles being slapped down as smug refugees from the northern chill glugged ouzo in the warm Spring sunshine?

Not here. All I heard was the griping of the pink-faced Brit abroad bemoaning the lack of decent bacon, fluffy sliced white bread, editions of the *Daily Express* less than three days old, people wot spoke proper Inglish and declining standards in Ingerland thanks to all them bloody immigrants. Somehow it had escaped their attention that they could now be tarred with the same brush.

With a civil war just getting underway in Syria a couple of hundred miles away – a war that could spill over into Cyprus any time – it didn't seem unreasonable to expect there to be some discussion on whether the international community should intervene. But from their responses when pressed on the subject one could be forgiven for thinking they hadn't actually noticed. And when one simply opined that bombing the fuck out of the place would be good practice for pilots stationed at Britain's Cyprus military base of Akrotiri, I walked away. A considered analysis of the Syria situation seemed unlikely from a group who'd clearly graduated from the University of Umbrage with honours degrees in failing to see there was little actual difference between the expat settler and those they classified as bloodsucking immigrants.

With any hope of finding anyone who did looking as distant as Syria obviously looked to the regular Paphos flea market stallholder, I made to make a rapid retreat. But only until spotting a group of mainly English-speaking folk drinking tea in the market cafe set up to raise funds for mistreated animals.

Suddenly my hopes were rekindled. Animal rights-ists were people with a conscience who kept an eye on current affairs, right? Surely they'd offer a better conversation prospect.

A quick earwigging of the chatter at the nearest table and my education was complete. There'd be no intelligent conversation today without resorting to guile. With the group more intent on discussing the knotty problems of where to find a good washing machine mechanic and why it was impossible to find ANY decent cheese in Cyprus, the only way into the conversation was clearly to await mention of anything of greater import than mere domestic inconveniences.

It was worth the wait. Another cup of tea later and the talk had turned to the bankrupting cost of Paphos's veterinary services. A-ha. At last a way to direct the conversation towards more expansive territory. Now animals had at last been mentioned, could the group enlighten me on an animal issue that'd come to my notice that very morning?

Cycling down to the flea market I'd passed such a hideous example of animal mistreatment I'd had to stop and take pictures. Confined to a muddy grassless pen no bigger than the average British garden was a suicidal-looking ostrich pacing back and forth like a lion deranged by a life of long-term captivity. Did the animal welfare society know of it? And if they did, was anything being done to get it re-housed in more humane conditions?

My intervention failed to prompt the response I'd hoped for. Instead of the group collectively rising outraged to the defence of the giant bird, everything went quiet. Without exception the tea-sippers clammed up and sat staring into their cups as if they were about to reveal some great universal truth. Was it something I'd said?

The answer came from the cafe's less-than convivial owner. In a response that, in light of the subject being discussed, could hardly have been more comically ironic I was roundly told to ignore the ostrich and mind my own business. They had enough to do saving the country's cats and anyway, drawing attention to the bird – which they knew all about – would be bad for tourism.

Excuse me? Was I being told that some tacit agreement existed between the animal welfare-ists and the local government? That some trade-off had been agreed in which the authorities wouldn't interfere in their activities providing they didn't embarrass Cyprus?

I'd have asked outright but since that was hardly likely to inspire full transparency I decided to try a less direct approach. The owner herself had planted the seed. Would she join with me in seeing the comedy in what she was asking me to do?

'So let me get this straight,' I asked. 'You're saying it'd be best if I buried my head in the sand about the ostrich?'

The owner's unsmiling silent stare by way of response to my attempt at levity told me all I needed to know. A sense of humour, a bit of light-hearted banter and any hope of having a half-decent conversation were only likely to be found by abandoning the park, the flea market and the bicycle and taking to the bus.

* * *

Why hadn't I thought of it before? Probably because I'd had trouble believing it. But it was true. The buses really were that cheap. The fare for going anywhere on the Paphos provincial bus service – just one stop or right to the end of the line in Polis thirty-five kilometres away – really was just one euro and once I had it confirmed that was it. Sundays from now on were sorted. For virtually no cost I could not only explore this part of the island to exhaustion but do so in the company of what I was sure would turn out to be kindred spirits.

Long distance buses and trains tend to attract the footloose, the inquisitive and the barking eccentric. In other words, people looking for the same distractions as me. And one could almost guarantee there'd be not one humourless hypocritical cat person amongst them. Sunday was their day for whining about Cyprus at the flea market.

It took just one trip to Polis to discover what I'd been missing. During a two-hour ride through the craggy sand-blasted Paphos hills I found myself discussing everything from where to get a decent meze, Cyprus's standard dish, to China's growing presence in the island's property market to Russia's plans for developing a huge offshore gas find between Cyprus and Syria. It was a sanity saver and the discussions weren't just with conversation deprived itinerants like me. Diversity came as standard right down to the Methuselah of a grizzled old Cypriot man who claimed to have been incarcerated in a German prisoner of war camp in World War Two before taking refuge in Cardiff on his release.

I'd expected my 'which was worse?' quip to be met with bemusement or outright hostility. But after a short pause to absorb the comment my new friend exploded in thigh-slapping mirth and even joined in the spirit of the thing with a mock serious defence of the Welsh capital. So welcoming had he found it that he'd stayed far longer than intended and it was only on his return to Cyprus many years later that he'd found his land taken over by Turks. He'd been away when Turkey invaded Cyprus in 1974.

'I wasn't,' I told him. 'I was in the Greek islands. Trapped there until the emergency subsided.'

'That makes us blood brothers!' he insisted playfully as he hopped nimbly off halfway to Polis.

Thanks old man, I thought. For the rest of the trip I'm going to be plagued by the image of the faces of my long-departed parents on being informed they had another son. One about the same age as they'd now be.

Fortunately the image didn't last that long. Two young Brits in the seat behind shattered it with a question. How, they were intrigued to know, had it been for a foreigner unable to escape from somewhere being invaded? They could scarcely imagine it.

Rarely given the chance to reminisce at length without interruption about my past I considered giving vent to every verse of every chapter of the Greek islands incarceration but on reflection thought better of it. Knowing from empirical research of the younger traveller's average thirty seconds attention span, I pared the story to the bone. The guilt of being responsible for the withdrawal symptoms they'd suffer from being kept from their mobile phones too long would be too much to bear.

To my amazement, as my half-minute presentation came to a close they demanded more. In my experience that made them almost unique amongst those of an age group known to be more comfortable in the company of electronic screens than people and I took full advantage of it. By the end of the trip they not only had the full story but addenda contributed by Cypriots on the bus in varying degrees of fractured English leaving no one under any illusion as to the effect the invasion had had on the island's Greek population and how they yearned for the reunification of north and south.

It was just the sort of education I'd been longing for and left me with a yearning of my own. I wanted more and the only way to get it was to take the same bus at the same time every weekend. The destination – an unremarkable tourist trap of a town hosting little more than bijou bars, gift shops and a muddy seaside campsite populated by the sort of clientele I'd fled Paphos to avoid – was all but irrelevant. It was the bus ride that was the thing, a sort of university on wheels which finally brought some meaning to the otherwise deathly Paphos Sunday.

Just how deathly I was to discover on deciding to try a different route one Sunday, ending up in Cyprus' very own Costa Geriatrica.

On first sight of Coral Bay not far from Paphos, the town seemed indistinguishable from Paphos's downtown tourist centre, every other building a sports bar crammed with people making a valiant effort to drink themselves to death.

But then I discovered the difference. Coral Bay's residents were winning hands down in this regard and the closer to the beach I got the more success it looked like they were having. At the beach cafe itself you could be forgiven for thinking you'd arrived in Lourdes, the able-bodied having to pick their way between the crutches, Zimmer frames and wheelchairs to find a menu whose contents seemed designed to finish the job.

Cholesterol-with-everything was the cafe's exclusive choice of fare and the primary reason for it being full to overflowing with the medical lost cause abroad. If they were on their way out they were going out with a full English breakfast inside them and a hearty vote of thanks to their tour company for what, from its name, seemed to be the company's policy of helping them fulfil their every last wish.

'Asbestos Tours', I decided, was chosen for a reason. This was the Cypriotic way of advertising their primary mission was the taking of the heat out of dying and they weren't being coy about it. The name was emblazoned in three-foot high block letters on the side of the full English breakfast scoffers' coach in the cafe car park.

Frozen in mid-stride after having to do a double-take on seeing it I felt the presence of others similarly stopped dead, as it were, in their tracks. Just behind me, a group of wide-eyed, open-mouthed Africans had materialised from nowhere not knowing how to react. As our eyes met it was clear they were in need of guidance and that I'd been singled out as the chosen one.

'Your guess is as good as mine,' was the look they got back. I'd have propounded the taking the heat out of dying theory but, after spending the better part of my working life in Africa and knowing something of the African's reverence for the dead, didn't. They could well have reacted by walking away in disgust and I had a burning question to ask. What, I wanted to know, was such a group doing in Cyprus?

So...

'I suppose Asbestos could be a place,' I mused without conviction. As unlikely as it was it seemed to satisfy them and as we turned to collectively board the bus back to Paphos I listened intently for clues as to their own heritage. Was that Swahili they were speaking? After being away from East Africa for over a decade mine was a bit rusty but I tried it anyway. Result – stunned silence and more open mouths and dinner plate eyes.

'You know Swahili?' said one, astounded.

'*Kidogo sana.*'

Suddenly we were no longer strangers on a bus and as the journey progressed I worried that I was about to gain a whole job lot of blood brothers and sisters to add to my fraternity with the old Cypriot man.

By the time the bus pulled into the Paphos bus station I knew three things. One, that they were a group of mature students from Kenya studying at university in Nicosia. Two, the life story of each and every one of them. Three, that if I ever felt the need to go back to Kenya I need look no further for accommodation. Their families would take me to their bosoms and cater for my every need.

Well now, I thought as my head hit the pillow that night. That IS a thought. Going back to Africa had never occurred to me. It hadn't been exactly kind to me at times. But there again, neither had Cyprus. Yes, in Paphos I'd found a fairly cheap place to travel to and live. And yes, there was no problem with either visas or currency exchange. But no, it wasn't the warmest place in winter. Swimming comfortably had been possible for just half my time here and that in a sea that'd been all but fished out. The price of seafood bore testimony to it. What was left of the fish stock was on offer at premium prices and when I did dig deep to afford it I regretted it. Some dodgy prawns left me in need of treatment at a medical centre which all but turned up its nose at my EU health card.

But fair's fair. Given time I'd probably settle down to the Cypriot way and maybe even come across the odd conversation partner or two.

But did I want to? Now that my African friends had planted the seed in my mind, I knew if I didn't check Kenya out, I'd be left forever wondering if it'd changed over the past decade.

Dammit. I had no option. I HAD to go back.

POST-CYPRUS WINTER SANCTUARY CRITERIA ADDENDA

CRITERIA	ITEM	REASONING
Location	Sub-tropical at least	Even at its most southerly extremes it can get bloody cold in temperate/Mediterranean zones in winter.
	Warm sea	See above.
	Plentiful seafood	For an affordable alternative to meat and vegan.
	Cosmopolitan	For an alternative to the xenophobic griping and bitching one's own sun-seeking countrymen seem to thrive on.
Accommodation	Decent bed	In order to avoid spending every day recovering from the night before.

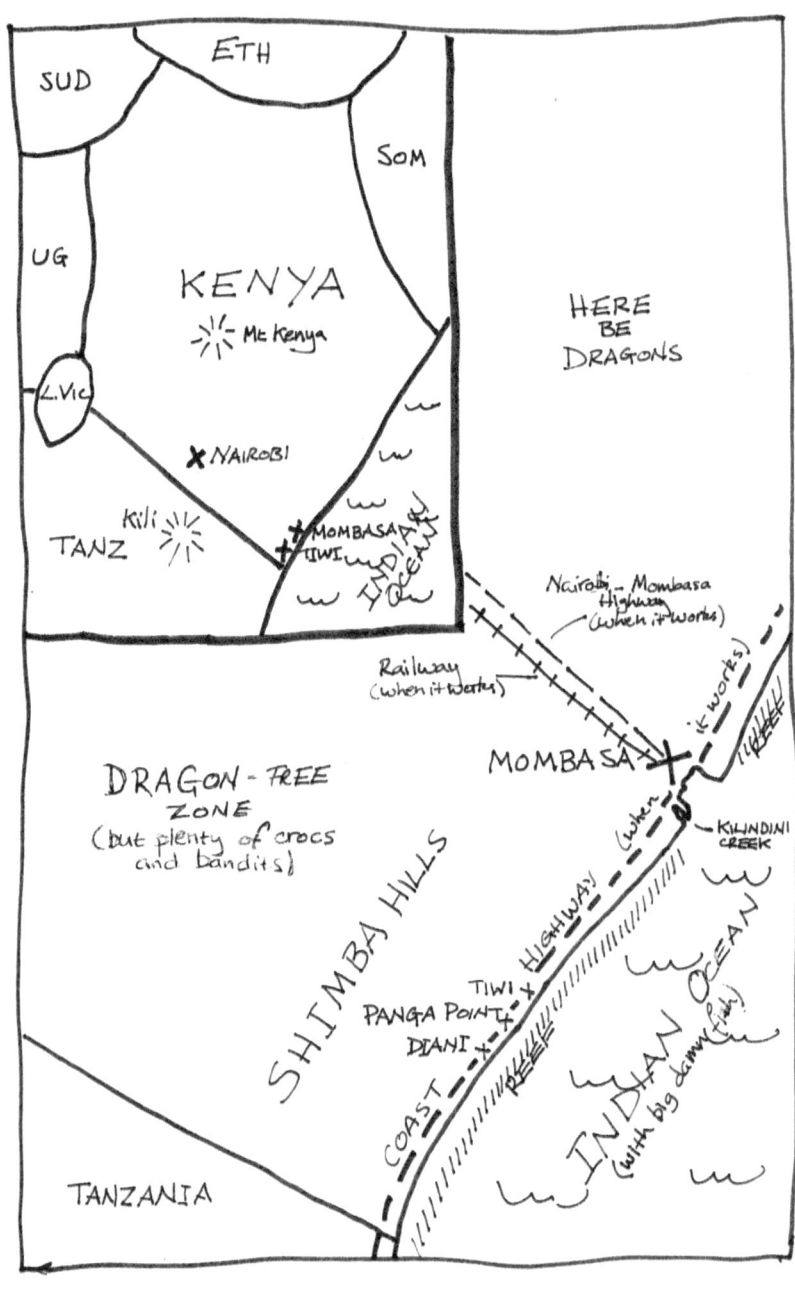

6

KENYA
Palms, qualms and Kalashnikovs

Phew. In. On arriving I'd half-expected to be told by immigration to 'go with this man' for a 'chat'. OK, it was thirteen full years since filing my last, not over-complimentary, newspaper report on Kenya but there was still the chance of a nose or two remaining out of joint and if any still were I couldn't bank on arriving to an altogether cordial welcome.

So rather more prudence than usual seemed appropriate in preparing for this trip. Prudence bordering on out and out subterfuge. Probably best, I decided, to refrain from applying for a visa prior to travelling and fly direct to Mombasa, avoiding the capital Nairobi altogether. The less the Kenyan authorities knew of my travel plans the better and more muted immigration vigilance was pretty much assured in the steaming equatorial conditions of Kenya's coastal city airport.

It was a wise decision. The only official greetings committee there to meet me was the massed ranks of airport taxi drivers jamming the arrivals hall and crushing in on exhausted newcomers until in desperation they dived into the first taxi they saw just to get away from the heaving, clamouring mob.

With the horror of some of those past arrivals still fresh in my mind this time I'd made sure I was ready for them. This time I had a trump card with me – a print-out of something that simply wasn't in existence in the nineties and was undeniable evidence of landmark change coming to Kenya in my absence. Courtesy of the internet I possessed proof of a pre-booked ride to my chosen destination, a vampire taxi driver repellent to rival any religious cross Van Helsing might have used to keep Dracula at bay.

To my astonishment it worked. That single sheet of paper had the taxi driver cabal shrinking hissingly back to allow unobstructed passage to the open air where I settled smugly down to wait for that promised ride to materialise.

And wait and wait. While there was no doubt that the arrival of the internet had revolutionised both room and taxi booking procedures – when last here it'd been a matter of picking up an antiquated landline telephone and praying there'd be a dialling tone – it was clear there'd been no equivalent cultural revolution with Kenyan time-keeping.

As infuriating as this was, on reflection it was oddly reassuring. I'd been worried that the place selected as my 2013/14 winter refuge might not have been able to resist the ravages of time and technology and to have changed out of all proportion to the way I remembered it in the nineties. Now, here was an indication that change in Kenya was but skin deep and if that was the case it was entirely possible that Tiwi beach some thirty kilometres south of Mombasa would still be a pristine white strand devoid of the sort of facility the regular tourist seems unable to live without.

Nestling amongst coconut groves at the end of an interminable bone-jarring rocky track winding through dense coastal plain vegetation, the small habitation of bungalows, bar and campsite that comprised the Tiwi beach community had long been the almost sacred refuge of Kenya residents seeking respite from the country's heaving urban sprawls and tourist millions. To be accepted here one almost had to take an oath of secrecy to prevent it being discovered by genus tour group and since only the more hardcore traveller was ever likely to take on the challenge of mounting a veritable safari to reach it, it had largely been spared the fatcat camera-toting bling tripper whose idea of a challenge was finding space for the five meals a day being force-fed them at the Diani Beach resorts further along the coast.

On occasion one or two did make it but they didn't stay long. Finding their bar room chatter of kitchen design, flashy cars and whatever was in Hello magazine this week failing to impress the regulars it wasn't long before they moved on to somewhere less full of grizzled beards swapping tales of crossing deserts in death trap Land Rovers, narrowly escaping ambush by Nairobi's carjackers or dodging sharks out on the reef to speargun yellow fin tuna for their dinner.

As the wait for my ride to Tiwi passed from one hour to two I entered a sort of floating reverie, travelling back in time to the eighties and nineties to relive days and nights spent in the company of such wayward adventurers and of sinking without trace into the blissful, time-defying atmosphere of the Tiwi of those days. So steeped in the reverie in fact that I almost missed the call from my errant driver blaming the delay on a broken down ferry across the creek near Mombasa.

The call was received with mixed feelings. While news of Kenya persisting with a ferry that'd been in use so long its fabrication date plate could no longer be read was further evidence of lack of real change, the fact that a humble, previously unconnected, taxi driver could now communicate with every part of the world from the comfort of his driving seat at the punch of a mobile phone button was quite the opposite. If there'd been such a tectonic shift in communications how could the beach I was heading for possibly have escaped an equivalent atmospheric upheaval?

If I was expecting reassurance from Mbarak the driver on the way there I was to be disappointed. Uncharacteristically taciturn for a Kenyan for the entire ninety-minute sunrise drive through the urban mess that was Mombasa, across the Kilindini creek on the amazingly still functioning ferry and south along the coast road to Tiwi, he remained mumblingly schtum. It was as though I was either keeping him from some other more enjoyable activity or that he was under orders not to forewarn his fare as to what he was about to encounter at the beach. It was as disconcerting as it was intriguing.

As we pulled off the coast road onto the track leading down to Tiwi it was clear I'd had no need to worry. Still as tooth-loosening as it'd been in the nineties the only change I could see was that the vegetation enclosing the track had grown more dense and remained that way all the way to Coral Cove Bungalows, an enclave of some eight thatched beachside cottages at Tiwi, one of which I'd booked for a full three months.

Grinning from ear to ear over the prospect of moving into a temporary home I'd only been able to view with envy from afar last time I was here, all fears of finding the place irreparably changed evaporated the moment we pulled into the compound. With the sun just coming up over the treetops Coral Cove looked as if it'd been preserved in aspic. Even the dilapidated furniture on the cottage terraces looked the same and as I watched Mbarak disappearing back up the track to his next job I sank into a sagging wicker armchair and sighed. It was like coming home.

* * *

Or it would have been had there been someone there to greet me. I wasn't expecting the red carpet treatment but considering I'd paid the whole period up front, to arrive to find the compound doing an impression of the Marie Celeste left me scratching my head.

Yes, it was early and yes it was still a few weeks til Christmas but surely business and the consequent activity on the compound should be picking up by now. It always had in the past and the owner's proclamation that only payment in full in advance could guarantee residency for the whole of the Christmas/New Year period tended to confirm a lack of change.

So where was everybody then? Somewhere else it seemed and

the more I gazed out on the lifeless compound from my cottage terrace the more convinced I became there was something someone wasn't telling me about Coral Cove.

When at last she did come shuffling through the vegetation to inspect the new arrival the compound's shambling Swedish shipwreck of an owner was about as forthcoming over the lack of activity as Mbarak the taxi driver had been about Tiwi in general. Questions were received with a shrug and an avoidance of eye contact and as Ms Shipwreck sloped off back to her own bungalow after going through the regulation new arrival formalities, I was left wondering if it was my own recall that was at fault.

Tiwi could do that to you. So blissfully other worldly, one's mind could be left skating over the imperfections of the place. Things like trying without success to keep sand and mosquitoes out of your tent on the campsite, the ever-present risk of having your brains bashed in by full-size coconut bombs plunging without warning onto the site from the towering palms above and, when you really really needed to go, finding every other campsite resident in front of you in the queue for the hopelessly inadequate supply of choleric toilets. All these and, when being completely honest about Tiwi, quite a few more would combine at times to prompt the odd, longing gaze from impecunious campers towards Coral Cove and its convocation of moneybags residents whooping it up in all mod cons splendour. One day, you could hear the campers thinking, that'll be me.

Well that one day for me had now arrived and all was not living up to how I remembered it. Had I let imagination get the better of me? Had I misread the compound's grandeur and popularity when I used to camp next door? With few on the campsite ever being invited to sample the delights of Coral Cove bungalow life all we mostly had to go on was rumour and speculation. Had I let that colour my perception of the place?

Perhaps. But there'd been no fantasy attached to the general tenor of contentment oozing from the place back in the day. Nor of the demand for the bungalows making early booking essential. No matter how much they offered, latecomers never got a look in at peak season.

So what had happened? Had demand dried up? If so, why? Had somewhere even better opened up nearby? Or was it simply down to the general state the bungalows were now in? On close inspection while unpacking it was clear the passing years hadn't been especially kind to either of us. It wasn't just the furniture that hadn't been renewed since my last trip here. Neither had anything else, right down to the kitchen equipment and a shower room that might even have left the apparently unembarrassable campsite owner aghast.

With Ms Shipwreck unlikely to provide complete enlightenment on the matter it was clear I'd need an alternative source of information and as I made my way to the beach for my first dip in the Indian Ocean for far too long into view came the only place that qualified – the campsite bar.

Settling down later with my first Tusker beer of the trip in a bar that had thankfully remained as decrepitly homely as when I last saw it, I gazed out over the dazzling white beach to the turbulent reef beyond and began listening out for hints as to how Coral Cove and Tiwi in general had fared without me.

Three beers in and I was still none the wiser. Listening in requires there to be others to listen in to and apart from a small complement of sleepy bar staff both the bar and the campsite had remained as unpopulated as the Coral Cove compound. OK, it was mid-week and Christmas was still a few weeks away but in my experience such desolation was unheard of. There were plenty of people living locally year-round, there'd always been a happy camper or two on site and Tiwi had the only beach bar and restaurant for miles. Where was everybody?

The bar tender had just shrugged when I asked. Communing with his phone seemed to take precedence over passing the time of day with the single lone drinker in the place, especially one keen to skip the light fandango down memory lane to bygone Tiwi days years before the bar tender was born.

In the end I just shrugged too. Still suffering the effects of a Turkish Airlines flight which had included a Mumbai airport-competing flight transfer at Istanbul and an unscheduled, unannounced stop at the Mount Kilimanjaro airstrip where a night-time arrival made viewing Africa's highest peak impossible, I gave up and sloped disconsolately off to bed. With nothing in the bungalow kitchen cupboards save for some stained cracked crockery and a selection of pots and pans that looked like they'd last been used by Macbeth's witches the priority was to be up in good time to make sure there was.

* * *

'Nakumatt,' said Mbarak the taciturn taxi man when I asked where was likely to have the things I needed.

'Really? That place still going?' Kenya's most chaotic supermarket chain had been an institution back in the day but surely something must have taken its place since then. It never looked like turning a profit.

'Yes, *mzee*,' he said in the manner reserved for those seen as having left their best years behind them. 'It has all.'

Well, all the budget shopper needed to contract a nasty dose of salmonella poisoning, I thought but didn't say. Unless it'd been on the receiving end of a serious investigation by Kenya's food standards authorities and had acted on the inevitable warnings it wouldn't be my first choice for picking up supplies. I'd get a speargun and go fishing on the reef first.

But Mbarak was insistent. Nowhere in Diani, the region's prime tourist resort and Coral Cove's closest shopping centre some fifteen kilometres distant, came close to competing on price or variety.

More to test the claim than to actually shop there I tentatively agreed to Mbarak chauffeuring me to it, another luxury I'd awarded myself after all those years of enviously watching the better heeled being ferried about with no worries over the state of their own transport. I'd lost track of the number of times I'd watched from under the bonnet of a temperamental geriatric Land Rover as worry-free chauffeur-driven fortunates from Coral Cove glided nonchalantly by. Now, I'd decided, it was my turn.

Anyway, I had little choice. A good three kilometres off the main coast road through a virtual jungle known to be populated by bands of local ne'er-do-wells ever on the lookout for unwary visitors to prey on, Tiwi was poorly served by public transport. Not served at all in fact, a major impediment duly noted when it came to consideration of Coral Cove's potential as a regular winter flight destination.

That hadn't been a problem when I lived in Kenya. I'd had my own wheels, unreliable as they were. Now I was fully dependent on getting a signal on my phone to call either Mbarak or one of the ubiquitous deathtrap boda boda motorbikes, named after the fleet of vehicles requisitioned by Ugandan Asians shouting 'Border! Border!' when that country's murderous dictatorial madman Idi Amin gave them twenty-four hours to leave the country in the seventies.

With crash helmets, insurance and a limit on the number of passengers riding pillion at any one time as foreign to the drivers as ensuring they always had petrol in the tank, boda bodas were the transport of choice of only the desperate and the penniless. And after being treated to the third account of a tourist-hired boda boda running out of fuel, allegedly, halfway down the track to Tiwi leaving its passenger(s) limping into camp bereft of all possessions after an encounter with locals more interested in their belongings than their welfare, I felt my decision to restrict myself to Mbarak's services was as justified as

Mbarak's Nakumatt recommendation had turned out to be.

Although chaos still reigned there was no doubt that both the range and quality of goods available had improved and now almost everything came vacuum-packed with identification labels translated into English from their original Chinese.

This was both good and bad. While the contents were probably less life-threatening than Nakumatt's offerings of yesteryear, here was proof positive that Kenya hadn't escaped China's indefatigable lust for world trade domination. Sighing over what felt like aiding and abetting China's deflowering of Africa's maidenhead, I loaded the keenly-priced Chinese imported necessities into a shopping trolley and paid with a credit card, another major advance in a country so notorious for fraud and corruption that credit card companies laughed in the face of anyone wanting to use their services when I'd last been here.

My state of disbelief over the change turned to elation on finding it simplicity itself to purchase a local SIM card from one of the plethora of mobile phone companies now operating and ultimately to astonishment as Mbarak moved on to what proved to be the biggest shock of the entire trip – a working ATM.

The relief of finding it cooperative was palpable. Getting cash from a bank just a few years earlier had involved planning of safari-preparation proportions making this the part of the trip I dreaded most. So indolent, hostile and nit-picking were the tellers in those days it seemed to be badge of honour to see who could outdo the others in accumulating swarms of dehydrated, increasingly irate customers in the ovens that masqueraded as banks. And that was just for cashing a bank cheque. Add in the extra customer apoplexy points they could accumulate on being presented with a foreigner trying to cash a traveller's cheque and every other teller just sighed. That, they knew, was game, set and match.

Mbarak was almost as ecstatic as me over the addition of working ATMs to Kenya's antediluvian banking system. They almost guaranteed a rapid and successful cash collection turnaround and since we'd agreed a price for his taxi services based on distance not time he now knew he'd have time to go hunting other fares and I'd have no excuse not to pay him. From his vantage point close to the machine, positioned there by myself as a deterrent against the ranks of boda boda drivers lounging too close for comfort, he'd seen the ATM do exactly as it'd been asked.

There was only one problem. The Kenya shilling notes dispensed were in denominations so big it gave anyone I did cash business with a built-in excuse for adding *kito kidogu* – something small – to the bill.

'No change, *bwana*. I give discount next time.' Grrr. And a note to self. Use cash at supermarket checkouts in future and ask for the change in small bills, a strategy which would sort two problems in one. Apart from neutralising the 'something small' issue it would set my uneasy mind at rest over the use of credit cards in Kenya. Yes, the card companies were now here but I'd been on the wrong end of too many scams across Africa in the past for me to match their confidence in preventing fraudulent card use.

The decision to go exclusively cash proved perspicacious. It took no more than a cursory glance at my card statement on arriving home in the UK to see that on the same day I'd used the card at Nakumatt I'd apparently also used it on an Indian gambling website. I wonder if I won?

A couple of weeks into my stay at a still deserted bungalow compound I began to regret not having been so foresighted over paying in advance for my accommodation. As the Christmas holidays approached it was clear that Ms Shipwreck's claim of Coral Cove being fully booked over the peak period had been made either in jest or desperation. For the entirety of that time I'd remained in splendid isolation save for an indolent *askari* night watchman, a mute gardener, a shuffling cleaning lady, a gang of thieving vervet monkeys and Dung, the manic compound cat I'd named after former Chinese leader Deng Xiaoping who'd had a thing or two to say about cats.

So isolated in fact that had it not been for the ever-entertaining Dung and its habit of presenting me with squirming venomous snakes whenever I was padding round barefoot on the bungalow terrace, I was in serious danger of getting down to writing a book I was studiously avoiding starting and the still empty campsite and bar weren't helping.

The desolation defied understanding. Here was a lovely beach with all the attributes for total relaxation in almost unspoilt surroundings, the reason why the Kenya expat community flocked here, or used to. Had they found somewhere better or was it more to do with something I fervently hoped was way off the mark?

* * *

The answer, when it eventually came, confirmed my darkest fears. It wasn't that there was anywhere better. Avoidance of Tiwi as a holiday hang-out was all down to security – or the lack of it – and paranoia.

It was something I'd already started suspecting after emerging from one of my regular morning wars with the pounding surf to see a uniformed policeman patrolling the beach with a Kalashnikov AK47 rifle slung over his shoulder. The message in that sight seemed clear. Not only was local insecurity now such an issue it warranted the presence of armed police on the beach but this was 2013, just a couple of years after the Arab Spring and a time when Islamic fundamentalism was all the rage in the Middle East, threatening to spill over to affect the whole of Africa.

To the north, not that far up the coast, Somalia was already being terrorised by the Al Shabab fundamentalist lookalike group, there'd been attacks on targets in northern Kenya and no matter how unthinkable anyone thought it to be, it wasn't beyond the bounds of possibility that holiday centres like Tiwi and Diani might eventually find their way on to Al Shabab's radar. We were in the largely Moslem Coast Province and for all anyone knew local Al Shabab cells could already be gearing up for attacks on tourist hotspots.

In fact, such attacks might already have started. Never the most secure of countries – Nairobi had long since been re-dubbed Nairobbery by long-term expats – it was quite possible that some of the inexorably rising incidents of violent crime weren't just regular incidents of violent crime.

No one wanted to believe it, of course. To admit to them being the product of fundamentalist insurgency would have been to sign the death warrant of tourism, one of Kenya's prime sources of foreign currency. But there was no doubt that Coast Province in particular was wide open to attack, and although no one was saying so outright everyone knew it.

Should I too be worried? Having danced around the elephant in the room for two lip-loosening beers, halfway through the third I could hold it in no longer and found myself putting the question more directly than intended to a couple of barfly expats who hadn't abandoned Tiwi and fled elsewhere for Christmas.

My approach was not best appreciated. They hadn't come all this way to be reminded of something they were clearly in full denial about and as much as told me so. Which, of course, told me everything I needed to know and I was soon weaving my beery night-time way back to my bungalow to get relievedly in and lock the door.

To date my own paranoia had been similarly locked in. But as the lights failed for the third night in a row – something else that hadn't changed at Tiwi – it burst joyfully out of its box and began rampaging noisily around the blacked out room.

Was this it? Had the first two nights' power failures been dry runs for the real thing on the third? If it was, I just hoped the insurgents would begin with the one other occupied compound bungalow to give me a chance to escape out of the rear window.

Which was when paranoia really kicked in. The unintended consequence of having security bars on all the windows was, I realised, the prevention of escape by anyone inside and I made a mental note to add escape hatches to the list of winter retreat accommodation criteria.

I was still groping around for candles to light when the bungalow bulbs flickered dimly back on and stayed on. It hadn't been a patch on the record blackout to date but it was no less memorable and I couldn't wait to raise the issue – a trifle more delicately this time – with the people who'd just moved into the bungalow on the other side of the compound, a lively Spanish couple judging by the snippets of conversation picked up as I edged gingerly along the darkened path past their lounge window on my way back from the bar.

* * *

Raul wasn't Spanish as it turned out. He was Cuban and a teacher of English of all things at a school in Nairobi, booked to stay at Tiwi with his visiting Spanish girlfriend for a full two weeks. Africa had become his new home some years before after tiring of Cuba's officialdom and somehow – I never did discover how – he'd relocated to Kenya.

Every Christmas holiday since, he'd taken a Coral Cove bungalow for the duration and this year was no exception.

I could scarcely contain my relief. Without any other longer term residents on the compound since my arrival – or booked anytime soon it seemed – I was beginning to feel not a little vulnerable. Apart from being a lone potential target for unwanted night time visitors I'd been the only compound customer for the daily tide of door-to-door hawkers touting everything from fruit to seafood and the attention they paid me was becoming tiresome.

Sure, being the only customer on site gave me an unrivalled

haggling advantage but I could only eat so much fish and once fully stocked there then followed the tricky task of refusing the advances of others – a decidedly delicate procedure when trying to explain the situation to brawny African fishermen brandishing spearguns in less-than perfect Swahili.

So thank God for Raul. With an apparently unlimited capacity for seafood and beer he not only took the heat off me but proved to be a fount of valuable information into the bargain. I had Raul to thank for confirming the suspicion the sight of that policeman on the beach had engraved on my mind concerning the absence of fellow expats.

'Feelthy running dog capitalitht media!' he spat with a fire in his eyes that told me he might not yet have totally abandoned his Cuban roots and that it might be prudent to keep my own links with the media quiet until we knew each other better. 'They the wonth to blame!'

'How tho... so?'

'Thoth dogth keepth printing bad thtuff about Kenya. Nothing but bad sheet about violenth and corruption and thtuff and people keepth leaving. Can't hack it, bloody wimpth. No backbone theeth dayth. Didn't uthed to be like that. People coming to work in Africa uthed to have... how you thay... bottle. That right?'

I nodded. This was getting interesting and words – or pronunciation corrections – might interrupt his flow.

'Not any more. Especially with teacherth. They takth one look at the paperth and runth like bloody hell! Fuck, man. What the fuck do they ecthpect? Theeth eeth bloody Africa. Violenth goth with the territory. Don't they teach keedz in the Wetht anything theeth dayth? They comth ath if they're going to work in Thalthbury or thumwhere.'

'Salisbury?'

'Thi. Worked there wonth. Long thtory,' he muttered in the manner of one not caring to be pressed further on the subject.

I made a mental note to do just that in due course but not right now. Of more interest was the loss of Kenya's expat community.

'So they don't last long.'

'I've had beerth that latht longer,' he said, draining one bottle and reaching into the cool box beside him for another. 'Eeth why I have to teach Eengleesh. No one elth to do it. They keepth running away.'

Hmmm, I thought. That didn't really compute. When I lived in Kenya I knew lots of expat teachers who'd come for the long haul and wouldn't get rattled by a few gory newspaper reports. Must be any number of them still here.

'What about the teachers who've been here a while?'

'Don't know any. Maybe finished contractth and gone. I'm one of the longetht therving at my thchool.'

Well, I thought, that seems to be pretty much that then. If Raul, with just a few years residency under his belt, was one of the longest serving expat teachers left that meant the old hands had found the insecurity threat – real or perceived – in the place they'd adopted as their new home sufficiently worrying to up sticks and leave. And, as I knew from contact with them in the past, it'd take some pretty serious shit for that to happen. Any number had had houses broken into at dead of night, been mugged on the street or found themselves dumped by the roadside by carjackers and still couldn't be shifted.

So surely SOME were still around. The ones who'd effectively burned their boats with their homelands and, with nowhere else to go, couldn't leave. Just like those two expats who'd given me short shrift at the bar. From the tenor of their conversation, bordering on the sort of racist neo-nazi rant that was becoming disturbingly unrestrained on some football terraces around the world, newcomers they most definitely were not. Had they been, it was hardly likely one would have got a laugh from the other with the quip 'What's the difference between a tourist and a racist? About two weeks.'

I'd have pressed them further for a reason why Tiwi was all but empty but after what I'd heard decided their views would likely be about as considered as an Arsenal supporter's views on arch rivals Tottenham Hotspur. More productive would be waiting to see who else showed up. It was still a few days before Christmas and there was still a chance of some remaining old hands arriving, unable to resist the lure of the beach.

It was a good decision. Some did trickle in. But it was just a trickle and they didn't stay long. They too were as dismayed by the change at Tiwi as me and had begun, reluctantly, to arrive at the same conclusion. Especially one I vaguely recall meeting years before. A friend of a friend who'd long since quit Kenya, she'd hung grimly on in the hope that the burgeoning insecurity and disrespect for Europeans who were trying to help the country develop was a passing phase. But even she was on the verge of giving up. With her contract about to expire, her Tiwi visit was her means of gathering her thoughts and deciding if she wanted to renew. But from what she'd seen of the place that looked unlikely and she'd soon be disposing of her scant possessions and boarding the plane out. Yes, she'd be sorry to leave but what choice did she have?

'Back in the day I used to feel welcome and valued,' she reflected. 'But that respect seems to be fading. I've even started feeling like an intruder at times... sometimes even an infidel. The whole atmosphere had changed, especially at the coast. Locals here always used to have a smile in their eye when fleecing you. Not any more. More and more I've noticed it being replaced with a sort of stone-eyed look of contempt and if that's the way things are going I'm thinking the time has probably come to go.'

The way things were going? In what direction, exactly?

There was a growth in Islamic influence, of that there was no doubt. But that wasn't all of it. She'd sensed an upsurge in anti-expat nationalist sentiment and even though she and her ilk could in no way be accused of harbouring racial superiority tendencies, she and many like her were beginning to feel targeted. No matter how wide of the mark it was, in the eyes of a growing number of Kenyans being white and European made you rich and privileged and many had taken to venting their feelings on the internet.

'It's all down to the growth in smart phones,' was her summation. 'They've been both a boon and a disaster for this country. Thanks to them you don't need a computer to get on the internet and it's something the extremists have realised and taken full advantage of. It's a fantastic way of messing with the minds of the impressionable and poorly educated.'

While her explanation for the absence of expats at Tiwi did sound reasonable was that just her talking or was it the general feeling growing amongst Kenya's expat community? I needed to isolate myself from the bar hubbub and think. So I relocated to a beachside table well away from the bar and gazed out, beer in hand, towards the surf-battered reef.

* * *

My solitude didn't last long.

'Anything out there?' a heavily-accented voice said from behind me.

Without asking if I minded, a burly bewhiskered behemoth of a man had planted himself in the table's only other chair and begun matching my gaze out to sea.

'Usually quite active this time of day,' he informed me by way of effectively announcing his long term residency in this part of the world.

'Saw a swordfish jump the reef once. Must have got trapped in the shallows this side as the tide went out. Magnificent sight. Good eating too. You have tried?'

I had. And just about everything else on the bar's severely limited menu in a failed attempt to find something that didn't taste exactly the same as the meal before. With the contents of every dish salvaged either deep frozen or half-thawed from a dilapidated freezer devoid of permanent power thanks to incessant power cuts and the absence of a restaurant generator the chef was clearly under orders to avoid salmonella outbreaks by subjecting everything he cooked to the fires of hell.

'Brave man,' he said on hearing my review of the restaurant. 'I don't eat here unless I know it's fresh. Except the chips. They do good chips here. Think I'll have some now. You want?'

Since he was buying it seemed churlish to decline. And since it'd be a bar regular doing the ordering, I could be pretty sure the chips wouldn't be being cooked in engine oil, the way they did it for non-regulars by the taste of them.

By the time some quite palatable chips arrived Henri, my uninvited guest, had gleaned all he wanted to know about me and had embarked on the story of his own, not unvaried, life.

A businessman in Belgium for longer than he cared to think, he'd finally sold up and taken off on a voyage of discovery around the world until he'd washed up at Tiwi a decade earlier.

This was it, he'd decided. Nowhere he'd seen could offer him the sort of lifestyle he wanted at a price he could afford without having to work again and he'd bought a sizeable house just down the coast and settled in.

As the story unfolded I found myself listening with jaw gradually falling agape. The man was effectively telling me my own story... with three important exceptions. First, he'd actually found somewhere that fitted all his criteria. Second, once found, the plan had always been to stay in the place year round and forever. Third, he wasn't averse to sharing.

Sharing? Didn't that undermine the whole project? Importing anyone into your own dream, I'd long since decided, was fraught with pitfalls. Your dream rarely coincided exactly with someone else's.

'Ah, but that's only a problem if you share with someone from the outside who's also on a paradise-seeking quest. That's why I haven't imported anyone. I've gone local.'

The woman who used to be his housekeeper, to be precise. And a bunch of wayward Kenyan orphans.

'It sort of happened by accident,' he said in the way he might have been explaining the situation to a magistrate. 'I showed kindness to one kid and it just sort of snowballed. But I love it. It's great having them around even if they do come with problems. They aren't the easiest of kids.'

I could imagine. It wouldn't have been part of my plan.

But Henri seemed happy with the arrangement and his life in general, even managing to float above all the insecurity and crime that, yes it was true, was growing by the day.

'Sure I've been robbed. It goes with the territory. This is Africa, man. Shit happens. You just need to accept it's just a redistribution of wealth thing and move on. If you don't, well, you're fucked.'

Which, later that evening, is what he almost was.

Staying longer than his usual two or three beers it was dark by the time he left me waiting for what he confidently predicted would be a better swordfish steak having ordered it for me himself.

It wasn't and I was making a mental note to question his confidence in long-term residents being less of a rip-off target than visitors when the message was delivered for me.

Still sitting at the beachside table watching the night time ocean waters dance and effervesce and enjoying one last beer before bed I became vaguely aware of a commotion in the bar behind me. Henri was back giving the staff hell while the other barflies shrank back on their stools and watched in awestruck silence.

He had, apparently, got about a kilometre up the track into bandit territory when one of the wheels of his Toyota Land Cruiser dropped off and he'd been forced to walk back to the bar in the pitch dark to seek help leaving the car and its belongings at the mercy of the night.

He was under no illusion what would happen now and how it'd happened in the first place.

'One of you fuckers loosened the fucking wheel nuts didn't you!' he started screaming at the assembled gawping throng. It wasn't a question. 'You're all in fucking league with each other, you and those bushwhackers up there. I know. I'm not a fucking idiot!'

Well, maybe just a bit of a one, I silently told him from a distance, draining my bottle and slipping silently away into the night. The last thing I needed with a bellyful of beer was to be dragged into an involvement with him, them or the squad of police he was threatening to call. Especially when I was secretly thinking that the man just might have had it coming.

Shit happens in Africa right enough. He was spot on about that. But it doesn't help to encourage it happening by setting up in the big house like lord of the manor, throwing your considerable foreign weight around and shacking up with a local who's probably someone's sister. That might not win you the respect you were hoping for and filling your house with wayward children was unlikely to be seen as an act of altruism in the eyes of some in these parts.

Indeed, I'd felt my own narrowing as his informal orphanage story unfolded. Without knowing anything about the man or his set-up I felt every sense tense. Stay wary and alert, they screamed. For all you know you might be drinking with a local kiddie fiddler with friends in high places. So, as the bar room mêlée swelled, I decided it'd be best for all concerned if he was left to fight his own battles, make myself scarce and leave what may or may not be about to transpire to those with a direct interest in the affair. The greater the distance I put between him and me the better.

* * *

Trouble was, I had to know. If I didn't I wouldn't know if I should be avoiding him should our paths cross again. So next morning, as I popped into the restaurant to pay the previous night's bill, I broached the subject with the restaurant staff as offhandedly as my intrigued curiosity would allow.

No dice. What had happened after I vacated my table and ran for the hills was clearly out of bounds. All I got was a look telling me that in alluding to the subject I was not only wasting my time but treading on thin ice. Some things were for local ears only.

But I wasn't finished yet. Overnight a small encampment had appeared on the campsite just close enough to the bar to have overheard the kerfuffle and I was sure they needed welcoming to Tiwi.

'Sorry man. Didn't hear anything,' drawled the only camper who'd so far emerged from his tent. 'Bit out of it last night. Still recovering from the trip down.'

Damn. Dead end. But maybe if I hung around a while sipping at the mug of campfire coffee he'd thrust into my hand one of the others might prove more informative.

They weren't, except to confirm another suspicion in my mind. The campsite's latest arrivals weren't the Americans I'd first thought them to be. The 'ow' in their 'down', 'out' and 'about' – words which got a good airing during our campfire-side conversation – gave them away. As spoken by Canadians it always reminded me of British West Country yokel-speak.

They weren't, of course, either British or yokels. What they were, this little knot of intrepid travellers, was a band of brothers and sisters so laid back they were virtually horizontal and their presence immediately had the effect of reminding me how tense and wound up I'd become in my few weeks here – the exact opposite of how I'd used to feel at Tiwi.

In the past, the moment I stepped onto the beach I was Tiwi-ed. All the travails of getting to it and all the woes of the outside world would float away and stay away until circumstance demanded a return to pre-Tiwi life. As anyone who got sucked into the Tiwi vortex in those days could attest, that was the worst and most difficult thing about the place – having to leave it.

But that was then. Now, just about everything about the place screamed caution in my ears and the wheel nut loosening affair and its aftermath – about which all concerned remained determinedly uncommunicative for the rest of my stay – didn't do a lot to alleviate my darkest fears.

Was it the same for the Canadians? This was far from their first visit to Kenya and Tiwi.

Yes and no. Or rather yup and nope.

'Number of people camping has definitely gone down over the years,' said my host topping up my coffee, 'but it's still a great place to escape the big freeze. Not many places in the world we could afford to stay a few weeks.'

Didn't the increase in security incidents worry him? A bomb had just gone off on a bus in Nairobi and there were reports of factional Islamic unrest in Mombasa.

'Don't really bother with the news while we're here. Escaping all the bad shit is why we come. Tiwi is like a little oasis in the middle of all that. Time seems to stop here,' he said with a look that told me my line of inquiry wasn't helping keep it that way.

Message received, I decided. I wouldn't press the matter further. I had no wish to mess with his mellow. But inside the feeling still lingered that this airhead in the sand – almost literally – approach could come back to bite them. I knew. That same approach had almost been my own undoing a few years before.

After a week or so one time at Tiwi I'd lost sufficient connection with reality to join a small group wandering mindlessly off down the beach for a picnic. A group who, in their reverie, failed to realise they were passing Panga Point, a place that got its name from any number stories of beach wanderers being mugged there at the point of a machete, panga in the local language.

Rule one amongst Tiwi's time-servers was that the only thing you took with you to the beach was a smile. Anything else and you were just tempting fate. So when I noticed one of the younger, newer members of the group carrying a camera I was suddenly jerked back into the here and now. Too late. The panga gang had spotted us.

Had we resisted it could have ended badly. But rule two – don't argue – forced itself into our collective consciousness and we made it back to the campsite camera and picnic-less but otherwise unscathed. Had we had the wit to appoint one of the group as designated keeper of wits before setting off, the kid with the camera would have been sent back and an incident that left us stripped of our Tiwi anaesthesia would never have happened.

It took a while to get it back and as I took my leave from the Robinsons – the nickname they'd adopted after the fictional family of that name marooned on a desert island – I hoped they'd never find themselves faced with having to undergo a similar rehab process. Their presence at Tiwi was precious to me. It reminded me of my own early Tiwi days and was a sanctuary from having to speak Spanglish at Coral Cove.

* * *

While it was just me, Raul and his girlfriend there, a mix of English and Kiswahili had become the lingua franca once Raul had finished laughing at my attempt to speak his language... but only until a bunch of his mates from South America arrived. Deprived of the chance to use his native tongue in largely English-speaking Kenya, Raul had grasped the opportunity to dive headlong into it with his compadres leaving me an illiterate onlooker.

I didn't really mind. If I'd been deprived of my mother tongue for as long as him I'd probably have done much the same. But as I watched, fascinated at the way every statement seemed to be a declaration of war, I had to smile at the irony of the situation.

The reason you won't find any South American country

making an entry into this book is that my lack of conversational Spanish made that continent a non-runner in my search for a regular winter retreat. Now, here was I in a country whose official languages were Kiswahili and English faced with understanding not one word in ten of the chatter in a compound I'd selected to be my home for the next few weeks. It was enough to send a bloke sloping off with an amused shake of the head.

Which, in the end, is pretty much what happened. Raul, bless him, was neither upset nor surprised by my eventual announcement that I'd decided to leave them to it and spend more time with my book and the Canadians. At least I could hold my own in French if the Robinsons lapsed into that at times.

They didn't, but only because they didn't lapse into anything much. They seemed to know one another so well that language of any kind was deemed unnecessary for communication most of the time.

When it did come it came with a drawl and a bottle in the hand, much the way it did when I was invited to join them for a barbeque at their camp.

With Christmas upon us and New Year looming the campsite had filled up a bit with the Robinsons as the focal point. Result, a veritable United Nations of happy campers at their barbeques, exactly the sort I'd hoped to find at Tiwi.

As the sun fell out of the sky they started drifting towards the Robinson's and settling in around the campfire. Here, a couple of Austrians on their way around Africa in a beaten up VW camper van. There, an ageing Swiss just arrived in a fancy four-by-four by way of Jordan and Saudi Arabia after finding his cross-Sahara way blocked by a war in Sudan. Yonder, floating around in an alcoholic haze, a British woman who didn't seem to have a tent and was happy to crash in any she found unoccupied. And close to me, seated quietly by the fire not speaking unless they were spoken to, a young couple who, to my immense surprise, turned out to be Americans.

Why surprised? Because the whole of the USA seemed to have been put off travelling anywhere by reports of the horrors coming out of places occupied by Islamic State. The Americans, went the reports, were top of the IS hit list and the resultant paranoia left places like Tiwi devoid of tents flying the stars and stripes.

So what were these two doing here? These Hansel and Gretel lookalikes seemed the very essence of the type of American who'd do anything NOT to venture beyond the confines of their fifty states.

It just went to show how appearances can deceive. They were, in fact, the son and daughter of an American missionary posted to Kenya years back to save the African from himself. After growing up in Nairobi they'd returned to the US when it was time for college. Now, like me, they'd come back on a brief visit to see what'd changed in their absence.

Their impression? Much the same as mine. There had been progress but it was only skin-deep. Peel it back and you'd find virtually the same lawless pockmarked country it was when they'd left and they'd pretty much come to the conclusion that there was only one hope for it.

'Re-colonisation?' I quipped and immediately regretted it. It was a rare American that got such attempts at humour and these two were no exception.

'No,' the girl reprimanded me sharply. 'Of course not. Jesus Christ our Lord!' she beamed with those orthodontically manicured snow-white teeth common amongst all who've been 'saved', the light of the holy virgin gleaming in her clear blue wrinkle-free eyes. 'The word of God Almighty!'

Oh Christ. The night was still young and somehow I'd not only managed to get trapped by a pair of happy clappies but a pair of the worst sort of happy clappy. The American Christian evangelical in Africa sort. In my experience, once they got a redemption resistant sinner cornered they went at him like hyenas on a fresh carcass until he gave in and begged to be allowed to repent. It was the only way to get them to stop and resistance, I knew, was futile. The only alternative was to find a distraction.

Thank God for the Robinsons. The panic in my eyes hadn't gone unnoticed by one who immediately scurried to my rescue with a plate of campfire-grilled jumbo prawns and a lengthy explanation of how they'd come by them, how long they'd been marinated in garlic and how critical it was that they weren't left on the barbeque too long.

Taste buds salivating, I grabbed a couple and greedily tucked in.

Hansel and Gretel didn't. Were they vegetarian or was it the sight of a sumptuous mix of garlic, prawn juice and saliva dribbling down my chin? The former I hoped. All the more for me.

The answer, when I finally prised it out of them, had me shaking my head and growling in irreligious fury all the way back to Coral Cove.

Yes, they did eat prawns but only ready-peeled ones.

Eh? Some sort of American health kick thing?

Er, no... (pregnant pause of embarrassment). Having never actually peeled a prawn, they, er, didn't know how.

So they'd only ever seen ready-peeled ones?

No, they'd seen unpeeled ones but hadn't actually peeled them. They'd always had someone to do that for them.

The whole campfire ensemble went suddenly quiet. Jaws dropped, eyes widened and prawns froze in mid-air between plate and mouth.

Had they heard that right? These two were the offspring of missionaries, surely the sort of people who'd be the first to eschew the old Kenya hand practise of paying locals a pittance to wait on them hand and foot while treating them like slaves. Surely becoming a missionary was to devote one's life to helping one's fellow man, not taking advantage of one's fellow man's penury and lowly position in life.

But these two seemed to be telling us just that and I could tell by the campfire-lit look in my other companion's eyes I wasn't alone in thinking the obvious. There was more to this missionary stuff than we thought. Rather a lot more.

The first things that come to most people's minds when the word missionary is mentioned are Mother Theresa, the film 'The Mission' and the most conventional of sexual intercourse positions, but not necessarily in that order. What didn't was a family lauding it over a complement of black skivvies whose meal after all the prawn peeling, I wouldn't be at all surprise to learn, was the leftover skins. If this was the reality of missionary life I, and everyone else around the campfire, had been seriously misinformed.

Well, everyone except Hansel and Grettel. The message in the look of innocence and incomprehension on their well-scrubbed faces wasn't difficult to decipher. Surely, it said, everyone had someone to peel prawns for them... didn't they?

To avoid that look, the only thing to do was get another beer from the cool box and find someone – anyone – else to talk to. Should I get so much as another glimpse of it I wasn't sure I could trust myself not to suggest to them it was a good night for a stroll along to Panga Point.

* * *

In the end, with the temptation to resist making the suggestion becoming too great it was me, not them that left. Not in the direction of the panga gang but over to Raul's place to recover my poise with one or two of the Cuban's *cervesas* and the inevitable semi-inebriated discussion on whether the real, underlying mission of American missionaries was cultural colonialism conducted via the insidious use of religious texts presented as proof of God's endorsement of the Great American Dream.

Thanks to a combination of beer and the ineradicable residue of reverence for things religious left by the Conquistadores across the entirety of South and Central America, we never did reach full accord on the question leaving me no option but to continue having the discussion with myself, largely because soon there'd be no one else to have it with.

Almost as soon as New Year was done with, Tiwi reverted to its pre-Christmas desolation leaving me back in dreaded isolation. After what had been a decidedly low-key holiday by Tiwi's previous uproarious standards, both the neo-Conquistadores and the Robinsons had sloped off back to their real lives, Henri hadn't reappeared and Dung the manic cat was proving a poor conversation substitute no matter how much I tried to engage it.

I'd been hoping we'd begun to understand one another, Dung and I. I needed its help in determining whether a small group of new, short-term, arrivals at Coral Cove were Chinese or Japanese. Named after a former Chinese leader, I thought it might be able to offer an insight. But if it knew it wasn't saying and I was about to consign the conundrum to the archives when a question from the compound cleaning lady brought it starkly back into focus. Was the foreign bank note the Japanese, as they'd styled themselves, had tipped her with on leaving worth anything?

It wasn't. The Kenya shilling equivalent of a five Chinese yuan note wouldn't have bought a loaf of bread at Nakumatt.

But in another regard it was priceless. It told me their claim to be from Japan was about as truthful as the Chinese government's declaration of having no interest in involving itself in African affairs.

Passing their bungalow one day I thought I'd heard snippets of Mandarin coming from inside. Now, their meanness in passing off a worthless note as a generous tip confirmed it. They were definitely Chinese. But why? Why would they want to have people believe they weren't?

It didn't take much working out. The Chinese had been flooding into Africa for a number of years on the trail of the continent's mineral wealth and hadn't made themselves over-popular in the process. Locals in their employ reported working conditions, wage levels and a degree of racial disrespect to rival any seen at the height of colonial rule.

Even so, Kenya's government was doing little to discourage their presence largely due to a Chinese policy that had proved so successful across Africa and the rest of the developing world.

In short, the Chinese came bearing gifts. Infrastructural development sweeteners doled out in return for rights to whatever they could dig up and cart away. Hence all the improvement work they'd carried out on the coast road close to Tiwi. A sizeable deposit of titanium had been discovered south of Tiwi near the Tanzania border and China needed good road links to get it to a dedicated ore handling terminal near Mombasa. And since China also needed good links to inland 'investment areas' it was about to inject a good whack of cash into rebuilding road and rail routes linking Nairobi with Mombasa.

To say these links could benefit from some improvement was as much a truism as Coral Cove's very survival being wholly dependent on attracting more – or even some – visitors and that the two things were inextricably linked. As the shipwrecked Swede had grizzled to me in one of her more communicative moments, people who'd been coming for years had been scared off by the state of the road, the railway and the barely functioning power and water supply networks. Where once the trip down from Nairobi used to take a few hours either by car or overnight on the sleeper train, now it wasn't unusual for either to take a couple of days – something confirmed to me by the odd arrival who had risked it, ending up dragging themselves into the campsite griping loudly that that was the last time they did THAT trip.

So, despite their hard taskmaster reputation, there wasn't much local resistance to China's offers of help, some Kenyans I spoke to even going so far as to infer that they'd actually welcome a far greater degree of Chinese influence in Kenyan affairs. Chinese money might be the only thing that'd save their tattered tourism industry.

Coral Cove and the campsite were prime examples of businesses that could well be on the Chinese takeover radar. A vicious circle of lack of business causing lack of upkeep causing lack of business had set in and it didn't need much imagination to see their respective owners biting the hand off anyone making an offer.

They'd have to have deep pockets though, not for the purchase, for the renovation. My bungalow wasn't the only one with a leaking roof, bug-infested beds, collapsing furniture, a malfunctioning cooker and a water supply so salty it left your post-shower hair like straw and your toothbrush devoid of brush.

In short, both establishments were about twenty years past their save-by dates and needed pulling down before they saved everyone the trouble and did it on their own. Maybe that's what that little group of Chinese had in mind. Since they seemed to have no interest in the beach, staying close to their bungalow for their entire weekend, it wouldn't have surprised me. China had been rampaging through the developing world buying up likely spots for redevelopment as tropical resorts for its surging numbers of nouveau riche so why not Coral Cove if not the whole of Tiwi?

The very thought had me breaking out in a cold sweat. After a couple of years working in China I'd seen what their idea of tourist resort was and it was nothing like the Tiwi I'd known and loved. Get their claws into it and almost overnight it'd be a strip of concrete casinos and neon-lit monosodium glutamate-with-everything restaurants devoid of anything not imported from China.

The very thought of that happening was soul-destroying. Gone would be any old world charm Tiwi still possessed, the tranquil ambience (on a good day) of the Tiwi community, the luxuriant plant life and any hope of seeing the beautiful shy black and white long-haired Colobus monkeys who called by the compound on occasion. I'd even mourn the loss of the thieving troupe of vervets which rampaged regularly through on a mission to demonstrate there was no such thing as monkey-proofing.

But it'd probably never happen anyway. The growing security threat would probably scare off any potential Chinese developer, much as it had done to me in the final days of my stay. A bomb had gone off in a nightclub in Diani, there'd been more deaths in factional fighting at a Mombasa mosque, someone had chucked a grenade on the very ferry I was due to board to get across Kilindini creek en route to the airport and I'd made a decision. The few days remaining until I left would be my last in this fracturing country. Life was too short for all this and there were other, less relaxation-threatened places to check out.

If I ever got to see them. Courtesy of those insecurity reports, paranoia was not now restricted to night-time power outages and the Coral Cove cleaning lady's news of being violently mugged at a coast road bus stop didn't help, almost tipping paranoia over to religious faith. If there was a God, I found myself mumbling to no one in particular, perhaps he she or it would be so kind as to direct the violence elsewhere until I was in the air and out of this benighted place.

Up to the moment Mbarak and I arrived at the creek in the pitch black on my way to the airport for an early morning flight out, it appeared that someone or something had been taking notice of my 'prayers'. Despite an increasing rash of power cuts there'd been no uninvited night-time guests or brushes with local intransigents and for the first time on this trip I began to think I might have been over-egging the insecurity pudding.

Then rule one about Africa – never underestimate its capacity to surprise – interjected forcibly and that thinking was rapidly revised. There was every possibility that Africa was saving the best til last, lulling me into a false sense of security before reminding me who was boss. We still had the ferry ride to come and the thought left my head ringing with images of all the possible grand finale scenarios Africa might have up its sleeve for me.

As the ferry pulled away from the shore imagination transformed to trepidation, trepidation to bowel-loosening dread and then, on reaching the other side without mishap, to Mbarak-hugging relief. But not for long. Horrified at the thought of a close embrace with an infidel, the Islam-orientated Mbarak shrank out of reach and I was left hugging thin air.

No matter. We'd made it and all I had to do now was navigate my way through airport formalities and get me gone. That was it, I'd decided. The last time I'd set foot on African soil until someone – probably the Chinese – took it by the scruff of the neck and did some serious work on it.

But even then I couldn't see myself returning. The security the Chinese would undoubtedly install to counter any real or imagined threat to their investments would likely be worse than quaking in my flipflops every time the Coral Cove lights went out.

So now what? With Kenya now out of the picture and Kenya being one of the least under-developed of African countries, that meant the rest of Africa was too.

Which left where? All the way home I scratched my head. But only until the realisation dawned that almost every possibility on my winter retreat criteria-fulfilling list had been tested and, for various reasons, rejected.

So selecting the following winter's destination should be simplicity itself. The number of possibilities remaining could be counted on the testes of the blue-bollocked alpha male vervet who'd watched me pack while monkeying around in the bungalow rafters before stopping to celebrate his ultimate victory over this territorial intruder by peeing with pinpoint accuracy onto every item of his rival's homeward-bound luggage.

POST-KENYA WINTER SANCTUARY CRITERIA ADDENDA

CRITERIA	ITEM	REASONING
Location	Security	Not just desirable, paramount. Getting home more stressed than before leaving defeats the object of the exercise.
	Religious nutcase-free	See above.
	Populated	Not overly-so but just enough to prevent talking-to-self syndrome taking over completely.
	Modern banking system	Without working ATMs and credit card facilities you're left with traveller's cheques and banks to contend with. Not always the easiest or most pleasurable of experiences in the more remote parts of the world.
Accommodation	Public transport-connected	Crucial to avoid costly private transport hire necessary in isolated locations.
	Reliable power and water supplies	You don't realise how important these are until they're suddenly not there.
	Not on the ground floor	Especially in dodgy areas. High up rooms have less need of window bars which don't just prevent insurgent entry but also resident's escape. Anyway, the higher up the rooms the better the view and the better the chance of catching a cooling breeze.

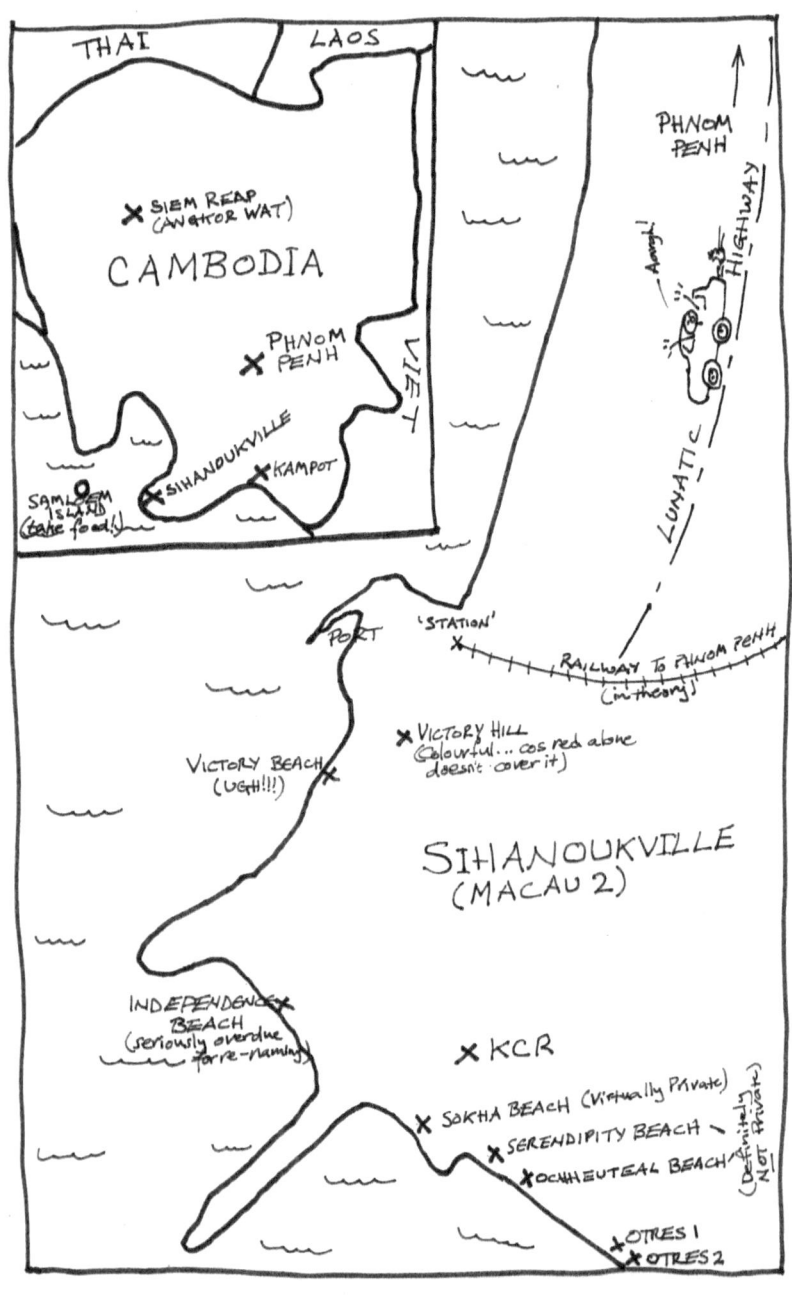

7
CAMBODIA
Din by name...

Right. So the Indian sub-continent, Europe and Africa had all been tested to distraction and been found wanting. Which left where?

The Americas and South-East Asia. So far I'd only dipped my toe in both with trips to the USA, Canada and Malaysia many years earlier and Thailand more recently. Maybe the time had come for a return to one of them. But which?

It was proving a tricky choice until I joined a group of UK friends drinking rum.

Ting! Of course. The answer was in a similar night's entertainment with Raul at Tiwi. Cuba. Why hadn't I thought of it before?

Probably because of the assumed language barrier.

'But eeth no problem!' Raul had assured me. 'Many people now thspeak Eeengleeesh in tourithst platheth.'

'Pardon. Not sure I got that.'

'I thaid many people now thpeak Eeeengleesh. I can give you thum contactth to get you thtarted.'

Cool. As long as they spoke Eeeengleeesh as well as Raul, I'm sure the Cubans and me would get along fine. And having a few contacts to get me thtarted would be an invaluable leg-up for someone knowing more about Donald Trump's tax affairs than he did about Castro's Caribbean kingdom.

'Jutht one thing though. Betht not to mention my name,'

he said with a look that left me in no doubt as to what might transpire if I did.

Message received. His secret was safe with me even though that did pose problems. How was I to introduce myself to the contacts he'd offered to provide without mentioning his name? Ah well. I'm sure I could muddle through.

The same could not be said of the pre-trip paperwork.

If you wanted to go on a two-week package holiday to Cuba the process was pretty straightforward. You just booked through a travel agent who'd do all the heavy lifting for you. But anything else and you were on your own, wading through such a swamp of obfuscation, ambiguity and regulatory red tape that I ended up convinced that since Cuba was banned from having a nuclear deterrent, to repel boarders it'd resorted to planting a minefield of immigration regulations instead.

First, there seemed to be no way in other than by a circuitous route via at least two other countries one of which must not be the USA. Then, if you did make it onto the island, new arrivals/intending subversives were confronted with such a baffling array of restrictions covering which currency you could use, where you could stay and when you could log on to the internet you'd end up wishing you hadn't bothered.

By the end of a complete day of being sucked down into this bureaucratic quicksand I was beginning to think just that. But I wasn't done yet. Driving me on was the little matter of Cuba's winter climate and affordable cost of living. Ticking every winter retreat box in both regards it'd take something mighty off-putting for Cuba to be scratched from the list entirely. What would it be?

Its eventual discovery left me thumping the desk and screaming at the screen in fits of hair-tearing frustration. Buried under a rotting pile of regulatory landfill was a limit on length of stay that made all my research to date redundant. Initial visas were limited to one month renewable for a maximum of one further month meaning that even if I did survive the visa application and renewal torture I'd have to return to the UK before winter was over.

Buggerbuggerbugger. That did it. If that's the way they wanted it, I decided, they could keep bloody Cuba. And the rest of the Americas. There were other places. Places that didn't put hidden visa tripwires in the departure lounge. But where? After the Cuban officialdom minefield experience, the absence of anything similar was now top of my winter retreat criteria list. Was there ANYWHERE as allergic to such things as me?

* * *

Cambodia, said one respondent to the near-desperate advice-seeking email I'd put out to anyone who'd been round the houses. I'd apparently have trouble finding a country less wrapped in red tape.

Seriously? Knowing little about the place other than that it'd had its guts well and truly kicked out in a very uncivil war in the seventies I'd need a lot more convincing... particularly in light of the source of the recommendation. Giving Cambodia the five-star treatment was the German layabout I'd first met in Sri Lanka and then been seriously misguided by in Thailand. A fleet of jumbos could get through the gap between his idea of a winter escape perfection and my own.

'Absolutely,' he persisted. 'And not just that. Weather's good that time of year, it's cheap, food's good, US dollars are in widespread parallel use to the worthless Cambodian rial, the ATMs work and you can stay as long as you like. What's not to like?'

When he put it like that it did sound promising. But there had to be a catch. What was it?

'If there is one, it's corruption. Nothing gets done without a sweetener,' he finally admitted. 'But if you've got the cash you can do pretty much anything you like.'

Hmmm. This was beginning to sound like a tourist office

promotional and a faraway voice told me to stay very very wary. Any moment now, it said, he'll be offering you a non-refundable plane ticket he just happens to have kicking around at a knock-down price.

He didn't but probably only because that, he knew, would be an inducement too far. I knew him too well. Anyway, from the tone of my emails he could tell he had my attention. If corruption really was the only problem, Cambodia was a definite candidate for the 2014/15 winter escape. The practise of palm-greasing and diversion of funds in the direction of Cambodia's not-so-needy couldn't possibly be a patch on Kenya, the place I suspected invented it if the information contained in a receipt obtained at Mombasa airport on the way out was anything to go by.

It wasn't that the coffee I'd bought in the departure lounge had cost me twice the usual Kenya price, it was the discovery that someone else was pocketing the change. Rather a lot of it. The sum of 149,850 Kenya shillings to be precise.

According to the deceit, sorry, receipt as payment for the one hundred and fifty shillings coffee – about two dollars – I'd apparently proffered the princely sum of one hundred and fifty THOUSAND shillings and had received that, less the cost of the coffee, in return.

Funny, I thought. I don't recall having to buy a wheelbarrow to carry the change in. Nor being thrown in jail for trying to export more than the few small shilling notes foreigners were allowed to take out of the country.

What I do recall is the refreshment bar assistant not meeting my eye when I thanked her for the coffee. You usually got at least a smile out of Kenyans you did business with. Maybe she was distracted by the thought of how she was going to get the equivalent of an entire year's wages out of the building without having her collar felt or how she was going to accumulate it in the first place. There'd have to be some pretty serious coffee drinkers passing through the departure lounge for her to fill her till with anything like that amount during the day.

I was still sniggering inwardly at the apparent stupidity of the scheme when, finally, the penny dropped. I was, of course, being hopelessly naive. This was an African airport, dork brain. Home of the scammiest of the continent's scamsters, aka politicians, where they operated with complete immunity, aka untouchability, and where a few hundred thousand shillings would be small beer in the overall scheme of African money laundering things. Cambodia, I thought, would have to go some to match this level of scamming ingenuity, so inventive was it at times in Africa that were similar effort devoted to national development the continent's standard of living would now be indistinguishable from Switzerland's.

The GL wasn't convinced. Cambodia could match anything Africa could do, he insisted. After all, its current crop of leaders had inherited a blank canvas to work with. Taking power after the murderous Khmer Rouge Marxists had been obliterated by Vietnam's in the seventies, they found themselves in charge of a country boasting zero education, government or organisational skills. The KR's Return to Year Zero policy of taking things back to absolute agrarian basics had ensured that anyone with any intellect or ability ended up in the killing fields leaving the country wide open to anyone with the brains to have kept their educated heads down during the KR's tyrannical rule.

'Yeah, but Africa's had centuries of practice,' I argued. 'Cambodia's just starting out.'

'They're quick learners,' the GL insisted. 'That's why they've kept regulatory barriers to a minimum. They've realised that the more rich foreigners they can attract into the country, the more there are to rip off in other ways. Cunning, huh?'

I had to agree. It was the sort of pernicious deviousness you'd never find in Africa. There, it seemed to be a given that the only way to make hay out of outsiders was to hit them with such a raft of unmeetable regulations it wasn't possible to keep the gatekeepers happy without greasing a few palms.

After that, Cambodia sounded like a breath of fresh air.

'So come,' said the GL. 'You can stay in my house.'

* * *

Ah-ha. So that was it. The GL had quit Thailand, moved to Cambodia and was trying to make money out of his spare room. I should have twigged. But I'd been blinded by the PR blitz and by the time I realised it, it was too late. I'd booked my flight.

Ah well, in for a penny...

What tipped the balance was unexpectedly not having to get a visa in advance. I could, apparently, get one on arrival at the airport for just a few dollars. 'But make sure you get a business visa,' said my host-to-be. 'Both the tourist visa and business visa are for one month but the only one you can renew without having to leave the country is the business one – for anything up to a year. There are agents here who'll do all the legwork for you so you don't have to do all that queuing at the immigration office. Neat, huh?'

If that was true I was in. Despite my reservations the GL could have my custom at his house until I got my bearings. It would at least save me the trouble of casting around for my first bed before I flew in. Anyway, he did make it sound appealing. Big place with all mod cons just outside the coastal city of Sihanoukville and a stone's throw from one of the best beaches in the country. What more could a boy want?

Rather a lot as it happened. Once more, the GL had misinterpreted my idea of accommodation perfection. He'd assumed I was OK with being all-but marooned in an isolated, virtually deserted concrete gulag whose only other occupants were a large group of apparently insomniac hearing-deprived Indonesian ruffians incapable of communicating in any way other than by shouting, especially in the early hours of the morning. Had they been housed on the other side of the vast, sprawling 'resort', as the GL had imaginatively styled it, I'd have hardly noticed them. But being right next door and adding to the cacophony with the importation of a large howling dog into a room not a metre from my bedroom window, they were a tad difficult to ignore.

The GL seemed genuinely taken aback when I announced I'd be seeking alternative accommodation, preferably somewhere within walking distance of the shops and which tuk tuk drivers could actually find when called to come and pick me up. So identical were the 'resort's' monstrosities masquerading as houses and so confusing the compound's layout that after the third tuk tuk driver had failed to find the house and gone away without being paid, others stopped answering my calls. Word seemed to have got round that this number belonged to a foreigner with a time-wasting obsession who was probably being paid by a rival taxi firm to tie up their services without recompense.

Although he never admitted it, I suspected the GL's number was also on the tuk tuk time-waster list which was why he'd resorted to renting a monstrous deathtrap motorcycle.

'I can arrange one for you too,' he offered.

Thanks but no thanks. I was still recovering from my single, helmetless, wall-of-death ride into town on the back of his and had long since decided to entrust my health to the ubiquitous, if only marginally less crash-proof, tuk tuk. At least they didn't have the engine capacity to try to break the sound barrier and once you found a driver with a smattering of English who could find your location and destination, at the pittance they charged it was clear this was by far the better option. The only problem was choosing from the collection of driver phone number cards I'd started building. And remembering their names, never in English on the card.

Actually that became less of a problem once I discovered they pretty much all had Din in their name, a particularly appropriate identifier given the average decibel level at any time of day or night anywhere in Cambodia. If it wasn't tuk tuks tukking frantically past your door day and night it was dogs or cockerels. If it wasn't raucous television racket it was families shrieking at one another over the incessant pounding of nearby construction sites. And if it wasn't booming night clubs it was funerals or bloody weddings, days long every one of them and every one to the accompaniment of the same, level-eleven distortion blasted out by banks of the cheapest, shrillest amplifiers the event organisers could lay their hands on.

The moment I landed in Cambodia I knew my foresight in having invested in a job lot of ear plugs was one of my most perspicacious purchases ever made. Without them, the book I'd made some progress with in Kenya would still be more a thing of the imagination than of actuality. They even dulled the pain of the hilltop Buddhist monastery's daily attempt to initiate an earthquake.

Before arriving in Cambodia I had no idea Buddhists were even capable of generating such an invasive racket. The low murmur of meditational mumblings coupled with the odd bit of gong bashing was about all I'd ever heard from monasteries in Sri Lanka and Thailand. But Cambodian Buddhists seemed to be of a different mindset. One that considered apocalyptic cacophony an integral part of the enlightenment-gaining process. And not just for themselves. For the whole city.

Which was why they'd planted themselves and their antediluvian, brain-shredding amplification system atop the hill overlooking Sihanoukville. From this position they had a clear, uninterrupted line of noise across the entire expanse of the city and its unfortunate, presumably hearing-impaired, residents. Me included. Every morning. At daybreak. For an hour at least.

The only respite from what sounded like an avalanche of cosmic ice cream vans cascading over a cliff to a cacophonic death in the reverberating valley below was when the wind got up and carried the din in the other direction. The relief when this happened would have been palpable had it not been for the fact that I'd started to become conditioned to being startled out of sleep by it. When it wasn't there I'd wake up worrying that the end of the world it seemed to be portending had actually happened and I'd missed it.

But such days were few and far between and in the end I fled from the crumby, city-centre guesthouse I'd taken refuge in from the German layabout house experience and headed for the beach. Somewhere on the casuarinas tree-lined strand a few kilometres out of town and behind the hill from which the Buddhists were intent on waking the dead had to be a sanctuary from all this. Somewhere I could bunk down and sleep until the heat of the sun, not the end of the world, woke me up.

* * *

It took a while to find. Otres beach, highlighted by the guidebooks as the most restful of Sihanoukville's beaches, was a great deal longer than the guidebooks led me to believe and had moved on a bit since it'd last been reviewed. A couple of kilometres apart, Otres was actually now two beaches, the second having been fled to and colonised by Otres's initial hippy settlers after someone had blabbed and news of their discovery had found its way to the fleshpots of Ibiza.

Five minutes in the booming mêlée of bars that was now Otres One was enough to have me following the hippies' lead and ordering my tuk tuk driver to head with all speed to the sanctuary of Otres Two.

Good decision. Although the hippies were now largely gone – moved to Otres village on the banks of the muddy, mosquito-infested river that flowed out into Otres Bay – they'd left behind a haphazard encampment of sleepy low rise guesthouses and restaurants, their thatched roofs blending neatly in with the verdant tree cover along the beach. And in place of the incessant thump of Otres One drum and bass, the Otres Two soundtrack was mostly a combination of lapping waves and the dreamy meditational hum of the happy, flip-flopped camper drifting randomly along the golden strand in search of nothing in particular. Bliss.

Yes, I thought, this would do nicely. This is where I could see myself whiling away the next few weeks as long as the price for this tranquillity didn't break the bank. In my experience, the only places that had managed to avoid being turned into commercial hellholes were those charging through the nose to keep the drum and bassers out. Could I dare hope that Otres Two hadn't succumbed to like money-grubbing eliteness?

First impressions were not encouraging.

Faced with having to select from a veritable chocolate box of guesthouse choices I decided to let instinct take over and only investigate the ones its compass needle swung strongly towards.

In the past the technique had served me well, gut feeling rarely sending me down rabbit holes to nowhere. But after directing me to a smart designer boutique hotel charging over a hundred dollars a night I reluctantly admitted that on this occasion instinct was having an off day and, as much to stop it laughing as anything, transferred the job to the hard-nosed realist in me.

Within minutes it had guided me to the equally laughably-named Honeymoon Hotel, largely thanks to a sign outside offering rooms at eleven dollars a night. Sprawling but basic, on first encounter with its interior it seemed to tick just enough boxes to at least warrant a short stay while I checked out other possibilities at my leisure.

One night was all that was needed to realise its name could only have come from its honey pot colour and lunatic design. Only a groom wishing to test his bride's resolve would book in here. It wasn't just that its rooms were either scorched by the sun or left in total darkness the whole day, it was that the only ventilation in those rooms was via the large gap left between the top of the rooms' dividing walls and the roof. Privacy and sound proofing – a likely requirement for the average newly-wed – were virtually non-existent and after being kept awake all night by the owner's snoring I crawled blearily out into the street to start looking with some urgency for an alternative.

Early investigations were not promising. A good eighty percent of the guesthouses along Otres Two's golden mile could be scratched from consideration on the grounds of price, noise, location or simple horror. Rather more than one or two had streams of raw, untreated sewage running through their grounds to empty into the sea and rather more than one or two of their owners seemed oblivious to the effect this might have on prospective guests. Their only expressions of surprise came on seeing me turn on my heel and walk quickly away muttering about the need to be careful where I swam and to restrict my fish-eating to species only found in deep water well away from the shore.

Having exhausted almost all the likely accommodation possibilities the prospect of having to go back to Honeymoon cap in hand and beg to be given my old room back began to loom large. Compared to the other places I'd seen, the Honeymoon owner's snoring was now looking the least environmentally worst option.

But what was that? A place I'd not noticed before seemed to be *pssssting* at me – a place I'd previously passed by thinking it to be a restaurant but now realised was a real contender.

Behind its eating house frontage White Beach Bungalows offered a small selection of rooms to rent that even a real estate agent would have trouble describing as bungalows. White Beach had both a ground and an upper floor.

To some, such a misrepresentation in the name might be good reason for rejecting it out of hand. But to one still mindful of the Coral Cove blackout experiences in Kenya it was pure gold. Being anywhere but the ground floor hadn't just risen up my list of winter retreat priorities, it almost topped it. Yes, I know a determined insurgent wouldn't be put off by the need to creep soundlessly up the stairway but since White Beach's stairway was more unevenly-stepped step ladder than proper staircase, the chances of one making it to the upper floor in the dark undetected and unhurt were slim to nil thus elevating my chances of getting a good, uninterrupted night's sleep in direct inverse proportion.

First sight of those invader-repelling steps had me revising earlier uncharitable thoughts concerning Cambodians and their apparent innate inability to fabricate evenly-spaced stairway risers. Maybe they were cunningly designed that way to deter invading forces. Maybe that was the reason the rise of every step up the concrete edifice that was the staircase at the German layabout's house was different and why the top step was a good five centimetres higher than any other. Like me one bleary still jet-lagged morning, uninvited guests could well find that difference the cause of their own unexpectedly swift and noisy descent to the hard marbled floor below.

The longer I stayed in Cambodia the more I came to think insurgent deterrence was indeed the reason for the uneven nature of almost every staircase encountered. But only until witnessing the construction process of a four-storey building opposite another accommodation possibility I was testing for acceptability.

If this construction was anything to go by design consideration was clearly the subordinate of keeping costs to the minimum, the developers relying mostly on semi-literate migrant workers brought in to live on site with their families and leaving them to it. The only time they seemed to check on progress was when they brought in lorry loads of sand and cement to be mixed exclusively by hand as the workforce inched its way upwards without any obvious form of plans, mechanical aid or measuring equipment.

With children gambolling around in the construction site chaos and with no concrete pouring or agitating equipment anywhere to be seen, the set structure would be so full of air holes it'd have all the strength of an Aero chocolate bar reinforced only with the skeletal remains of a child or two gone missing from the worker's vast families without them noticing.

The process – as I was to witness during succeeding winter stays at a place I'd eventually decided couldn't be bettered in Sihanoukville – took three years before they'd even reached the fitting out stage and left me questioning the wisdom of choosing as my ultimate choice of accommodation an apartment on the top floor of a residential hotel built, I had no doubt, in like fashion.

* * *

Even so, I had no plans to leave. It'd taken some effort to find something that fitted the bulk of my accommodation criteria and anyway, there were precious few buildings in the city that weren't collapse-prone.

Except White Beach Bungalows perhaps. At only two storeys high it'd probably be spared that and, on first sight, had seemed an ideal accommodation choice.

Affordable, quite well run, friendly, sanitary, close to all amenities, not mosquito-infested and so close to the beach you could almost jump from the rickety balcony into the sea, White Beach ticked a lot of boxes and my first week in residence passed in a state of contented harmony with the world. After a great deal of tail chasing I'd discovered somewhere I could sit back and relax in the knowledge that I could probably find nowhere better.

But then my inner realist made a determined reappearance thrusting my criteria list under my nose and suddenly I was back to square one. After a week in residence the White Beach short-comings were no longer so easy to overlook. It wasn't just that none of the rooms had kitchen facilities, there was also the small matter of a nightclub away in the distance equipped with such powerful amplification it shook White Beach to its minimalist foundations. All night long.

If the nightclub's intrusions into Otres Two's tranquillity had been a nightly occurrence I wouldn't have lasted the week. But since it was largely limited to weekends it was just this side of tolerable.

Living without cooking facilities was not. Yes, a wealth of affordable eateries was available close by but once you'd seen one selection of Cambodia's limited culinary offerings you'd pretty much seen them all and it wasn't long before I began yearning to be able to go to the fridge and pull out the ingredients for something, well, else.

So that was that. As sad as I'd be to leave White Beach, this shortcoming was a shortcoming too far and, as much as I loathed the very idea, meant the hunt for accommodation perfection was on again, this time for a short-let apartment at an affordable price.

Under normal circumstances finding one would simply involve selecting the right letting agent and perusing their properties.

But this was Cambodia, a place where the definition of normal was not finding things in the places 'normal' countries put them. Hence, not one letting agent anywhere at Otres or at any town-based shopping centre I visited and nothing like a property section in any newspaper I came across. Everything seemed to be done via ads on noticeboards or by word of mouth leaving me with something of a problem. Knowing nobody other than the German layabout, that reduced my range of options to one.

So now the hunt was on for noticeboards and the obvious place to look was shopping centres. Only one problem with that. It meant a return trip to town.

As my tuk tuk fought its way through the thickening traffic on Sihanoukville's outskirts the full extent of my habituation to the glacial Otres pace of life gradually dawned on me. The closer we got to the centre the more I felt like a country bumpkin making a rare trip to the bright lights only to find them way too bright for comfort.

But it had to be done and on discovering a noticeboard at the entrance of the first shopping centre the tuk tuk pulled into I breathed a sigh of relief and muttered a small prayer of thanks.

Then an oath on discovering no ads on the board for short-let apartments. Damn. That meant going deeper into the heaving Sihanoukville morass and I was grudgingly about to give the order when a thought struck. While I'd stood perusing the board any number of foreigners had passed by carrying shopping bags full of provisions. THEY must have kitchens. How had they done it?

Exactly as I thought. Word of mouth, said the first shopper I asked, an ageing Canadian gent living in an apartment block nearby which, he told me, had a range of places to let. Wonderful, I said. Let's go.

Spirits high on finding this so easy, they gradually sagged and then sank without trace on being shown what the Cambodian owner had on offer.

Yes, he had some newly-renovated places in his block but no they weren't for short termers, he said. People wanting somewhere for just a few weeks seemed happy with slightly less well-appointed rooms.

For less well-appointed read dungeons.

Hidden away round the back of the main block was a natural light-deprived yard containing a selection of almost windowless monk-like cells seemingly chiselled out of solid concrete. Just one look at the interior of one with its single unmade bed, its bare concrete cooking shelf and its lightless concrete shower room was enough to raise images of the tomb from which Christ is said to have risen again. How appropriate, I thought. There'd be a very good motivation for rising again if you ever found yourself with no option but to move in here and my face must have betrayed my feelings.

'But is cheap,' said the owner. 'Just hundred dollar.'

'That what you'll pay me to live here?' I thought but didn't say.

Message received his face told me back as he muttered something in the local dialect and sloped disconsolately off.

So all in all, not such a good start after all. Back to the drawing board.

Or maybe not. This exchange brought the drawing board to me in the form of another Cambodian who'd been earwigging our 'conversation'.

'You want apartment? I fix,' said a roly-poly woman with a wicked glint in her eye. 'How much you pay?'

Maybe a bit more than a hundred dollars a month if this is what it got you.

'No have hundred dollar apartments. Have hundred fifty. You like?'

Show me.

Two hours and several hair-raising trips later on the back of her son's motorbike through Sihanoukville's drug-crazed traffic and I'd seen and rejected five apartments, every one of them fabricated for people almost as desperate as those who'd be tempted to take up residence in one of the downtown tombs. It was time to reappraise things, perhaps by raising the price.

The woman's son's eyes lit up on hearing I might go higher than a hundred and fifty for the right place and without pause began calling numbers on his phone.

'Wait here,' he told me speeding off and leaving me stranded in the courtyard of a grubby filling station in an even grubbier district I didn't recognise. 'Man come.'

He'd bloody better, I thought. With no idea where I was other than that it wasn't the most salubrious of Sihanoukville's neighbourhoods, I felt a tad exposed. For all I knew the eyes of every hoodlum lurking in every dark corner of the district were glued to the shoulder bag that went everywhere I did.

Thank God for 'The Man'. Not only did he show up in five

minutes flat but wasn't riding a motorcycle. My luck with the Sihanoukville traffic was wearing thin and I had no desire to test the facilities of the local hospital. The tuk tuk he was in looked only marginally less accident prone but at least you had some protection from the madness around you and I clambered in to join him.

Three dehydrating hours later and we'd finally narrowed the search down to one place, the one I finally decided could not be bettered within the price limit I'd set for Sihanoukville.

Getting to that point, though, was an education. Cambodians, I began to suspect, were different to everyone else. Before this guy, any letting agent I'd ever encountered started by trying to interest you in properties at the top end of your budget range, only grudgingly agreeing to guide you to the cheaper ones later. Not this one. His technique was to start at the bottom and work up.

* * *

By bottom I mean bottom. Concrete bunker after concrete bunker was looked at and summarily rejected and I was about to call it a day and return to square one when he urged me to give him one last chance. Although it was getting late and I was more than ready for some beachside refreshment I agreed, but only because the place he had in mind was on the way back to Otres.

The intriguingly named Khmer Camelot Resort was not what I was expecting. Not one of the places he'd showed me resembled my ideal for regular longish winter stays and there seemed no reason to think this one, closer to the top of my budget range, would be any different. To find somewhere in a decent quiet location away from main-road hullabaloo and pollution, within striking distance of a beach and amenities, equipped with acceptable cooking facilities and sporting a pool to cool off in looked like a dream too far in my price range and I'd begun to think I'd have to dig a bit deeper into the reserves.

KCR was to prove me wrong.

Almost the moment the tuk tuk swung into its airy, verdant courtyard off a rocky back road at the end of which was one of Sihanoukville's best-kept beaches I knew the search was over. In front of me was a horseshoe-shaped compound comprising a small office on one side, a three-storey block of balconied apartments topped with an ornate traditional Khmer style roof opposite and a curious brick-built rotunda housing a restaurant in between. And the moment I realised there was a fair-sized swimming pool hiding behind the apartment block I knew I need look no further.

YES! Providing I could afford it, this is where I could see myself settling in for the long haul and in relief I all but hugged the agent and his driver. Why the hell hadn't he shown me this one first? Presumably because his property letting technique had been culled from those 'Escape to the Sun' TV programmes, the ones that use the formulaic technique of teasing participants with properties unlikely to receive approval as the means of softening them up for the coup de grâce – the one they'd pay anything to get.

If this was the man's strategy, it worked. I was sold before even seeing the rooms. And when I did, I was pulling money out of my pocket to pay the deposit before we'd even discussed the rent. Although they weren't big, the rooms were sizeable enough for my modest needs and each had a reasonably-equipped kitchenette with a decent-sized fridge, a well-appointed shower room and a small shady balcony containing a table and easy chairs positioned to look out over Sihanoukville's tree-covered hills away in the distance.

In short, compared to the string of hovels they'd tried to sell me all day this was Shangri-La, morphing into nirvana the moment the manager told me the price. Even on my meagre pension three hundred dollars a month was do-able. So do-able, in fact, that I caught myself beaming at the manager and ignoring the inner hard-nosed realist desperately trying to get my attention. This is sounding a bit too good to be true, it nagged. Aren't there any problems?

'Well, just the one,' the Cambodian manager told it in the best English I'd heard on this trip. 'We don't have any rooms available.'

So that's what an imploding world sounded like. Not the apocalyptic thunderclap you might expect but the simple, complete and immediate descent into utter, deafening silence. The agent and the manager had become goldfish, opening and closing their mouths with nothing coming out and me frozen in time unable to open mine.

NOOOOO! Fifteen long travel-wearied years it had taken to find somewhere like this and now the prize was being snatched away just inches from the winning tape. My poor exploding head could take it no more and suddenly the absolute aphasia the news had triggered was put to the sword by a crescendo-ing rush of screeching brakes. Ha, they seemed to be taunting. Gotcha!

Bastards! Was this the Cambodian idea of a jolly jape? If it was, someone – most likely the agent for bringing me to a place that had no rooms available – was in danger of losing his front teeth. Which were now grinning at me. Good. That'd make them an easier target.

If they'd just stop moving that is. Why would they be doing that, grinning and moving at the same time? Were they trying to tell me something?

They were. The manager hadn't finished his sentence. Through the scream of cranial brakes I managed to decipher three words coming after 'available'. And when the brain re-engaged long enough to take them in and analyse their meaning, I all but kissed him. 'At the moment' he was adding.

'So... er... you will have an availability soon?' I managed to stutter.

'Yes. January one.'

'I'll take it,' I croaked, probably a bit too loudly, almost before he'd finished speaking.

'OK,' he replied. 'But not this one. This taken from tomorrow.'

'OK. I'll take the one that IS available.'

'You don't want to see?'

'Is it different to this?'

'No. Same same. Just down there,' he said pointing along the rear walkway off which the rooms were accessed. 'But someone in til end-December.'

Fourteen days. That's all I had to wait. I could do that. It wasn't as if staying on a while at White Beach was an especial hardship. Just frustrating. I wanted in and I wanted in NOW and it didn't matter what the other room looked like. It was MINE and all I wanted to do was move in, crack open a chilled beer by the pool and smile back on the events that had led, finally, to a place all my senses were telling me was THE place. The one I now realised I'd been searching for the whole of my adult life.

Ah well, I consoled myself. Guess I'll just have to make do with a sun lounger on a beautiful golden beach and dinner at the one restaurant that did have some variety on its menu. It wouldn't match up to being able to pull my own choice of food from my very own fridge in my very own kitchen in my very own very affordable flat but it'd do. For now.

* * *

It was the longest two weeks of my life. Until I was in, even though I'd paid the first month's rent in advance plus a one-month deposit, there was still the chance of things going horribly, brain-manglingly awry. This was the developing world, the place where, in my experience, a confirmed booking meant only one thing – that someone else had your money and you had nothing but their practised 'no problem' smile in return.

It was a source of stress that made relaxing on the beach all but impossible. The entire time my mind's eye saw nothing but that smile, the one I knew could be interpreted as it not being a problem for one of you, just not necessarily you.

What I needed was a distraction. Without one I knew my head might actually explode and it was with some urgency that I started casting around for something a good deal more diverting than just kicking my heels at Otres.

The trouble was that the beach – like all beaches in the region – was simply too inactive. Usually in the tropics, changing weather and sea conditions at least produced the occasional swimming challenge. Not at Otres. Every day at this time of year the weather was the same unblemished sunny sky with the occasional heavy shower and the sea the same warm balmy bath with hardly a lap of a wave. Coupled with the gently sloping bottom, if you forgot about the raw sewage draining into them, the waters at Otres were a toddler's dream. You needed to swim a very long way out to get out of your depth and the lack of any obvious form of non-human life in it made it highly unlikely you'd bump into anything bigger than the odd plastic bag.

'Is it the same on the islands?' I asked the White Beach manager.

Before he could answer, another guest at the bungalows interjected.

'We've just been wondering der same ting,' said a thirty-something Irishman, recently arrived with his wife. 'Let's go find out!'

Easier said than, as it turned out, done. On paper, getting out to the islands seemed as simple as hailing a tuk tuk in the street. There were any number of agents offering trips to Koh Rong about twenty kilometres from Sihanoukville's ferry harbour and it was just a matter of choosing a boat and the place you wanted to stay when you got there.

For when read if. In Cambodia you need to make generous allowance for the TWAT factor, the Third World Alternative Truth advisory well known amongst seasoned travellers and never more applicable than in this particular case.

Sure, they said. Nice boat go Koh Rong nine in morning. Take an hour. Can be at nice place for lunch. Then go nap at nice bungalow. I fix?

The nice aforementioned boat turned out to be a party boat which left at ten thirty, fired up its apocalyptic drum and bass 'music' at ten thirty-five and didn't turn it off even when the boat dropped anchor just off Otres beach to serve a lunch of soggy white bread and spam and to make an announcement that the boat was going no further. Instead, it'd be staying right here – in sight of White Beach Bungalows – where the mostly Chinese teenage passengers were invited to go snorkelling.

Few took up the offer. They either failed to understand the broken English announcement made largely inaudible by the disco racket or, like us, they'd pre-paid for rooms on Koh Rong and would really rather prefer to continue to the island forthwith.

'No have,' said the only member of the boat's crew who was identifiable as such. 'Weather bad. No dock Koh Rong this boat. Need go speedboat from Sihanoukville.'

'How?' I enquired. 'We here.'

'You many?'

Me and them I indicated.

'OK. I get boat.'

A great deal of phoning and gesticulating to the shore later and we were clambering aboard a longtail fishing boat to be ferried back to port. First just me and the Irish couple, then a few other non-Orientals who'd figured out what was going on and also wanted to get to the islands, then half the population of the People's Republic of China who hadn't and didn't but who'd had second thoughts about staying on a party boat with no edible food.

First it was one, then two, then virtually the entire complement of passengers on a hundred foot, three-storey ferry boat, all trying to get onto our twenty-foot skiff. It mattered not to them that the skiff was getting low in the water nor that there were no lifejackets. The lemmings had decided that the party boat must be sinking and the single 'lifeboat' was their only chance of survival.

With no action being taken by the skiff's spaced-out 'captain' to prevent an imminent sea-borne disaster, the time had come to mutiny and, having heard me testing my smattering of Mandarin on our fellow Chinese passengers earlier, all eyes fell on me.

In the end, it wasn't the few threatening words of Mandarin I knew that prompted the invaders to retrace their steps back to the party boat, it was the look in the eyes of the wall of Europeans towering over the Chinese who joined me to drive the bastards back. You have two options, the look said. Go back and stay dry or try to stay and get very very wet. Your choice.

In the end they chose wisely and we were soon on our way back to port, the now closely-knit group of Chinese invasion repellers trying not to think about what might have happened had we not stepped in to take control.

'Never a problem,' said Mick the Irishman waving away our fears and nimbly defusing the tension. 'Dey was always going to back off once I told 'em to feck off. Everyone in de world knows dat word.'

True. And he proved it later on finding the booking agent at the harbour less than co-operative over changing our tickets to the speedboat ferry. When trying to be reasonable didn't work he switched to a string of Irish expletives and within moments we were on our way.

Right into the next agent fabrication.

Eventually landing exhausted at Koh Rong Samloem, the smaller of the twin Koh Rong islands, late in the evening all we wanted to do was get to our luxury chalets, as the agent had styled them, get a beer and a meal in the nearby bar and crash out.

Stymied on all counts. The only things true about the agent claims were that they were chalets and there was a bar nearby.

What wasn't included in the brochure was that, like prison cells, the chalet rooms weren't separate but joined at the hip with paper-thin walls, their sliding glass front doors impossible to close properly leaving the subsequent night time mosquito invasion rubbing their mandibles on finding the room unequipped with mosquito nets. It wasn't even possible to take refuge in the toilet without baring all to the world. Like the chalet's frontage the toilet door was also transparent glass.

Under normal conditions all the above would probably have been met with little more than a resigned shrug. This was situation normal in the developing world and, after all, it was only a couple of nights. But having narrowly escaped drowning, getting into two separate fist fights, dying of thirst at sea and finding the speedboat crossing unexpectedly stomach churning, our collective sense of humour was wearing a little thin.

On finding the bar next to the so-called resort had no food it collapsed altogether, not even being rejuvenated on the ironic news that the shortage was down to the bar's supplies being aboard the weather-delayed party boat.

All we could do was look at one another and crawl off to bed in envy at the mosquitoes. They'd be the only ones getting a feed tonight.

And the next night.

After spending the entire next day hunting for sustenance with only partial success, we once again took refuge in beds we hoped not to expire from hunger in during the night.

Prior to that point of desperation we thought we'd cracked it. Along the main beach was a place offering a seafood barbeque. Ah-ha. Here was a place that seemed to have had the foresight to stock up on locally-caught fish for moments like this. This was, after all, an island in a highly productive sea and there was no good reason why there shouldn't be a healthy supply of seafood at all times.

No good reason except for the fact that no one apart from this place seemed to have thought of it. Or of stockpiling essential supplies from the mainland on which the island was fully and completely dependent, even for vegetables.

But at least someone had had the sense to get the fishermen on the job and grabbing the opportunity we all but ran towards the place – to be met with a tiny plate of prawns and squid each and a bill that could only be covered through a highly reluctant use of my credit card.

No amount of pleading could win either more food or a price reduction and in the end, weak from under-nourishment, we feebly gave in and paid up.

'And how much shall I add for service, sir?' the waiter had the barefaced gall to ask without blushing.

'Here's my tip,' I managed to restrain myself to saying on rising frailly from the table to leave. 'Plan ahead.'

It was advice I'd decided I'd be following a lot more rigorously myself when – if – I ever made it back to White Beach and my ultimate Cambodian sanctuary, the sumptuous by comparison, Khmer Camelot Resort.

POST-CAMBODIA WINTER SANCTUARY CRITERIA ADDENDA

CRITERIA	ITEM	REASONING
Location	Easy visa	What is it about the developing world and visas? Such restrictions are counter-productive in attracting tourists and their hard currency and countries heavily dependent on the tourist dollar could do a lot worse than follow Cambodia's easy visa example.
	Din-free	What is it about the developing world and noise? Doing anything without attendant pandemonium seems to be a concept foreign to the developing world mentality and if the world's prime ear plug manufacturers aren't already located there to take advantage of a ready-made insatiable market for their product they should seriously consider it.
Accommodation	Kitchen!	You don't realise how necessary this is until it's missing.
	Non-collapsible	Almost non-existent in the poorer regions of the world but gold dust if you can find one. Saves on coffin-repatriation costs.
	Upper floor	Less chance of the tensile strength of bars on windows being tested by night time insurgents and greater chance of getting a decent, invader uninterrupted, night's sleep.

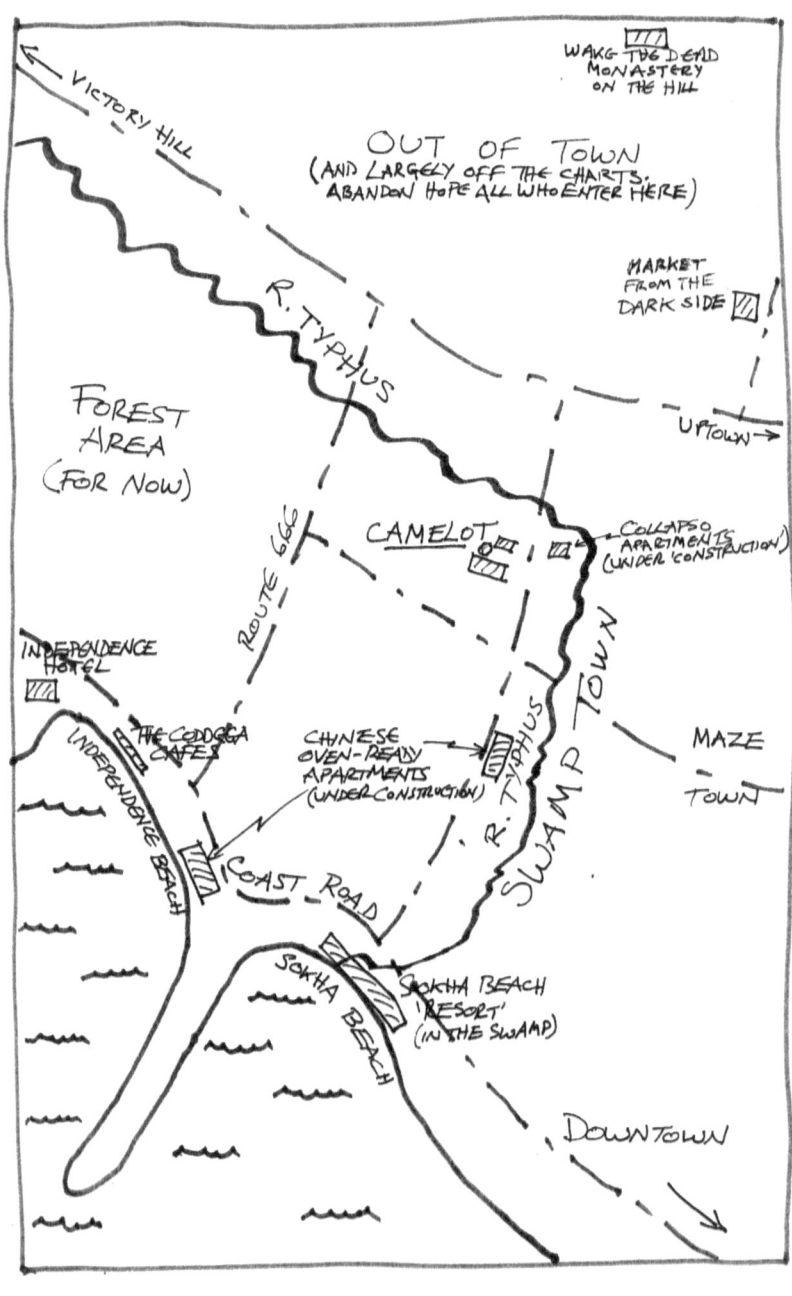

8

CAMELOT
AKA Scambodia

Once finally in and occupied, early indications were so promising there seemed nothing I could fault the Khmer Camelot Resort on.

Except, perhaps, its name.

No matter how much I tried to ignore it, a Jeremiah voice nagged in the back of my head reminding me that KCR's namesake hadn't turned out to be quite the thing of substance believers in King Arthur and his knights of the round table thought it to be.

The intervention was not well received.

'Oh purrrlease!' I snapped back. 'Just because the owner is so fixated with the Arthurian legend he's named his hotel after Arthur's mythological domain, that's a good enough reason to be concerned this place will turn out to be a Camelotian castle-in-the-air? Seriously?'

'Just sayin',' mumbled the suitably-chastened voice in response.

'Well don't. Unless you've something a bloody sight better than a fairy story to offer as advice against becoming complacent with my choice, just leave it. Know how long it's taken to find somewhere that ticks most of my winter retreat boxes? Fifteen bloody years. That's fourteen years longer than I expected to be travelling this road and frankly, the tyres are wearing a bit thin.

'Truth be told,' I continued mumbling feebly to myself, 'the fabric is showing through in places and I'm not sure they have many more miles left in them. So please voice, just butt out and let me park up for a while will you? If there are any serious drawbacks to this place they'll show up in good time. OK?'

Stunned silence. The inner Fault-Finder General in me wasn't used to having its voice of caution challenged and wasn't quite sure how to react. So probably best to slink off into the shadows, lick one's wounds of humiliation and wait to see how things unfolded.

The weary traveller in me was relieved to see it go. But only until noticing the backward glance thrown over its shoulder as it faded from sight.

'OK,' it said. 'Have it your way. But I'll be ready to accept your apology when the time comes.'

Bastard.

* * *

As days turned to weeks with nothing of substance emerging to support the voice's concerns it began to look like I'd be thumbing my nose at Mr Sceptic. Somewhat to my surprise, on this occasion it looked like I'd been right and his nagging warnings had been without foundation. KCR, it seemed, did have it all. Facilities were good, the place was well-run, it was close to all amenities and the beach and it was all within budget. What was not to like?

Well, maybe that the road alongside and the building site opposite were a bit busier and noisier than expected. And the heaps of rotting garbage dumped on the roadside and turning the nearby creek purple were proving more of a pungent eyesore than my senses had first detected. But apart from these minor inconveniences, what was not to like?

Er, maybe that the management expected guests to pay for toilet paper, didn't clean the pool as often as one might have liked and filled the hotel with hordes of shrieking out-of-town families at weekends?

Yes, OK, such things did detract a bit. But apart from the road, the building site, the garbage, the extra costs, the sometimes-cloudy pool and the lack of weekend privacy, what was not to like?

The place being in the direct line of fire of that hilltop monastery, perhaps?

Oh God. Yes. That thing. That was going to intrude on the overall ambience somewhat. But with the judicious use of earplugs...

'Seriously? What are you? Some kind of ostrich?' Oh dear. The inner hard-nosed realist I thought I had under control was back and refusing to be fobbed-off.

'Have you become so burned out with looking for the perfect place you're now prepared to stick plugs in your ears and your head in the sand so you can't see or hear the sort of imperfections that'd have had you fleeing from similar places just a year earlier?'

Oh crap. Yes. He could well have a point there. Judging by what was obviously going on all around me it was beginning to look like I might have lapsed into denial mode.

But wait a minute. Wasn't it also possible that having tried everywhere else I'd actually found the one place whose imperfections, whilst being annoying, weren't SO annoying they couldn't be tolerated in the short term and acclimatised to in the fullness of time?

Yes, that could be it. Casting my mind back over the years there hadn't been one place whose faults wouldn't have eventually penetrated my ostrich ear. But KCR was different. Here, there didn't seem to be an itch that couldn't be scratched.

'Sure about that?' interjected the voice. 'Aren't you forgetting the state of the local market?'

Oh bugger. Yes. That. It was true. That could be an itch too far. To keep living costs down and satisfy the ethical man in me, having a local market to shop in was high on the location criteria list. But so was staying healthy, something that would be coming under serious threat if there was no alternative to obtaining supplies from the vilest, filthiest, darkest, most mediaeval example of apocalyptic environmental decay I'd ever seen.

Even by developing world standards that steaming market was enough to have arch purgatory-made-flesh painter Hieronymus Bosch gagging. Mixed in with dumpsters overflowing with a cocktail of rotting remains and what smelled like the detritus of a cat refuge were bank upon bank of blacked-out fruit and veg stalls, chopping blocks running with the blood of indeterminate species being hacked to shreds by equally-bloodied cigarette-lipped men wielding monstrous cleavers and tank after tank of writhing unidentifiable sea creatures waiting to have their entrails ripped from their bodies and unceremoniously tossed into an open gutter of blood, guts, flies and pestilential street cats, probably the only reason why I saw no rats unless they too were part of the butchers' offerings.

Frozen in mid-stride on ducking into this rancid, lightless, airless chamber of horrors, three things came immediately to mind – I'd been in African bushmeat markets less hazardous to health than this, if I placed any value on my own health an alternative shopping venue had to be found tout suite and nowhere was the term black market more applicable. Whatever alternative I chose it should at least be somewhere I could see what I was buying.

Grinning broadly as he listened to the story of my shopping expedition to the market from hell the man on the KCR reception desk thought for a moment then suggested Samudera, a mishmash supermarket to rival Kenya's Nakumatt for haphazard product placement and which turned out to be the place similarly market-repelled expats ultimately gravitated to.

It was with a sizeable sigh of relief that I finally found it. Not just because it was an ideal alternative to the market from the dark side but because I'd got there and back in one piece. Not until I'd already parted with sixty dollars for a secondhand bike for use in the hunt for Samudera was I to learn that Cambodia's truck drivers regarded anything on two wheels as fair game.

Three near-misses and several exhaust fume-induced choking fits later I reluctantly decided a plan revision was required. Maybe best to leave the bike un-ridden until I'd not only got a good mask but had developed the bat-like senses local two-wheelers relied on to preserve life and limb.

This enforced change of strategy was regrettable. Not only had I found a bike to be by far the best way of discovering parts of a city new to you but two wheels could get you out of 'situations' way quicker than two legs – a vital ingredient in the exploration of a city's darker corners where encounters with those of dubious intent and packs of rabid street dogs could almost be relied upon. But for the sake of self-preservation it had to be done and in the end, to placate my grumbling inner pioneer spirit, I eventually plumped for a middle way. Tuk tuks for expeditions to the teeming city centre and the bike for safaris into quieter neighbourhoods and the beach.

Especially the beach. Two in fact, both accessible via relatively quiet roads which was handy once I discovered the closest, Sokha Beach, was privately-owned by the luxurious Sokha Beach Resort where the price of a lime juice alone was more than the daily rate for my apartment.

So that, in reality, just left Independence Beach a couple of kilometres further on.

Surprisingly under-trafficked, the road to it meandered out into Sihanoukville's sparsely-populated rural backwater where reminders of Cambodia's French colonial history and pre-Khmer Rouge habitation leapt out from every field. Around every one were the remains of substantial brick-built enclosure walls, many so intricately constructed they could only have been the brainchild of long-gone well-heeled landowners intent on keeping riffraff out while flaunting their wealth at one and the same time.

Here and there the odd lazy cow munched mindlessly at the scrubby vegetation but by and large the fields seemed to have been left to run wild, almost as if what was left of Cambodia's population after the ruthless Khmer Rouge tide had swept viciously across the landscape regarded the fields as tainted.

It was much the same at Independence Beach. Judging by the crumbling portico-ed edifice guarding its entrance, here had once been a well-manicured beach frontage where flouncy-frocked madames twirling parasols would once have promenaded with their linen-suited mustachio-ed beaus through a myriad of scented tropical plants before taking tea and cocktails on the now long-disappeared marbled beachside cafe terraces.

The evocative remains – and ghosts – of that fabled era were everywhere, left to rot back to the land with no obvious attempt being made to either conserve or remove them. It was as if decay was simply part of normal existence in Cambodia or that no one in the country could see any value in conserving anything. Even the mind-boggling temple ruins at Angkor, the most extensive in the world and which Cambodians must have known about for centuries, had only relatively recently started receiving both tourist board attention and visitors – together with their tourist dollar millions – by the lorry load.

Or then again it could have been that the country just didn't have the money to spend on such frivolous niceties. From what I could see the only hard currency coming into the country was from international donors, tourists like me and from the export of textiles and pepper. Damn good pepper it has to be said, picked and sorted by hand at a little place called Kampot not far from Sihanoukville, but hardly the stuff fortunes are made of.

Hence the shanty of decrepit shacks masquerading as restaurants at Independence Beach dotted along what must once have been a magnificent, money-spinning strand of golden sand sheltered from the blazing sun by towering shady mango trees. No one seemed to have any spare cash to re-invent Independence leaving its undoubted potential as a lucrative tourist dollar earning machine all but untapped.

One or two of the shacks were making a bit of an effort by producing menus in languages other than Khmer. But for the most part it was a matter of either learning the Khmer words for noodles, rice, squid, fish, coconut and beer or pointing at dishes being served up to the smattering of locals arriving for lunch during the week, growing to mass shrieking family invasions at weekends.

The moment I discovered it I knew I need look no further for a regular weekday hang-out. With the food and drink costing pennies, a beach the generally smiley cafe owners at least made a token effort to keep free of detritus, waters not over-obviously choleric and no apparent plans to turn Independence into a Copacabana lookalike, this was what I'd been looking for so long and I wasn't alone in thinking so.

Rooted in Cambodia so long they gave the impression of having been brought in by the tide and left to shrivel in the sun, a gaggle of 'mature' European, American and Canadian 'gentlemen' encountered here made their way to the beach daily to eke out tiny pensions and even tinier savings through 'meals' of fifty cent-a-glass local beer and heavily-scented exotic 'cigarettes'.

Here, unless I was very much mistaken, was the very embodiment of the CODDGGAA, representatives of the ubiquitous tribe of coffin-dodging dyspeptics, drunks, geriatric gits and assorted addicts to be found in every corner of the developing world keeping the owners of the shadiest bars in business. I'd never been in such a bar and not encountered one, mostly male but not exclusively, with a tale – invariably tall – to tell at both length and repetitive frequency and of which I could see myself becoming a paid-up card-carrying member unless I was very very careful.

I could see it coming. The signs were all there. Agreement with the Independence Beach entourage over this being the perfect venue for our respective needs tended, unfortunately, to confirm it. All it needed was for me to double my alcohol intake, develop an unhealthy drug dependency and move downmarket into one of the tomblike hundred dollar-a-month rooms I'd seen at the outset of my accommodation search. Rooms I could easily see any one of these gentlemen of the beach flopping insensibly out in at the end of each drinking day.

It was the horror of that mental image that, I think, was my salvation. I'd grown accustomed to something rather more accommodating at KCR and the thought of having to leave it and descend to such depths through an over-indulgence in Cambodia's plentiful supply of gut rot hooch and mind-altering drugs was about as appealing as having no option but to shop at 'that' market.

Reeling at the prospect, I thought nothing could supplant the memory of that place for aversion therapy until an even more shudder-inducing thought occurred. Those tomblike rooms must have become just that to some of their occupants over the years. Without funds for health insurance and with no option but to rely on public medical facilities only marginally more sanitary than the asphyxiating Independence Beach toilets, I could imagine this tomb-dwelling coterie providing the Sihanoukville mortuary with a flow of business the country's bartenders could only dream of.

Once the thought was implanted it just kept getting more vivid with every trip to the beach and in the end I knew only one thing was going to quell my growing fears of being sucked down to CODDGGAA level without realising it. My custom had to be transferred to the one cafe on the beach no fully-fledged CODDGGAA could afford. It might not help keep within my daily budget but it would at least reduce the likelihood of becoming a contributor to the mortuary's attendance records myself.

* * *

Reduce, yes. Eliminate, unfortunately not.

It might have been the extra few metres of cycling needed to reach my chosen cafe or the richer diet encountered there but shortly after migrating away from the CODDGGAAs the prospect of being in need of the mortuary's attentions before any of my erstwhile companions leapt out to waylay me with a grin of vengeful mischief.

Smiling smugly at the thought of having escaped the mortuary's clutches on collapsing in the KCR pool at the end of a particularly hot cycle ride back from Independence, a strange sensation in my ankle prompted me to clamber out and inspect it. For no apparent reason a vein I'd never previously noticed was now very blue, very swollen and throbbing in a manner suggesting cause for concern.

'Zut alors!' gasped the Canadian Quebecoise I was sharing the pool with. *'Ne bouge pas! Restez la!'*

A quick dredge of my very underused French and I had it. For some reason he was warning me to stay very still, a reason that was to become all too clear when he deigned reluctantly to switch to English to recount his own experience with blood clots.

Suddenly very tired on a walk downtown he'd decided to get a check up at a local private clinic. He went no further with his walk that day. Just hours later he was in the capital Phnom Penh being seen by a specialist heart surgeon. A blood clot in the leg was diagnosed and he was told to lie very very still while the operating theatre was prepared. Any moment the clot could shift to the brain and kill him.

'The vein in my leg looked very much like that,' he said, pointing at my ankle. 'It might be nothing but I'd suggest you get it checked out. Shall I call the consultant?' The look on his face suggested no was not an answer. The last thing he needed was to have to deal with a corpse in the pool. Especially one that hadn't even had the decency to let him speak French.

With the consultant warned of my imminent arrival, the Quebecoise mobilised others – of which there were many at KCR, all escaping the midwinter Canadian deep freeze – to pack a bag with hospitalisation essentials and organise a taxi to take me straight to Phnom Penh. The consultant could see me at his clinic in the city's Calmette hospital tout suite.

Expecting to be delivered to one of the shiny new private hospitals I'd noticed during an acclimatisation stay in the capital before moving to Sihanoukville I was somewhat taken aback to find myself queuing with half the population of Phnom Penh at the reception desk of one of the public hospitals, one in which every sign and all conversation was in French. The consultant, it turned out, was beset with a conscience that required him to help out at the public, formerly French colonial, hospital on occasion, today being one of them.

With no option but to await my turn to be seen I found a seat in the heaving waiting area and took in my surroundings. Beijing's central railway station at Chinese New Year, the time of the single biggest human migration in the world, sprang immediately to mind. As my eyes adjusted to the steaming, virtually lightless, paint-peeling room whose only form of ventilation was a single ceiling fan rotating almost imperceptibly overhead I could just make out who the competition for the consultant's attention was. I was, it seemed, in a room full to the rafters of the self-same people I'd last seen in Sihanoukville's typhus market.

'Figures,' I remember mumbling to myself as a nurse ushered me, the sole European in the place, through the throng to a consulting room. Considering the level of hygiene in the market the only surprise was that my fellow patients had lasted long enough to make it to a hospital.

Two hours, two consultants, one ultrasound scan, a lot of head scratching over the Cambodian-accented French, one visit to a dispensary and a forty-five dollar bill later I was out on the street hailing a tuk tuk. Unless I'd misinterpreted their French, it wasn't a life-threatening embolism after all. It was a minor case of varicose veins which could be treated with the drugs on the prescription they'd given me... after I'd handed over the money.

As relieved by the diagnosis as I was to be out of the hospital, I headed for the hotel I'd used as a stopover on first arriving in the country and to my bed. It'd been a long and exhausting day and all I wanted to do was take the drugs and sleep. But not before doing an internet search for the drugs prescribed.

The result was as surprising as the entry without knocking of the spitting image of the wicked witch of the West asking if I needed anything, as in ANY THING. I didn't. And neither did I need these drugs. Apart from the worry that I might have fallen victim to Cambodia's counterfeit drugs epidemic, Daflon was a treatment for haemorrhoids, as in bloody piles.

Well, I thought, at least I have a remedy handy for such an attack, something that wasn't beyond possibility during the next day's heart-stopping helter-skelter flight to Sihanoukville in the back of a suicidal driver's suspension-less taxi, both in urgent need of hospitalisation themselves. If one thing couldn't get me, I found myself thinking as he tore past a lumbering truck on a blind bend, it must be in the stars that something else would.

In the end this game with the constellations ended Newham 1 Astrology 0 but it could easily have gone the other way and my relief at arriving without mishap, haemorrhoid attack or something a great deal worse was only matched by the pleasure of being out of the Phnom Penh pressure cooker, off the highway and back in my Camelotian sanctuary. Despite the roadside trash, the fetid nearby creek, the construction site opposite, the incessant tuk tuk noise and having to share the pool with Canadians who knew full well how to speak English but wouldn't, it had become home. A place I knew I'd be coming back to next year, especially if the manager kept his promise and booked me into the room furthest away from a road that was now being torn apart by monstrous resurfacing trucks and out of earshot of the nightly howls of a neighbour's dog prone to panicking at the sound of any real or imaginary insurgent it sensed.

* * *

The manager's signature on a receipt for the month's deposit on the room sealed the deal and a week later I was on my way back to the UK a contented man. After a decade and a half of looking I'd found a place where I could happily leave my stash of personal stuff in the blissful knowledge that on my return, for the first time ever, I could dispense with all the fuss of sanctuary searching and simply head straight for it.

Stashed securely away, that receipt was my passport to one of the most joyous, carefree UK summers since childhood. For the first time in years my mind wasn't plagued with the fear of being caught in the impending winter doom before finding somewhere to escape to. Instead, the only thing occupying it was the choice of next winter's flight, something I was on to before even starting to unpack.

Rarely had I had so much pleasure in parting with money. The utter, unadulterated delight of locating the right flight at the right time at the right price and punching the 'buy' button before summer had even got started left me with a smile that was to last right up to the moment the stars decided to get their own back and teach me a lesson I wouldn't forget.

It was inevitable I suppose. Ever since beating the rap the day of that death-defying taxi ride down from Phnom Penh I'd been secretly worrying when retribution would arrive for thwarting the stars' best efforts to ruin my day and really should have guessed. The constellations would undoubtedly choose the moment when all had been arranged for my return, summer was done with, winter was all but on us and my thoughts had turned to whether my travel bag would hold together for one more trip.

With impeccable timing, the minute they saw me pull it from storage they struck. Into my email box the stars dropped a bombshell they knew would atone for all the disappointment of seeing me cheat fate.

'Remember that room you booked?' they said with a scarcely disguised smirk of vengeful satisfaction. 'Cancelled.'

And just to rub it in, don't even think about trying to book one of the other rooms. They're cancelled too. In fact the whole place is cancelled. So looks like you're back to square one, sunshine. Square minus one in fact since you're now stuck with no accommodation in a place you've a non-refundable ticket to.

'So now do you get it?' they smirked. 'No one beats the stars. Not in the long run. All you did in sidestepping our attempts to kill you was annoy us and make things worse. Now it's personal and we've decided a mere harming of the physical entity alone just won't cut it. So now we're going to spare you physical distress and mess with your psyche instead. Hence this email which should, if our assessment is correct, cause such a loss of hope and faith in human nature it'll cause so much long-term pain you'll wish you hadn't survived that taxi ride after all. Get it now?'

Bastards. They weren't wrong. Their assessment that I'd be left screaming inside at the KCR manager's email informing me of the owner's decision to let the whole hotel to a Chinese casino for use as staff accommodation for the next three years and to cancel all other bookings was faultless... with one exception. As if it pleased some vindictive streak in them to leave me in the dark over the full extent of despair the news would trigger, the stars had ensured that complete loss of faith and hope wouldn't be the whole of it. Once the initial shock and seething fury had subsided, I'd discover the full set included charity.

Up to this point I'd been prepared to give both KCR and Cambodia the benefit of the doubt over its foibles. Here was a country still trying to find its feet and, after due consideration, I'd managed to convince myself Cambodia's intentions to tackle the problems it faced were, by and large, honourable.

Well now I knew better. Now the true extent of my misreading of that cherubic face of innocence had been revealed to me all charitable feelings evaporated. Behind that smiley welcoming façade lurked a deceitful, callous, money-grubbing, unscrupulous leech that thought nothing of bleeding its victims dry before ratting them out to the highest bidder.

Whether it was a national trait that had its root in the country's horrific past I knew not and, after all feelings of understanding had dissipated, could now care less. Along with everyone else with upcoming bookings I'd just seen my immediate future summarily scuttled by a host with as much obvious respect for his guests as Cambodians had for the environment and there could be little doubt I wasn't the only one left grinding his teeth as he sat down to craft a suitably-worded TripAdvisor review I hoped would take the enamel off the owner's teeth. Prospective guests needed to be warned that should they make the mistake of booking in here they, like me, risked losing not only their sizeable room deposits but any stuff left there for safe-keeping, neither of which was deemed worthy of mention in the owner's deadpan, contrition-less, pro forma cancellation email.

That omission was duly corrected in one of the most difficult response emails I'd ever had to write. In order to retain any hope of getting my money and possessions back somehow I had to stay this side of business-like, resisting all and every expletive insertion temptation and any exhibition of the spittle-flecked paranoia now consuming me concerning all things Chinese, the ones at the root of this change of circumstance.

With relations between me and the People's Republic already what the diplomatic corps would describe as 'strained' after I'd published a less-than reverent book about life in the gearbox of the Chinese propaganda machine a few years earlier, anything with a Chinese connection was now enough to set my paranoia nerves jangling.

'Would it really be beyond the bounds of possibility,' my inner voice was now hissing conspiratorially in my ear, 'that as retribution for embarrassing China some super-sensitive little soul in Beijing has set their goons on you with a plan for getting their own back? Creeping up behind you and filling in the sanctuary-finding hole you've spent so long digging would be just the sort or sneaky spiteful stunt they'd pull, wouldn't it?'

It was a proposition I had difficulty arguing with. But surely my little book wasn't worthy of such an elaborate prank. The revelations within its covers had hardly set the world alight. So no. Surely this was just a coincidence. The Chinese couldn't be that cussed... could they?

Well, even if they could, bugger them. I had an airline ticket and was buggered if I was going to let it go to waste. There were winter retreat alternatives to KCR in Sihanoukville. I knew. I'd already checked them out during my pre KCR-finding sanctuary-seeking traipse around town.

'So up yours China,' I murmured as I boarded the flight to Phnom Penh. 'You don't get to screw me over that easily.' That was the speciality of the Sihanoukville tuk tuk drivers.

* * *

They started by trying to fleece me for the ride from the bus drop-off point to Backpacker Heaven up at Sihanoukville's Victory Hill fun spot, a place I'd recalled the German layabout giving a good review having used it himself on first arriving in town.

Yet another bum steer by a man I was starting to have serious doubts about. Yes, the rooms weren't bad and it was close to any number of decent eateries but in every other respect he must have been talking about somewhere else.

The rooms didn't, as he'd told me, have cooking facilities, the hotel's viewless bar and restaurant rated a 'meh' at best, the pool was so small that diving in meant risking brain damage on the opposite wall and the rooms were a good deal pricier than he'd led me to believe. In short, I was once again a victim of the GL's delusions.

And presumably his loss of hearing. Backpacker's next-door neighbour was a wedding-specialising restaurant with just a low boundary wall separating my room from the caterwauling, earplug-defeating, Cambodian wedding din which kicked-off at five in the morning and went on for days.

When the restaurant began cranking up for a third day running of cataclysmic connubial cacophony I knew the time had come to take urgent evasive action. Having already checked out the accommodation alternatives close by and declared them even more uninhabitable than Backpacker's, in desperation I called the GL.

'You can come and live in my house,' he enthused.

The flashback to my very first days in town this triggered left me mouthing a string of silent expletives at the phone, a fit of feather-spitting speechlessness he took as an invitation to launch into his latest room-letting spiel.

In short, he'd moved. No longer in the Stalag 14 compound of last year but in a bungalow close to Victory Beach just down the hill from where I now was, and he had two spare bedrooms he sublet to transient visitors. One was currently available and I could have it at a 'very reasonable' rate.

Right. I knew precisely what that meant but so desperate was I to get away from the weddings I agreed to give it a go and within the hour I was in.

Or rather, out. Out of Backpacker Heaven and into the GL's outhouse, a shabby little room off the bungalow's open porch completely unprotected against intending night-time invaders and in which I was locked out of the main house once the GL and his newly acquired Cambodian girlfriend had retired behind its double-locked barred metal doors.

Sheee-it. This was more precarious than my bungalow in Nairobi a bunch of dead-of-night insurgents had targeted some years back. That incident might have ended a good deal worse had there not been two sets of steel doors separating me from them. Here, there were none.

But at least the GL's new place was quiet and I revelled in the comparative tranquillity as I planned my next move.

Top priority was the retrieval of my belongings from KCR and two rather strange phone calls later I was on my way there to meet the manager.

My first call was received with some degree of surprise, as if he had no recollection of me despite our being on first name terms by the time I'd left the previous March.

'Oh. Yes. OK. Yes. You. Yes. I call back,' was the gist of the call. Then: 'Yes. Ah. Can be there later,' was a summary of the second.

Can be there later? Some mistake here, surely. With the needs of a full complement of Chinese casino mafiosi to cater for, surely he'd be there most of the time.

That he didn't and wasn't only became apparent on arriving at the appointed hour to find the place deserted, locked up and showing signs of being overrun by the plants that had received such tender loving care during my previous residency.

Although he deserved a great deal more, a simple quizzical look seemed sufficient for a man who'd sheepishly shown up ten minutes after me and had led me, with not a mention of this turn of events, to the storeroom.

In a country with a forty-year history of dictatorship and authoritarian rule, and where making direct reference to sensitive topics or querying the motives of those in positions of power could lead to consequences, his apparent blindness to both my look and the elephant in the room might have worked with a Cambodian.

Not with someone who was not only not Cambodian but had left a sizeable amount of money to cover the room deposit.

At the mention of it he went pale and seemed to stagger, a reaction I presumed to finding himself confronted by someone with enough brass neck to challenge the status quo and venture into minefield territory.

'Sorry,' I added quickly in an attempt to tiptoe back out of it, 'but it is rather a lot of money.'

'Ah. Yes. Of course. Yes. I can give refund but thought you might want to leave it to cover your booking.'

My turn to stagger now. Had he forgotten he'd cancelled it?

'Ah. This situation is changed. I send email last week. You did not get?'

No I bloody didn't. Or rather, thanks to rubbish internet connectivity at both Backpackers and the GL's house I hadn't been able to check my emails for a while and had no idea what was awaiting my attention in the inbox.

'What did it say?'

'Owner wants to open to visitors again in New Year. Must renovate first. Tenants not good to rooms. So am surprised you ask for return of your items. Thought you were happy here.'

'I am... was,' I managed to bluster through a jaw that had temporarily lost control of its faculties.

'So what, er, how, er...?'

* * *

Minutes later I was in a tuk tuk gleefully giving the stars and the Chinese the finger as we headed back to the GL's house in possession of all – or most of – the facts and a small bag of things I'd need while waiting to move into the room I thought I'd never see again.

'My point, I think,' I told them out loud to the driver's unconcealed consternation. He obviously didn't get many gesticulating foreigners with imaginary friends in his cab. All I could do was grin. If he'd heard what I'd just heard he'd be grinning and gesticulating too. The Chinese, the manager had just told me, had 'run away' leaving rent unpaid and every room and the grounds in a delapidated condition. They'd proved 'unreliable' and now the owner wanted to recoup his losses through re-opening KCR as it was before the Chinese moved in.

For glee read ecstasy. All I had to do was wait a couple of weeks and my chosen sanctuary would be mine again. Yes! If the manager hadn't backed away on seeing the look of manic triumph gleaming in my eyes I'd have hugged him.

'So I keep deposit?'

In my delight I almost doubled it before reality tapped me on the shoulder and coughed. I'd be needing that cash to cover the cost of my second choice of second home – the rather more expensive White Beach Bungalows at Otres Two.

Moving back into my old room there the next day I found myself laughing out loud to the bemusement of the White Beach manager. This, it had just occurred to me, was déjà vu all over again. In my journal for December 2015 I could, with one exception, simply write 'see December 2014', that exception being there'd be no repeat of the island excursion experience. As an old Sihanoukville hand now, I knew better.

Likewise with certain beaches tested as possible alternatives to Otres Two and Independence.

Simply put, there weren't any. If it had been noise and annoyance I'd been craving I couldn't have done better than the downtown Ochheuteal Beach or Otres One and had I been harbouring a perverse hankering for plain unadulterated filth none could outdo the unutterably disgusting Victory Beach for base pollution.

Straying onto it on my first day at the GL's nearby bungalow, all I could do was gasp. In all the places in all the countries in all the world, never had I come across a beach like it. So strewn with garbage was it that you needed aerial photographs to locate patches of clear sand and so well 'used' those patches they needed forensic inspection to ensure they were clear of raw excrement, used condoms and hypodermic needles, if I hadn't been in danger of over-heating I'd have turned on my heel and fled.

But with the need to cool off becoming urgent and the water looking surprisingly inviting for such a beach I decided to chance it with a quick in/out.

Big, big mistake. What looked like smooth sand on the bottom was in fact sludge and after sinking a few inches into it all thoughts of staying any longer were rapidly abandoned. I have no idea what my bare feet had sunk into and I had no burning desire to find out. But it undoubtedly had something to do with the beach's close proximity to the city's commercial port and I made a mental note to look a lot further afield than round here for a seafood meal.

'But you won't find a better meal deal than the restaurants at Victory Hill,' said the GL. 'I eat there all the time and I haven't suffered.'

Yeah, but that's because you counteract the effects of the food with massive doses of Cambodian brewery antidote while you're eating, I thought but didn't say. Taken in sufficient quantities the country's toxic beer could kill cancer cells and I was surprised the country hadn't marketed it as such. It wouldn't have looked out of place amidst Cambodia's standard range of product advertising.

It was probably why Victory Hill attracted so many CODDGGAAs, every one having been taken in by word-of-mouth reports of the beer's elixir of life properties. No matter whether it was late late evening or the dawning of the day the roadside bars at Victory Hill overflowed with elixir imbibers seeking to extend what would otherwise be drink-induced truncated lives with jug after jug of fifty cent-a-glass glug. Then undoing all the good work with plateload after plateload of chips-with-everything fried cholesterol while making determined attempts to catch HIV from the inexhaustible supply of scantily-clad come-hither hostesses swarming the Victory Hill streets.

The guidebooks weren't lying when they described Victory Hill as 'colourful'. Red alone didn't cover a district the police left largely to its own de-vices unless they too were on the pull or the take. If anything was out of bounds I missed it on trips there with the GL, a man now well on his way down desolation road himself and not keen on travelling it alone. Desperate for a travel companion, he'd fingered me as a kindred spirit and would not take no for an answer, even going so far as to offer to pay for my meal at his favourite hang-out.

I declined. Not on the grounds of not wanting to check the food and the place out but because acceptance would have inevitably led to a cementation in his addled brain of my acquiescence in becoming both his confidante and collaborative cohort.

It was not a label I was keen on having attached to me but I was intrigued. Surely, at the prices he said the restaurant charged, the food could not be anywhere near this side of edible.

I could not have been more wrong. For just a few Cambodian rials – charging in dollars seemed to be a step too far for the redoubtable Mrs Sim, the restaurant's no-nonsense proprietor – one could gorge the night away on anything from fresh fish to finger-licking fried fungi while tuning in to a cornucopia of cosmopolitan voices berating the Michelin guide for failing to give Mrs Sim the recognition she deserved.

OK, maybe Mrs Sim's roadside caff within nostril range of an open drain wasn't quite up to Michelin standards. But it was good enough for my modest culinary needs and I knew I'd be making regular forays to it from KCR once I was re-installed… but only in the early evening while the GL was sleeping the afternoon session off, before the red lights came fully on and the night time elixir drinking shift arrived. At that time of day, Victory Hill was almost genteel.

* * *

Well, genteel by Victory Hill standards anyway. For true gentility you needed Otres Two, the place I'd flee back to as soon as the first CODDGGAA was spotted weaving his unsteady way in the direction of Mrs Sim's.

Despite one or two changes Otres Two was still as laid-back and unruffled as I'd left it twelve months earlier. Kicking my heels there while waiting for KCR to re-open I noticed a couple of quite upmarket places – still building sites when I was last here – now up and running and peopled with designer-visitors called Tamsin and Jonquil from Paris or Milan or London or somewhere. But neither place detracted markedly from the overall Otres Two ambience, their occupants even seeming to turn a blind eye to the geriatric South African itinerant who'd set up his shanty beach camp within snoring distance of their bedroom windows. It was as if the Otres Two nouveaux had only been given permission to locate here providing they left their new brooms behind and promised not to mess with the beach's historic character.

How long that'd last I knew not. But it didn't really matter. Pretty soon I'd be back in KCR and cycling each day to an Independence Beach surely safe from the Tamsins and Jonquils of this world. Had to be. Apart from the sprawling high-priced Independence Hotel way down the other end of the bay with its own private beach, there was nowhere else to stay.

Or there hadn't been nine months earlier. The vast concrete skeleton that had landed next to the beach's shanty town in my absence suggested change of some sort was imminent.

What it was or was intended to be was a mystery to all. Not a sign or a billboard gave any clue as to its purpose and if they knew, the cafe owners weren't saying. Like every other Cambodian, they knew that talking out of turn carried consequences.

So discussion of its possible function – in every permutation – was left to those to whom Cambodian consequences carried little threat.

Now looking ever more likely that their shanty cafe days at Independence were numbered anyway, the CODDGAAs had little hesitation in imagining every application for the building their altered reality brains could dredge up.

Everything from secret service R&R quarters to a five-storey concrete zoo got an airing but in the end the general consensus was that it was earmarked to be another Chinese casino. Just like the ones at Victory Beach where punters from the People's Republic spent their entire holiday in darkened halls feeding roulette tables and slot machines and avoiding any contact with the air, sea, beach or the garbage the casino flung onto it in the full knowledge that no one inside gave a toss about what happened beyond the gambling hall's hallowed confines. Perhaps that's why they named it Victory Beach I mused on the cycle ride back to KCR. The place is a victory for those who know the price of everything and the value of nothing.

Which, sadly, is the way everyone in the town seemed headed. It wasn't just a suspicion. Contact with a couple of professional gamblers encountered in a downtown bar confirmed it.

Having moved here a few years earlier to take specific advantage of Sihanoukville's inexorable re-invention as Cambodia's Macau they had an insight into the direction Sihanoukville was going few others I came across there could match.

It wasn't just Victory Beach where Chinese casinos were springing up, they said. They were the length and breadth of the town providing the gamblers – one American, one Dane – with a lifestyle some notches above that enjoyed by the average foreign Sihanoukville resident. So bad at poker were the Chinese that these two had been picking them off at their leisure, eventually packing them off home devoid of shirts, trousers, socks and shoes. They were left their underpants. The pair weren't totally devoid of scruples.

Unlike the scamsters who'd taken over KCR in my absence, apparently. On mentioning the name of the place I was living, the faces of my two new friends registered a collective smirk and I was soon in possession of the whole, pure Sihanoukville, story.

The Chinese outfit that had thrown my whole world into disarray had, said the pair, landed in town to run an illicit phone gambling racket for punters in China where gambling was illegal. Put under pressure by the Chinese authorities to crack down on it, the Cambodian police had raided not just KCR but any number of other shady establishments in the hood and arrested several hundred Chinese who were now languishing in jail.

Any amount more – varying from hundreds to thousands depending who you talked to – had fled overnight and were still being hunted down by the police leaving the likes of KCR suddenly depopulated and the owner short of the eye-watering rents he'd been promised. I was, it seemed, now living at one of the city's most notorious addresses which would explain the crooked knowing smiles on the faces of the tuk tuk drivers when asked to take me to it. They now knew exactly where KCR was without me having to direct them.

This was both a blessing and a curse. Although I could now dispense with the map I always carried to help guide the drivers to my door, for some weeks it meant I was the only one in residence. Word had got around about the place and there was some reluctance amongst other long-termers to park themselves there. Result – the owner was equally reluctant to provide upkeep funds until he saw more rents coming in, little was done to reverse the decline and, on seeing how unkempt the place had become, potential guests on the hunt for accommodation came and left without making bookings leaving the owner even less enthusiastic about forking out to make it look habitable.

Something clearly had to be done to break this vicious cycle and, prompted by the discovery of algae in a swimming pool that'd started turning green, I like to think I was at least part responsible for KCR's eventual resurrection.

Faced with the prospect of becoming homeless again if the

owner began tiring of the whole palaver and decided to let the compound sink back into a state of ruin, it was with some relief that I bumped into a couple of the previous year's Quebecoise to be met with astonishment that Camelot had re-opened to visitors. The news had somehow eluded them.

Clearly relieved they could now escape whatever hovel they were now slumming it in, word spread quickly and within the week the whole place was pretty much booked out with Quebecoise... providing the owner promised to bring in the clean-up squad tout suite.

With a nice pot of room deposits in his pocket to fund the work the owner was as good as his word and, two weeks later, KCR was almost back up to its old standards. The Damoclesian sword of imminent eviction had been withdrawn from my neck and I was once again safe to lord it over Camelot from my ivory tower at the pinnacle of a place I was now sure would be my winter home for many years to come.

* * *

So certain of this was I that when the time came to return to the UK I hadn't even bothered taking a suitcase. No point. I'd only be hauling the self-same stuff back when winter came round again and if there had been any doubts in my mind about having finally found my Shangri-La, the sight of the manager smiling as he dangled my room keys at me as my taxi pulled into the KCR compound the following December served to dispel them.

'Know something,' I told myself on entering my old room to find he'd actually done as requested and re-installed my personal stash and loaded the fridge with fresh milk and wine, 'I think I've finally cracked it.' After so many years of working on the jigsaw the pieces seemed at last to be coming together.

Thirty minutes later and I was convinced of it. Stripped down to sarong and singlet, all northern winter clothing jettisoned,

I was back on the balcony as if I'd never left. Cold glass of Sauvignon Blanc in hand and listening to the local uh-oh gecko saying goodnight I sighed in contentment as I awaited delivery of the best takeaway curry I'd yet found in Sihanoukville. Even the prospect of being jolted out of my jet lag by the hilltop monastery at the crack of dawn the next day couldn't dent the feeling of having finally got this winter escape thing sorted.

So sorted in fact that this time I was fully prepared for the Buddhist onslaught. Earplugs at the ready, I almost dozed through it all confident that in a couple of hours relative tranquillity would return.

Try three. As if they knew I was back the monastery's inmates seemed to have decided to make up for lost time and to give it all they had. Their way of bringing me back on the path to enlightenment I mused as I boarded my bike later to set off for Independence Beach.

If that was their intention, it worked. By the time I pulled back into the KCR compound I was not only back on enlightenment road but a pretty fair distance down it. The lurking suspicion I'd been harbouring during my first two British winters here of Cambodia – Sihanoukville in particular – being earmarked for full-on Chinese economic invasion with the enthusiastic co-operation of the local powers-that-be had started transforming into full-blown fact. The road from KCR to Independence Beach confirmed it.

Gone were the fetid mountains of garbage flanking what had previously been little more than the promise of a road to the seaside. In their place were battalions of monster excavators carving meteoric craters out of waterlogged fields into which had been driven the first piles of the gleaming glass and steel tower blocks the site's billboards shrilled were destined to soar upwards from this newly-created man-made moonscape.

And the road? That was now an airport runway-width four-lane highway clogged with yet more heavy equipment just itching to get to grips with turning fantasy into unignorable fact. Tower blocks in a landscape of fields and cows would be difficult to miss.

Still blinking at this overnight devastation, I emerged out of it only to find this was just the *hors d'oeuvre* to the main event. War seemed also have been declared on Independence Beach, now clearly earmarked for imminent conversion into one of the city's premier centres of luxurious living and gaming excellence.

With construction of a skyscraping condo block complete with shopping mall, marina and 'entertainments' halls well underway on one side and the Independence Beach Hotel on the other the beach's shanty cafes' days were undoubtedly numbered. How long could it be before these flanking developments were unable to resist joining up in the middle?

Not long, I suspected. For as the text on the condo site's billboards and showroom office now admitted, this was a Chinese development and the Chinese weren't known for hanging about once they got started.

But neither were they especially well-known for taking local conditions into account and nothing in the complex's brochure suggested any early change in construction thinking was imminent. Planned to rise up out of the Independence Beach sands was a monstrosity that owed everything to construction speed and nothing to local design considerations.

If the designer was aware that his or her building was destined for a tropical location he or she showed little sign of it. With every one of the complex's quarter of a million dollar apartments facing either east or west there wasn't one that wasn't in the direct line of fire of the intense morning or afternoon sun, not one would have a balcony providing shade to the apartment below and the only thing preventing the apartments becoming people ovens were blackout blinds fitted to each dwelling's full length, unopenable, sun-intensifying plate glass windows.

Result – to prevent the occupants stewing quietly in their own hot sauce every one of the apartments would need to be plunged into semi-perpetual, blind-drawn gloom, air conditioning bills would be sky-high and those having to pay them would soon be discovering just how appropriate the term blinds was. For a good part of every day there'd be the unforeseen consequence, as it were, of them blinding occupants to the view of the ocean the developers were using as the apartments' prime selling point.

Having made the mistake of staying in a similarly-designed oven room elsewhere on my travels, orientation was now high up on my accommodation selection criteria, something I thought the apartment sales girl might appreciate hearing. For sheer professionalism, devotion to duty and ability to hide her horror on finding herself with no option but to give the show apartment guided tour to someone in sweaty shorts and T-shirt who'd just parked his bicycle outside, she deserved a suitable reward.

But she was the only one worthy of such generosity I told the sales staff before pedalling quickly away in an attempt to get to the shanty cafes before the developers beat me to it. The only thing they and their idiot architect deserved were lengthy jail terms for breaching every common sense design consideration in the book.

With smiles turning to gawps of astonishment at being treated to such an outspoken condemnation of their beloved epitome of luxurious living, a hasty exit was called for and it wasn't a moment too soon. By the looks of things at the cafe beach, I'd arrived in the nick of time.

Although 'development' work had started it was at least restricted to renovations of the entrance portico, the parking area, the beachside gardens and, to some extent, the cafes themselves. In what looked like some sort of sanitation blitz, of the twenty or so beachside cafes just two now had functioning kitchens, the rest being reduced to mere sitting areas with drinks fridges.

As track-stopping as this discovery was, in truth I wasn't

overly dismayed. I'd seen cleaner kitchens in African civil war refugee camps and, for self-preservation purposes, had already begun wondering if I should start bringing my own food to the beach.

Well now that decision had been made for me. But by who, I wondered? Who'd been reading my mind and, more importantly, was this the prelude to something far more 'cleansing'? If it was I sincerely hoped early attention would be being extended to the choleric toilets, places so disgusting they all but ensured those with complaining bladders chose the sea instead.

By the time I left after a dip in waters still surprisingly un-muddied by the condo site excavations not a mile down the beach, I was none the wiser. If the owners knew who was behind it they weren't saying and there'd be nothing forthcoming from the now absent CODDGGAA community. Packed up and left seemed to be the message in the less-than appreciative sign language of one of the cafe owners. Bloody wimps.

Cycling back I wondered how long it'd be before I joined them, wherever they were. For sure it wouldn't be Otres Two. Last time I checked the prices there were several notches above the CODDGGAA's pockets and that was before even more designer boutique hotels were ready for occupation. Construction had been well underway when I left earlier in the year. They must be finished by now. It was time to go and check... and to see if that beach too had succumbed to what was now looking like an unhealthy collaboration between the invading Chinese and local vested interests.

It hadn't but word was that the owners of some of the prime beach spots were coming under pressure to sell. So far they'd resisted and had kept the stretch much as it had been during my last visit. But for how long? If money couldn't tempt them no one was under any illusion that they'd soon be faced with having to deal with more underhand tactics.

It was a prescient prediction. Within the month there'd be

reports of a fire rampaging along the beach taking wooden constructed property after wooden constructed property with it. To be followed by the arrival of benefactors bearing inducement gifts? No one would be in the least surprised. As anyone who'd been in Cambodia for longer than the regular tourist visit knew, since surprise came as standard here nothing really came as much of a shock and one just got used to expecting the unexpected.

Take, for example, turning a corner and coming across a completely naked, heavily pregnant woman rolling around in a building site sand pile. That was unexpected but still rated a 'meh' at best from locals passing by. Just another day in Sihanoukville it seemed.

Likewise being gifted a one hundred US dollar note by a complete stranger on the street. That struck me as a bit out of the ordinary. But only until realising it was Chinese New Year, Cambodians also celebrated it by handing out good luck money to all and sundry, the note was counterfeit and the giver was just doing it to see the look on my face.

Yep, good joke it managed to say, a reaction that pleased the note-giver enormously.

* * *

The longer I stayed in Cambodia and the more events of similar ilk I came across the more the scales fell from my eyes and the more I started 'getting' this crazy country. Here was a place where the ordinary was something other people did, logic was seen as a bit of a joke and Cambodians liked a joke as much as the next man, especially if it could be had at a foreigner's expense. Which was why, towards the end of my third term here, I came to the conclusion that it was usually wise to factor in the Cambodian humour constant whenever falling into conversation with one.

Usually but not always. The police not unexpectedly had as much sense of humour as police anywhere and the same,

I eventually discovered, could be said of hotel proprietors – something that only came to light when a change, almost imperceptible at first, descended on KCR.

Something, it seemed, was afoot. Everyone could smell it. But was it just our imagination? Were we seeing a change in management attitude that didn't exist? Things still got done, issues still got sorted, staff still fussed about and life still seemed to chug on as normal. But was it chugging on with slightly less good grace than over the previous three months? Were the usual smiles a bit more strained than before? And could it be that the management's eyes really were starting to avoid ours?

Nah. Couldn't be. Everything was fine. This was just a blip in the otherwise cordial guest/management relations and the general consensus was that it was something that could be shrugged off.

Or it could be until the wifi went down and it emerged that the owner had changed the password without telling anyone. That was something that couldn't be ignored. Such an absence of consideration for the guests was completely out of character and for the first time during my stay murmurings of discontent became audible in the ranks.

Most died away once the wifi was restored but only until another disturbance in the KCR ionosphere gave rise to new mutterings. What was the owner doing putting Chinese friends in rooms usually kept free for Cambodian weekenders? And why had he started hosting large dinner parties for them in the KCR restaurant, a facility that hadn't been in operation since my first stay here? Something was definitely afoot and suddenly KCR was awash with rumour. The place was being expanded into the vacant plot next door. It was being sold. It was going to get a regular restaurant. Its prices were going up. It was going to start doing Cambodian weddings. Aaargh no! Anything but that!

With not a hint of what was going on filtering down to the regular guests it was left ultimately to chance for the real reason to emerge and by chance I was the one to chance upon it... to end up walking away shaking my head in disbelief and charged with the onerous responsibility of having to relay the news to the others.

It was news that'd first have them laughing out loud before seeing the look on my paled, unsmiling face and realising this was no laughing matter.

In the manager's office to arrange my accommodation dates for 2017/18 he dropped a bombshell that'd serve to make the likelihood of the place starting to do weddings look almost tolerable.

Faced with my re-booking request he said nothing for a moment before realising he had no option but to drop all pretence and come clean. He wasn't in a position to confirm my request, he said without meeting my eye. Not because he didn't want to but because he'd been told not to take any bookings at all for the foreseeable future. The owner, he said to the papers on his desk, had entered into an agreement to let the entire hotel to a Chinese casino... again... for the next five years.

Yeah, yeah. Good joke, I grinned back. But about my return dates...

The grin was met with a face as impassive as a magistrate's. The joke, if there was one, was on me and the rest of KCR's big winter-freeze escape community. The hotel, the manager repeated with no hint of a smile, would no longer be entertaining guests from anywhere but China, staff members of a new casino soon to be opening at Independence Beach.

Stunned silence. Dinner plate eyes. Mouth doing goldfish impressions. Blank look from the manager. What more could he say? Except to indicate by his manner that this wasn't his decision. It was the owner's alone and there was nothing more to say.

* * *

Shuffling back to my room barely able to put one foot in front of the other the only thing my addled brain could alight on was that at least now we knew. The owner really had lost his marbles. I was beginning to suspect as much after the wifi password thing. But this... after his previous experience with the Chinese, this was beyond madness and I was far from alone in thinking it.

Bumping into a neighbour on the stairway his reaction to the news was a mirror image of my own.

'Haha, nice joke! But seriously...' he smiled before seeing the look on my face and going slightly weak at the knees. 'Oh shit man! SERIOUSLY?'

It was the same with the others. Had the owner gone completely off his head? After being so comprehensively shat upon last time by the Chinese this was lunacy gone mad.

But there it was. The deal had apparently been done, was not about to be undone and in the days that followed KCR became a repository of trance-like zombies. No one seemed able to talk, least of all to the management, the entire complement drifting stunned and a bit tearful from place to place in clothes that seemed drained of all colour. It was as if we'd just been collectively informed of the wholly unexpected death of a loved one which, in a way, is what we had been. This was a bereavement but not just of the place itself. In an instant we'd seen all sense and trust and faith in humankind evaporate to be replaced with an all-consuming gnawing grief over the feeling that this was something from which we might never fully recover.

By the end of the week we had, of course, but only to find grief giving way to seething anger and feather-spitting exasperation.

This, went the collective furious response, was a déjà vu we hadn't needed once, let alone twice and what were we being left with? Nothing unless the enlightenment this mass eviction sparked counted as compensation. For some time China's focus on South-East Asia as an investment target had been intensifying and few were resisting its wooings. Was Cambodia now prepared to forget how Beijing supported the Khmer Rouge in the seventies and move on, accepting China's economic advances as a sort of reparation payment?

All was now clear. Cambodia had no intention of being left out of the Chinese gold rush. If there were Chinese billions to be had Phnom Penh wanted in and wasn't over-bothered about how it got in. If that meant trading the independence it'd won from the West for a new form of colonial rule from the East, so be it. The sparkle in China's baubles outshone any western trinket on offer, Cambodia couldn't wait to get its hands on them and if there was anyone doubting it, all they need do was take a trip to the Chinese-transformed Independence Beach, now a byword for a misnomer if ever there was one.

Gazing out to sea after one last disconsolate bicycle pilgrimage to the beach's shanty cafes, one thing alone occupied my thoughts. Having no wish to be around when the beach disappeared under Chinese concrete I'd already decided that was that for me in Cambodia. But what about the others? If any decided to stay on, how would they feel on finding they no longer pecked loudest in the country's most-valued visitor pecking order?

About the same as the marine life out there in the bay, I reckoned. Once the China syndrome kicked properly in, if those staying on weren't destined to become fish out of water valued more for the flesh on their backs than the contribution they made to the area's biodiversity I'd offer up the flesh on my own back and even consider returning myself.

But with such a prospect looking about as likely as the shanty cafes surviving the Chinese tsunami, for the time being there was nothing else for it. The search for the perfect winter retreat would have to be resumed elsewhere... with one crucial criteria addition. After the Cambodia experience even the merest hint of a serious Chinese presence would warrant any winter retreat contender being ripped unceremoniously from the page, torn into the tinniest shreds my shaking fingers could manage and fed without compunction to the ducks... all without meeting the eye of Mr Fault-Finder General. If eye contact was made, swift evasive action would be required on Mr FFG's behalf. One involving the look of smug satisfaction on the bastard's leering told-you-so face and the direction of travel of my tightly-clenched fist.

POST-CAMELOT WINTER SANCTUARY CRITERIA ADDENDA

CRITERIA	ITEM	REASONING
Location	Affordable edible food supply	Primarily for health preservation. Alternatives to mediaeval markets critical. Ditto restaurants knowing at least how to spell hygiene.
	Honourable medical facilities	For the avoidance of rip-off fake medicines and quacks with no qualifications other than the ability to wear a white coat convincingly.
	Free from wholesale redevelopment plans	For the preservation of the character that attracted one's attention in the first place. Some change over time is inevitable and often desirable... with one critical exception – any form of Chinese involvement.
Accommodation	Honest communicative management	Bloody good luck with that.

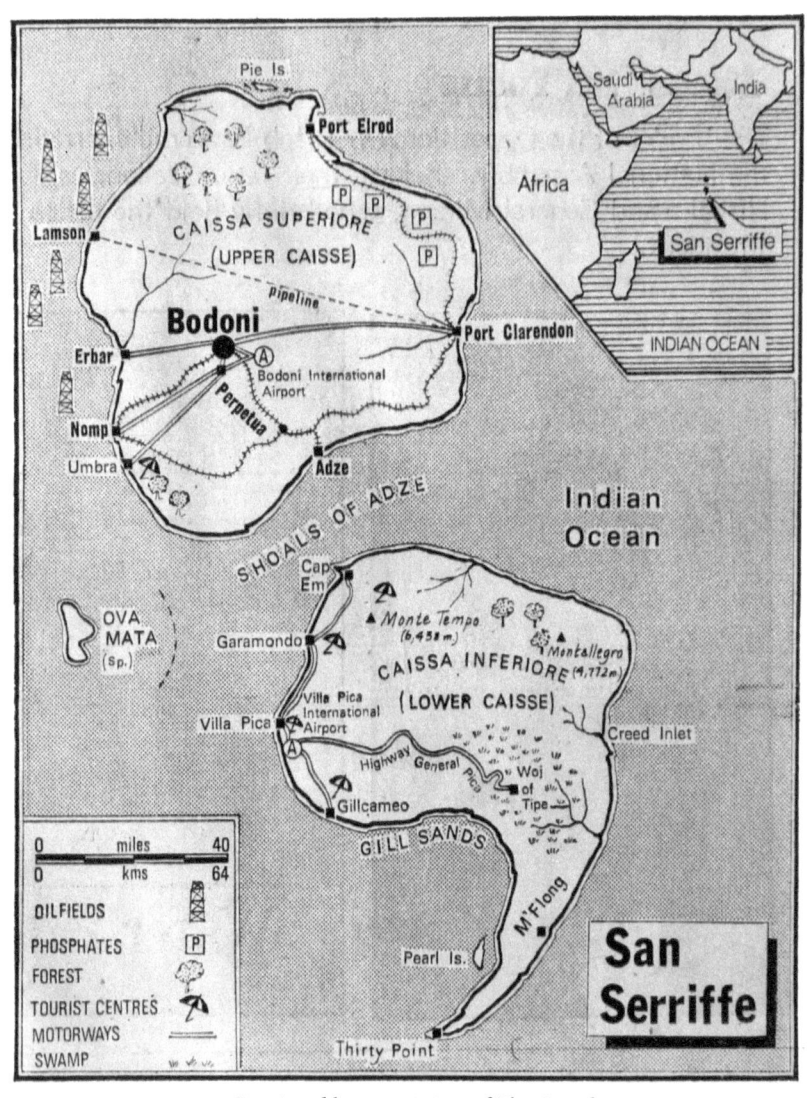

Reprinted by permission of *The Guardian*

9

SAN SERRIFFE
A goose, cooked

Madness, sell-out, betrayal – about the only printable things the KCR residents had to say about the hotel's management in the wake of the Chinese takeover announcement.

When they could bring themselves to say anything that is.

In the days leading up to eviction D-Day the compound fell eerily silent. Like a community resigned to losing their homes under a reservoir's inexorably rising waters, KCR's long-termers shrank inside themselves, what talk there was limited to low-tonal exchanges about practicalities as they listlessly started packing up and preparing to leave.

Well, low-tonal until the time came to settle their final bills. With each resident's visit to the management's office the glowering silence enveloping the compound became more deafening, echoing precisely the sentiments of the now job-threatened KCR workforce. With their futures as uncertain as our own the usual friendly smiles and jovial banter had sunk beneath a tide of sullen, grim-faced brooding and seething resentment. By the day it got harder to get them to carry out their duties until, in the final week before the coup de grâce, co-operation ceased altogether.

No one was surprised. Considering who the new occupants were to be, the only surprise was that the staff hadn't turned their entire attention to booby-trapping the place, welcome presents for a people who'd backed the murderous Khmer Rouge during their Cambodian killing spree of the seventies.

For all I knew that's exactly what they might have been doing. I was too taken up with other things to notice. Quite unexpectedly I'd found myself consumed with something I least thought would enter my head – whether this really was it for me and Cambodia.

Like most at KCR I'd initially reacted by declaring it was and by making plans to leave, never to return. But then I saw how a small minority were taking the news and began having second thoughts. Those who'd been coming long enough to have burned their boats and made Cambodia their second home were proving more philosophical about it all. Shit happens was the message in their impassive shrugs. Get over it.

Hmmm. Did they have a point? If others could accept their fate, move on and go in search of a KCR alternative here, could I? Having already trawled Sihanoukville for alternatives last time this happened and finding nothing to compete with KCR, repeating the procedure seemed like an exercise in futility.

But that was over a year ago. Long enough for some of the other possibilities to have improved. Maybe I should take a swift tour just so I'd know. If I didn't I wouldn't and that would never do. I'd be left forever wondering.

Well wonder no more, I told myself on returning from the only two I'd found with half-decent swimming pools. Yes, both had changed but not in the way I'd hoped. Not only had prices soared but the pool at one had turned green and the other possibility had become the accommodation of choice of the Russian drinking mafia, arriving every October the receptionist told me, to occupy every room and wait out the Russian winter in an alcoholic Cambodian haze.

So that was now definitely that. No more messing about. My first reaction had been proved right all along and I'd be able to board the flight out safe in the knowledge that everything else on offer in Sihanoukville made KCR look like the Ritz – probably the reason the Chinese had homed in on it in the first place and would be unlikely to give up so easily this time.

Which left what?

All the way back to the UK I wracked my brains for an answer and found nothing. Every potentially acceptable over-wintering spot I could think of had been tried and every one, for one reason or another, had been found wanting. In the past, whenever one was rejected another seemed to materialise out of the ether saying 'try me!' Not this time. All the ether did this time was swirl. Had it given up all it had to give? It was beginning to look very much like it.

* * *

Spring came. Spring went. Then summer and the only thing emerging from the ether was a growing sense of foreboding. Unless inspiration struck soon I'd be left high and dry to suffer the British winter chill with no prospect of escape from the cold, the damp, the gloom and the sort of people who considered it acceptable behaviour to invade quiet-designated train carriages with a boombox and turn my flight back from hell headache into a migraine.

Truth be told, I admitted to myself later, the music they were playing wasn't actually half bad. A sort of grunge and reggae fusion tinged with traditional Caribbean rhythms. Shame I was in no state to appreciate it at the time. Twenty-four hours in battery hen airliner incarceration when not kicking your heels in soulless airports can leave your capacity for musical appreciation a trifle drained.

Six months it took for that capacity to fully recover and when it did I was glad of it. You could always take refuge in music to dull a nagging pain, the sort that grew daily as the end of British Summer Time closed in and the going back of the clocks signalled that was that for another year.

Raking fallen leaves into piles the October gales would then gleefully redistribute around the cricket field I was helping put to bed for the winter, I found myself in need of musical solace and for some reason began humming the tunes the train carriage boomboxers had introduced me to.

Mid-tune I froze. Oh my God! Of course. Why hadn't I thought of it before? Maybe because the combination of high winds, cricket and reggae music hadn't presented itself before. But now it had I knew exactly where to go. There was an alternative to travelling south and east. One that'd been staring me in the face from the west all this time.

Why hadn't I factored it in before? Probably because the Caribbean was, in my book, part of the Americas and the Americas *per se* had long since been wiped from the escape possibilities list.

Anyway they had to be too expensive didn't they? The West Indies were the haunt of Richard Branson-esque fat cats, royal family layabouts and the descendants of eighteenth century sugar barons now returned to the islands to rob the progeny of the barons' former slave 'employees' of the land they'd 'inherited' at emancipation.

But did that really mean the region was beyond my limited means? Never having been there I'd had to rely on the reports of others and if there was one thing I'd learned from my travels such reports needed to be viewed in much the way I'd learned to view the German layabout's glowing accounts of his latest accommodation finds. How many times had I been to places 'known' to be expensive only to discover lesser-known bunking houses off the beaten track offering rooms at prices that made those on it look like economic insults to the intelligence?

So yes, why not? Only by being on the ground would I really know so let's give it a short, intensive go for the 2017/18 winter, starting with Barbados. As one of the pricier West Indies destinations it'd be a good place to test the off-the-beaten-track theory. If

I could find something affordable here, I could find it anywhere in the Caribbean. Anyway, with flight prices to Barbados a good deal cheaper than to any of the other islands, Barbados it had to be.

* * *

First impressions were, not to put too fine a point on it, unencouraging. After a manic British Airways flight to the island in which the attendants seemed to have little idea how to deal with a panic-stricken girl screeching she'd been poisoned by BA's food and refusing to come out of the toilet the last thing I needed was to be kept waiting two hours just to get into a country I'd come to help economically through the diminution of my own bank account. It was as if the lone slovenly immigration officer on duty at a peak arrival time had decided to wage a one-person war on the island's tourism promotions board and begin a rearguard action to put a stop to all this touristic madness.

Enough is enough, her glacial processing of every passport seemed to be telling their flagging, teeth-grinding owners as they stood fighting every instinct to punch this paragon of officialdom hard enough in the face to splatter the 'Welcome to Barbados' poster behind her with whatever flowed through her xenophobically-induced hardened arteries.

And this was just the start of the tourism high season. How long those coming after me would be kept waiting I didn't dare think but their treatment would probably be roughly on a par with that received at the hands of the Basil Fawlty-esque owner/manager of the apartment I'd booked on the outskirts of Bridgetown.

Located after a lengthy trawl of the internet and finding nothing else within my price range, if Angler Apartments had been a Barbadian flop house catering for the most budget conscious of budget travellers I could have understood the offhand brusqueness of a management which seemed to regard visitors as an occupational hazard.

But it wasn't. At the price they charged for a one-month self-catering stay I'd have been able to stay three times as long at KCR and that was without all the surreptitious add-ons mentioned neither on the Angler website or on arrival.

Use of washing machine, I was informed a week into my stay, fifteen US dollars (and bring your own detergent). Use of wifi, three dollars a day. Use of safe, two dollars fifty a day. The list went on and on and although there wasn't, I wouldn't have been surprised to find a charge added to the bill for the extra exercise you got running across the apartments' courtyard to beat a highly territorial dog with big snarling teeth to the gate, another unexpected aspect of Angler hospitality the owner had conveniently neglected to include in the establishment's promotional blurb.

Just a few days there was enough to prompt urgent alternative accommodation-finding action. Action that was to prove as rewarding as trying to find fresh fish at the local fish stall, a place you could get anything you wanted as long as it wasn't fish. Local waters had been so fished-out the stall only bothered rolling up its shutters when frozen supplies from elsewhere arrived and when the owner wasn't supplementing his income by charging twenty US dollars a day for a sun lounger on the one local beach that wasn't privately owned.

In short, after an intensive trawl of local letting agents I came to the inescapable conclusion that self-catering houses and flats let at affordable rates here were about as plentiful as swimming areas safe from maniacs on jet skis and after the third near-miss in as many days I reluctantly found myself admitting that I might possibly have miscalculated. Demand for just the sort of thing I was looking for had priced anyone not in possession of a healthy stock market portfolio and a company director's final salary pension out of the market.

And it wasn't just Barbados. Word was it was pretty much the same right across the Caribbean, and now I came to think about it just about everywhere else these days. I knew. I'd been there and found I'd been followed – and priced out of the market – by every nouveau riche Chinese newly-released from a previously locked-down authoritarian regime.

I blamed Deng Xiaoping. If it hadn't been for him and his opening-up policies on taking over from Mao in the seventies it's unlikely China would have become the world's factory, the newly enriched Chinese who'd made gazillions from it would still be scratching a living on collective farms and I'd still be sitting on my balcony in Sihanoukville sipping at a chilled Sauvignon Blanc and waiting for the curry delivery man to bring me my dinner.

Add in the fall of the Berlin wall, the disintegration of the Soviet Union, the rise and inexorable rise of the budget airline, wifi, internet, smart phones and bloody television travel programmes focusing on out of the way places and you have all the ingredients for mass transit to the very places I'd been seeking out for years and had assumed would always be there for me, reserved solely for the more adventurous breed of traveller.

Such complacency, it was now abundantly clear, was hopelessly misplaced and the fault was partly down to us, the people who'd blazed the trail in the first place. By not keeping schtum about the places we'd discovered we'd as much as invited the world's tour group operators to move in on our patch. With all the hard pioneering work done, all the tour operators needed do was keep an eye on social media and updates from the likes of the Lonely Planet guides, now as much a misnomer as Sihanoukville's Independence Beach. The only thing lonely about LP now was the feeling pre-LP travellers got on returning to precious, previously unpublicised places to find them overrun with Tamsins and Jonquils, Gavins and Staceys and sun loungers at twenty dollars a day.

Ah well, I sighed on boarding the flight back to a chilly UK New Year, I suppose it was inevitable. We'd had our fun. Maybe it was now time to leave the planet to those whose idea of adventure was travelling without being absolutely sure of there being a McDonalds at one's chosen paradise hideaway.

As if it had been reading my mind, British Airways decided to reinforce the thought and ensure it didn't go forgotten on my arrival at Gatwick airport. After surviving being buried alive on African bus rooftop luggage racks, dunkings in the bilges of Indian river steamers, the ham-fisted attentions of tuk tuk drivers throughout South-East Asia and granite-faced Chinese officials suspecting it contained hidden drug compartments, the battered old bag that'd been my faithful companion for years was delivered back to me so smashed-up its resurrection would have been beyond Jesus Christ himself. And just to make sure there was no misunderstanding, the replacement British Airways insisted I accept was a size smaller than the one they'd destroyed. Try getting your regular stash of travel stuff into that, seemed to be the message they were sending.

It was a message that did not fall on deaf ears. My bag wasn't the only thing that'd finally met its Waterloo. Fuck travel, I noted in my journal later. I'm done. My blazing-trousered old dad had been right all along. Abroad – travel in general, come to that – was overrated.

* * *

As if to cement the sentiment, almost as soon as my trusty travel companion went south so did any number of the places on my winter sanctuary possibilities list. It started with renewed vicious insurgency trouble in Sri Lanka, moved on to East Africa in the form of out of control locust invasions and the first hurricanes the region had ever experienced and then went viral.

First came a rash of workhorse 737-Max planes suddenly falling out of the sky for no apparent reason. Then air travel in all its forms (and those who used it) found it and themselves being pilloried for being major contributors to the climate emergency.

And finally, in case we still hadn't got the message, an unstoppable deadly virus emerged in 2019 to kill not just millions worldwide but international travel itself. It was as if the planet had decided it was tired of being trampled underfoot and had declared all-out war on those doing the trampling.

So that, it seemed, was that. Even if I could summon up the energy and enthusiasm to continue the search, the lack of countries accepting visitors from virus-infected countries and the lack of airlines now flying to them combined to bring the quest, voluntarily or not, to a shuddering, unplanned conclusion. The decision to call a halt had been taken out of my hands and there seemed little prospect of a return to normal service anytime soon.

In a way it was a comforting thought. Now I had no option but to bed down in the UK and just roll with it. My old dad would have been proud, and not a little smug.

'See?' I could hear him scoffing from the great beyond, 'I told you it'd all end in tears and you'd be back with your tail between your legs. Nowhere is better than home, young man, and I'm glad you've finally realised it.'

There was only one problem with that. Well, two. First, it wasn't my decision to call it a day. That had been foisted on me by forces beyond my control. Second, hearing my father scoff at being proved right was only ever going to have one outcome – renewed determination to make him eat his words. But how?

A lengthy walk in the woods later, I had it. With the woods all but deserted thanks to the virus making people so nervous about coming into contact with others they were mostly staying home, it was like the walks I used to take before these woods became popular.

My God! That, I realised, must now surely also apply to many of the places on the winter sanctuary list. There must now be any number of them so devoid of visitors that anyone making it there would not only be treated like gods but gods who could name their own price. It'd be like stepping straight back to the start of my quest. Further, in fact. There must be places so deserted they'd be like they were in the seventies, the time of my first forays into the back of beyond.

Oh fuck. The thought was so enticing that, for one fleeting moment, I even considered it seriously. There were precious few opportunities in life to start over. This was most definitely one. Could I? This needed another walk in the woods.

Deep in its interior and I was back in Ethiopia aged twenty-four, sent to help an oil prospecting crew out and taking my first hesitant steps along a fifty-year path of discovery that appeared to have now gone full circle. Anyone able to make it to such places would now have them all to themselves, untroubled by the battalions of sun-blocked, sun-hatted, camera-toting tour groupers in matching pristine safari suits stepping nervously from luxury air-conditioned buses onto scorched African earth crawling, they were sure, with man-eating wildlife and even wilder humanity to adventurously grab snaps of exotic wonders before returning to the lobster-with-everything buffet lunches awaiting them at their five-star safari lodges. Those lodges would now be all but mothballed, I was sure of it.

Bloody hell! Tempting or what?

* * *

'A-hem,' a little voice from nowhere intervened. 'Aren't you forgetting something? For one, you're not twenty-four any more. For two, it ain't the Ethiopia you knew back in 1974. Back then it had a coastline. Not any more. In the wake of a civil war lasting longer than the reign of the Queen of Sheba, all Ethiopia's beaches are now in the territory of Eritrea, somewhere no one can go now it's become Africa's version of North Korea.

'So you might find swimming opportunities in that part of the world a trifle limited, old son. Anyway, there's the little matter of a nasty little internal war just starting up in the north. That might restrict your movements a bit.'

Bugger. The voice was right. All the above did rather rule out a return to Asmara, the Eritrean capital that was bursting at the seams with grand old crumbling colonial houses built during Italy's brief occupation of Ethiopia where you used to be able to slum it for pennies. Without access to them and the islands and beaches along the country's Red Sea coast a return to Ethiopia wouldn't be much better than spending the winter in landlocked Uganda, a country where bathing came complete with crocodile companionship.

So maybe not Ethiopia. Or anywhere in the Horn of Africa for that matter. If it wasn't maniac Marxists running the show it was insane Islamists, a hazard not much different to Uganda's crocs and one now so endemic across the continent it pretty much put the whole of East and West Africa out of bounds.

So how about Southern Africa then? Nah. Don't think so. Never really got on with South Africans and anyway the whole region had been economically devastated by the combination of the virus, political cronyism and financial mismanagement.

Middle East? Not while the whole region was going up in flames, thank you very much.

South Asia? Sadly no. The only place getting anywhere near ticking the majority of boxes on my now extensive criteria list was Sri Lanka, but after a spate of bombings of churches and tourist hotels, massive pollution of the beaches thanks to a tanker blaze offshore and political and economic meltdown courtesy of the global energy crisis, that too had to be crossed off. Reports said life there had started returning to subsistence level and that meant every visiting foreigner would now be a rip-off target for those with a mind to rise above it.

Hong Kong? Unlikely. Now effectively under direct control from Beijing which hadn't been altogether appreciative of my writings about it.

Indonesia? Malaysia? Nope. The only areas not overrun with Chinese had introduced Sharia Law and I valued my hands and alcohol too much to risk it.

The Antipodes? Too expensive for a long stay without working, too damn far away and anyway there was the Strine hazard to consider across the entire Australia/New Zealand/Pacific Islands region.

The Americas? You really don't want to go there.

Which left where? Nowhere unless the bits of Europe I'd already tested to distraction and found wanting were put back on the list. But even then there was now a problem. Thanks to the Gavins and Staceys of the world falling for all the anti-EU nonsense spouted daily by Britain's media, the UK had voted by a short head to leave the EU – leaving every British person deprived of the right to stay in EU countries as long as they liked whether they'd voted to leave or not. So no more lengthy stays in Cyprus without a sodding visa, dammit.

And damn my own sodding criteria list too. All those additions to it over the years had effectively put the whole world out of bounds where, I was now realising, it would stay unless the list was subjected to a serious edit. Cut nothing and there was the very real prospect of having to face up to something so unpalatable the very thought would have had my younger self gagging in a paroxysm of furious, feather-spitting, head-shaking denial. The bunk, I'd have no option but to accept, really might now be history.

* * *

Even as recently as five years earlier such a thing looked so unimaginable that if any thought of it actually happening ever entered my head it was summarily dismissed as the ravings of one who'd partaken of a beer/vindaloo excess too close to bedtime. While heavy backpacks could still be hurled into the back of tuk tuks, bike pedals could still be turned fast enough to outrun rabid dogs, death-by-alcohol nights out didn't result in death-by-hangover mornings-after and chillies-with-everything roadside gloop didn't end in terminal trips to the toilet the likelihood of life on the road becoming beyond me had looked as remote as the chances of finding a fork in a Chinese chop house.

So what the hell happened? My own damned pickiness, that's what. Experience had dictated that stuff that could be tolerated in the early days now, well, couldn't. Result – a criteria list that'd taken on a life of its own and was now controlling me rather than the other way round. Like Dr Frankenstein or some artificial intelligence developer geek, I'd created a monster. One that'd become wilfully independent, refusing to be reprogrammed or restrained and with but one single purpose in mind – the ultimate destruction of its creator.

Shit. Was there nothing to be done? Looked very much like it. The monster had all but ensured nowhere could satisfy every requirement on the list and that meant having to face up to something so unpalatable I could scarcely bring myself to accept it.

Like it or not, the odyssey really was over.

Leaves stopped rustling, birds stopped singing, rivers stopped gurgling and my own footsteps stopped stepping through the woodland tranquillity mid-stride.

The end? Noooo. Can't be. I won't let it be! I'm not ready for the bath chair yet. All this is, surely, is some sort of late-life crisis. The one, I'd heard, that creeps silently up on you, pounces and pins you to the ground under the weight of creaking joints, medication, specialist appointments and age-related travel insurance premium hikes.

But wait. That can't be right. I hadn't had a mid-life one yet.

Or had I? Was that in fact what the quest had been all about? Was it actually my own equivalent of the fancy sports car, the hair implants, the plastic surgery, the chasing of girls forty years younger than one's own retrosexual self and the declarations of a liking – no, honestly! – for present day music?

Oh bugger. Now I came to think about it, that's exactly what it might have been. Somehow I'd fooled myself into believing the quest was a search for somewhere to escape the northern winter when all the time it was a search for lost youth. What else could explain all those returns to the playgrounds of bygone halcyon days?

Fair point. But hang on a minute. Not all the places tested were part of my youth. Factor that in and you'd undoubtedly see the compass needle start to waver, uncertain about pointing squarely at the urgent need to turn the clock back.

So if that wasn't the basic underlying reason for the quest that left what? The simple purpose of escaping winter. Had to be. What else was there?

Oh crap. There was something. A thing so disconcerting it'd been buried deep in my subconscious so it didn't have to be confronted too often.

Oh double crap. One of those confrontation times was now. Like having to return to the pub you'd disgraced yourself in to retrieve something indispensable, the moment could be put off no longer. The actual, real, undeniable fact of the matter lay in an affliction that'd plagued me from an early age. An affliction that leaves the afflicted one with permanently itchy feet.

Filed under 'just don't go there' in the subconscious was something I'd come to know as never satisfied syndrome, an incurable condition foisted on me by others insisting that some things in life were unattainable.

Er, why, seemed a reasonable enough response to their diktat that I might as well chase wild geese as chase after that girl who preferred the company of rock stars to mine. Surely, I said in the spirit of academic discourse, geese could be caught or there wouldn't be any domesticated ones or pâté de foie gras. All you needed was a bit of perseverance, some forward planning and a bloody big net.

With the point leaving the diktat-deliverers groping for words that seemed to be game, set and match and in the absence of any immediate coherent response I basked in my victory. But only until realising what it meant. Having delivered my own counter diktat that there wasn't a goose in the world that couldn't be caught, for the preservation of face I was now saddled with having to prove it. My life wouldn't be worth living if I couldn't continuously demonstrate there wasn't a dream that couldn't be bottled, a rainbow that couldn't be pinned down or a pie in the sky that couldn't be stuck with a fork.

After the first few failures – including having my face laughed in by both the girl and her rock star beau – you'd have thought I might get the message and decide to downgrade my perfection-seeking ambitions to something more achieveable.

You'd be wrong. All it did was make me more determined, ratcheting-up my goose-catching pursuits to the point of an obsession that even the embarrassment of being caught out by a twenty-four carat solid gold hoax couldn't dent.

* * *

Settling down for breakfast one fine Spring morning in 1977 I found myself engrossed in an eight-page *Guardian* newspaper pull-out travel supplement detailing every aspect of an unadulterated piece of paradise the tour companies had yet to move in on and wreck.

From the moment I started reading I was hooked. This was a place that had to be visited and here, thanks to the *Guardian*, was a chance to visit it. Anyone calling the paper before a certain cut-off time would be entered in a draw for a free ticket and my hand was already reaching for the phone when something stopped me. Something about this wasn't right. What was it?

Only the time, the date and the place.

Apart from every element of the utopian island of San Serriffe being connected in some way to typesetting terminology – right down to the name of the President, one General Pica – entries closed at midday sharp and the date on the supplement was 1 April.

Damn the bloody *Guardian*. Wonderful April Fool which should really have taught me a sharp perfection-chasing lesson but not only didn't but carried a consequence I'm (almost) sure was unintended. From the moment I first read the name, my pensive walk in the woods revealed to me, not only had everywhere I'd gone been compared to San Serriffe but I'd effectively dedicated my life to tracking down somewhere that measured up to a place of pure fiction. A place I now saw was utterly and completely responsible for a winter getaway criteria list that was about as realistic and tangible as San Serriffe itself.

'Oh Christ. Seriously?' I found myself saying out loud on the realisation. Is that what I'd been doing these past twenty odd years? Chasing shadows?

'Yep,' the tree nearest me nodded back, rustling its leaves in a slow handclap of sarcastic woodland applause. 'And, if you don't mind me saying so, it's about time you realised it. Did it not ever occur to you that perfection exists only in the moment and mostly in your head?'

Well, no. Not really.

'Well it should have. If you'd really thought about it you'd have realised long ago that perfection is, by definition, transient. Has to be. It has to adapt to every change in your circumstances and is therefore the ultimate in shape-shifting imps, changing its form to suit whatever frame of mind you happen to be in at any given moment in time. With things evolving constantly it simply isn't possible for perfection to have any permanent shape.'

Gulp. As haughty as the homily was there was no doubt that the mighty beech responsible for it had a point. Was there no riposte? Didn't look like it. Or it didn't until a laid-back willow listening in next door took advantage of the pause in the beech's grandiloquence to chip in with a bit of homespun philosophy of its own.

'Whoa, man. Heavy. And maybe a bit off-beam, I'd say. Aren't you forgetting something?'

'What?' sniffed the beech.

'Us, man. We haven't evolved for millions of years. Which means we must've already reached the point of perfection. Stands to reason.'

'OK,' said the beech, 'I'll give you that. But with the exception of us, perfection is both transient and ephemeral.'

'And sharks,' said the willow thoughtfully. 'They're pretty perfect. The ultimate in killing machines which haven't changed much since they first evolved.'

'OK. But with the exception of us and sharks, perfection only exists in the mind.'

'And crocs. Crocs haven't changed for just about ever.'

'Oh, all right. But apart from us and sharks and crocs, there's no such thing as perfection.'

'And turtles.'

'And ferns,' squeaked the fern I'd just trodden on while backing away from the developing beech/willow squabble.

'Oh, all RIGHT! But apart from us, sharks, crocs, turtles and ferns, perfection isn't a thing. It's a state of mind and the sooner you get that into your thick skull the better it'll be for all of us. We're getting a bit tired of all the self-indulgent psycho-whining you keep bringing down this path. Doing our canopies in, it is.'

'Like the Buddha, then,' said the willow playfully after a moment's thought.

'What?'

'The Buddha. He's said to have reached ultimate enlightenment, isn't he? That's a form of perfection. And it was all in his mind. So doesn't that make him kind of perfect?'

'Oh... shadap!' snapped the beech, losing patience with the upstart willow, folding its branches across its trunk and staring away into the distance to signal this particular exchange was terminated. The beech wasn't used to having its authority undermined.

The willow just smiled and winked as I walked past.

'Thanks', it said. 'Not every day we get the chance to poke the beech in the knot hole and bring him back down to earth, so to speak.'

* * *

No. Thank YOU willow, I murmured as I turned and headed for home. Whether it knew it or not, the willow had hit the nail on the head. While they both had a point, it was the willow's mention of the Buddha that'd really struck home. After years on the road seeking enlightenment and never quite finding it he'd finally sat down under a tree to think. And that's where he'd made the breakthrough. Just as the beech tree had said, perfection, the Buddha finally realised, only really exists in the mind. Everything else is ephemeral.

Bugger. So all that time I'd spent on the road in search of the perfect place was a waste of energy and precious resources? Should I have saved myself a lot of time and trouble and just settled for a local tree to sit under?

' 'Course not,' I could hear my old dad's voice intoning in my head. 'No matter how hard a time I gave you about all that travelling, you were right. You had to do it. It was all part of the Grand Plan. Very much like my own although I didn't know I had Grand Plan at the time. If I hadn't spent time away I'd never have been able to see how good it was to be home. A bit like the feeling you're having now...?'

He wasn't wrong. And finally I'd reached the point of being able to admit it. At the risk of sounding like a British Tourist Board promotional, home by comparison with any number of the places tried, tested and ultimately rejected as winter retreat boltholes, was actually pretty good. Apart from the winter warmth bit it ticked pretty much all the boxes on a criteria list that, I now realised, was based more on what I had at home than I'd previously been prepared to admit. But I couldn't see home's silver lining until I left it behind.

So was that it? Was that all there was at the root of my wanderlust? Knowing deep down that the only way to fully appreciate home was to leave it? As much as I tried to convince myself it was, something still nagged. This, I couldn't help shake the feeling, was too pat. Too simplistic. Something felt missing. What was it?

The willow knew. 'That old saying about it being the journey, not the arriving, that really matters,' it said. 'Simple.'

Gosh. Thanks again willow. Got it in one. Throughout all my time on the road, standing in the way of any place – home included – being awarded the 'perfect' accolade was that maxim. All that time, I now realised, it'd been lodged in my subconscious, nagging about it being a crime to put an end to the journeys while new things were still out there waiting to be discovered.

'Stop travelling and you might as well go brain dead,' was effectively the message in the guilt trip that homespun philosophy had been taking me on. One I now realised that had turned me into a sort of never satisfied life experience nymphomaniac. Or the male equivalent of one, whatever that was.

So no wonder nowhere had been given the big, unreserved, thumbs-up. Nowhere could be while there was still the remotest possibility of there being something out there not experienced before.

So what had happened? How was it that I was now more than prepared to call a halt to the whole new experience searching thing?

Simple. The reservoir of new experiences had dried up. With every day of the beard growing longer and greyer, the chances of encountering a new experience had shrunk in direct inverse proportion until, in the end, the point had been reached at which nothing but repetition of things experienced before was now being encountered and that meant only one scarcely palatable thing. An end to this road could and did exist and without warning that end of road had risen up out of nowhere to greet me.

The realisation left me all but speechless and immobile. Although I wasn't unaware that such a time could come, I never countenanced the possibility of that time actually coming before I was ready for the real care home and began running my mind back over recent events to try to pin down the moment tipping point had been reached.

Bloody Cambodia. Had to be. So bizarre had that eviction from my chosen resting place been that I doubted anything could ever match it for plumb, unbridled madness. It'd become increasingly clear that after that little episode nothing would ever surprise me again. Nothing could ever compete.

'Oh, good grief. Seriously?' I could hear myself gasping out loud. Is that all it took for my life on the road to be brought to an abrupt halt? An example of utter derangement I hadn't needed once in my life let alone twice?

'Yep,' replied the willow. 'Like the two little road scares in a week you had in Kenya that finally drove you to quit Africa, it's often not the big but the little things that ultimately tip the balance. Even the Buddha experienced that. Even he ran out of road in the end.'

Crikey. That was good company to be in. But surely mere mortals like me weren't worthy of it.

'Not a bit of it,' said the willow. 'The Buddha's biggest gift to the world was his teaching that everyone has the ability to achieve the kind of enlightenment he achieved if they have the determination to transcend to the state of mindlessness he managed. Even rank amateurs like you.'

Blimey, I thought, I could do that. Contrary to how the willow obviously saw me, rank amateur at mindlessness I most certainly was not. The technique needed to achieve this state of mental vacuum had come with absolutely no effort whatsoever the day the most uninspiring flatpack teacher who ever lived entered my life to try to teach me Latin in a dusty, lightless schoolroom on a Friday afternoon in the sixties and had stayed with me ever since. If that grounding didn't stand me in good stead for taking to Buddhist meditation like a monk to prayer I'd do the unthinkable and give Latin another go. And even if I could only master the first of an undoubted great number of steps down enlightenment road needed to get anywhere near Buddha level, surely it'd be enough to be able to conjure up a sort of other world perfection just about anywhere I pleased. Even right here on my own doorstep.

Oh, the relief of finally realising it! The relief of having the burden of HAVING to escape every winter lifted! Now, my own little bit of enlightenment revealed to me, there was no need. By employing certain meditational techniques, travel was still possible but without the associated torture of having to suffer apocalyptic airport departure halls, battery hen airliner incarceration, interminable immigration queues, third world cacophony, life-threatening road madness, world-beating officiousness, accommodation frustration and seriously suspect restaurant offerings. Put these together with finding nowhere was now spared invasions by that element of humanity who must have been on holiday when environmental consciences were being handed out and all the ingredients were in place for a swift and highly relieved departure from all that.

From what I'd seen of how the planet's unstoppably rising number of occupants had let their home rot under their feet and done nothing about it, they were welcome to it. Especially since things could only get worse. Once Covid pandemic-induced travel restrictions were lifted those who'd survived would be so desperate to get back in the air there wouldn't be an airport or a city or a road or a guesthouse or a beach anywhere in the world not resembling a scene from Soylent Green, a film that left all other dystopian storylines trailing in its wake.

* * *

By summer of 2022 – the very year in which the fifty year-old Soylent Green film was set – TV footage of the mayhem overwhelming airports worldwide confirmed my darkest fears. Once the effect of the virus vaccination had kicked in and people were allowed to travel again, hordes desperate to make up for two years of being denied sun and heat stroke on foreign Somme-lookalike beaches started flooding to airports that were now doing a fine impression of Kabul's in 2021, the day the Taliban marched in and began forcing their own brand of Islamic puritanism down people's throats, literally in some cases.

Airport staff numbers seriously depleted by the long-term effects of Covid and the airlines' total inability to attract back people sent on gardening duty during the pandemic became overrun by the invasion and virtually threw up their hands in surrender. Resistance was obviously as futile as trying to fight one's way through the seething mob to make it to a plane that could well be about to sit on the runway for half the mob's holiday depending on whether their bags had made it onboard before the plane's take-off slot expired.

Viewing the pictures smugly from the comfort of my armchair many many miles from this air equivalent of road rage, a thought occurred. Soylent Green wasn't only a remarkably prescient story but was at the base of a not exactly well-received theory I'd formulated on the means of tackling a global environmental crisis brought about by humankind's complete inability to stop breeding. The solution, as Soylent Green clearly showed us, surely rested not in veganism – as the greenies had been going out of their way to convince us – but cannibalism. Starting with shaven-headed pot-bellied members of genus football supporter whose drunken loudmouth cavortings on Thai beaches were driving locals into the arms of Islamic fundamentalists.

Sadly, with the environmental lobby considering my suggestion a tad too challenging to be included in its policies for saving the world, the view of it from my armchair vantage point looked bleak. If the world couldn't bring itself to adopt and implement fast-acting solutions of the sort I had in mind, airports and beaches would never return to somewhere near acceptable levels of occupation and there'd be no option but to have to face up to a highly distressing truth. Under current conditions there was no way my quest to find the perfect sanctuary from winter could ever be fulfilled and if that was the case only one other option was left open to me – taking the Buddha route.

By climbing aboard the mindlessness express, the willow had assured me, I could voyage to any location or dimension of my choice, no airline ticket, visa, money or hotel booking required. Bliss. Or it would be once I'd learned how to achieve the Buddha's level of enlightenment – and therein lay a problem. Having now attained what diplomatic folk are kind enough to describe as a certain age there was the distinct possibility of another, rather less-welcome, destination being arrived at before the one I was aiming to reach had been.

Seven years it took the Buddha to find what he was looking for. After a lifetime of bouncing along the developing world road less travelled my body had started telling me it might not even make it til lunchtime and that some means of speeding the enlightenment process might very well be needed. Supplementing it perhaps with the sort of out-of-body experience-assisting pharmaceutical products resorted to by those seeking an escape from the Soylent Green nightmare?

Well, yes. Maybe. While I had no burning desire to travel that route there was no doubt such products would help achieve the desired effect. And who knows, their use might even facilitate trips to places like, say, San Serriffe.

Well now, I thought. That did sound rather tempting. But even if I could find the right, er, 'travel agent' from whom to obtain the necessary 'ticket' I'd definitely be building in a condition – resorting to any form of pharmaceutical travel 'assistance' would only be considered if bagging the desired goose by the Buddha route failed. I wasn't blind to the dangers of accidentally exceeding the ticket's terms and conditions and ending up with one's goose, in a word, cooked.

So was I prepared to risk it? Quite possibly. What was there to lose? Twenty long years and more I'd been on the trail of that sodding bird and where had it got me? Not much closer than the odd tantalising glimpse of my quarry. If it was true that taking advantage of assisted passage 'packages' all but guaranteed finally pinning it down I knew I'd have trouble resisting them if all else failed.

Which was entirely possible. Deep down, my confidence in achieving anything like an out-of-body state of consciousness without pharmaceutical assistance was, at best, moderate and the only other option was going back on the road, a prospect that made me shudder just thinking about it. Given the rapidly deteriorating state of both the world and my travel-fatigued body that option had been consigned to the trash can of history. It was now a route closed off to me. A thing of the past. The end of that road had been reached, the journey terminalised and the book closed firmly shut. I was, I told myself from my armchair eyrie while viewing pictures of the airport chaos through splayed, quaking fingers, most definitely done with all that.

No, really. I was! This turn of events meant the quest was over and that was that.

Really and truly this time.

Definitely, completely and absolutely.

Probably.

END?

Other Works
by
Mark Newham

For sample chapters and availability
of all books see:
http://moriartimedia.com/theworks.htm

LIMP PIGS

"Unique... Inspiring... " *BBC*

China isn't changing. Well, it is, but not nearly as much as they'd have you believe. And unless real change comes to China soon, a long cold winter of social discontent looms. Years spent working in the gearbox of China's propaganda machine left Newham unable to conclude otherwise. Attached to two separate Chinese state news agencies between 2003 and 2008, Newham left the country convinced China is politically moribund – as authoritarian, as repressive and as unyielding as it was under Chairman Mao.

Set against China's staggering economic transformation of recent years, Newham says it's this disparity which could ultimately prove China's undoing. The country has become a child with legs growing at unequal rates. Unless something is done soon to address the political/economic inequity, ultimate imbalance is, he believes, inevitable.

Presented in the form of an irreverent memoir-with-attitude of his time working for the Xinhua News Agency and the Beijing Olympics News Service, *Limp Pigs and the Five-Ring Circus* was published in 2011 and ranked **Number One** in Amazon's censorship category for several weeks.

Revised on the inauguration of Xi Jinping as China's president in 2012, *Limp Pigs 2013* is the e-book update of the original.

COMETH THE YUAN

"Beautifully rendered... " *Guardian*

Published in 2014 and set in the not-too-distant future, *Cometh the Yuan* is a work of speculative satirical fiction envisaging the not unlikely growing extent of China's influence on the West.

Having already used its economic might to re-colonise most of the developing world, China is now eyeing more challenging targets. Chinese tendrils are already deep into western commerce and industry but that's not enough for China's ambitious leaders. Western political targets are now in China's spotlight and a campaign is launched to infiltrate western seats of power via the services of an unsuspecting multi-billionaire critic of China.

Hong Kong property magnate Harry Wong finds himself hoodwinked into participating in a takeover exercise *par excellence* courtesy of Chinese deceit and Wong's love of cricket. Inculcated into the game at Oxford University, Wong's greatest ambition is to become cricket's new supremo. The man to whom all cricket bows its head. With full Chinese support, Wong's takeover target is none other than Lord's Cricket Ground, the spiritual home of the game. China, it emerges, has confused Lord's with THE Lords – Britain's upper house of parliament.

Can Wong succeed in taking over one of Britain's national treasures? Not if the Marylebone Cricket Club can help it. Almost by accident the bungling historic guardian of Lord's finds itself at the forefront of a battle to combat China's attempt to worm its way into western politics by the back door.

PLUNDERLAND

"More gold from Mr Newham" – *Amazon review*

Kearney and Ryan have been in Africa so long they're becoming choc-ices in reverse.

That was never the plan. A year or two at most. Surely that'd be long enough to make the killing they know is out there. Then they'd be free. Out of Africa to enjoy the fruits of their dubious exploits at their leisure.

Thirty years on and Ireland's answer to Stanley and Livingstone are all but spent. Still no closer to unearthing that elusive pot of gold than the day they started looking both know their next hurrah will be their last.

So this time they're breaking the habit of a lifetime and doing some planning. They have something Africa's latest colonial invader China wants and, the pair are betting, will pay any price to get.

With all the bases covered, all eventualities foreseen, what could possibly go wrong?

What indeed.

**For sample chapters and availability of all books see:
http://moriartimedia.com/theworks.htm**

www.ingramcontent.com/pod-product-compliance
Lightning Source LLC
Chambersburg PA
CBHW030256100526
44590CB00012B/422